EVERYONE DESERVES TO KNOW WHAT I THINK

Collected Writings, 2003-2013

Joe Peacock

Hey that's me!
J-Pk
2013

Facebook: http://facebook.com/joethepeacock
Twitter: http://twitter.com/joethepeacock
Email: joe@joethepeacock.com
Talk to me, Goose.

Everyone Deserves To Know What I Think:
Collected Writings, 2003 - 2013
by Joe Peacock
Published by This Is Not Art! Productions in Atlanta, GA
Copyright © 2013 by Joe Peacock

The events, people and places described in this book are based on the actual things from my life. In some cases, names, locations and other descriptive factors have been changed to protect the innocent, and should be noted appropriately. In the case that I got something wrong or forgot to mention it, consider it fiction and move on with your life.

Peacock, Joe. Everyone Deserves To Know What I Think.
ISBN-13: 978-0615887319 (This Is Not Art! Productions)
ISBN-10: 0615887317
Version 1.0
OICU812

Dedicated to Casey Edwards, Jeremy Halvorsen, Mike Crawford, Shawn Hill, Liz Stricklen and Katie Black.

ABOUT THIS BOOK

This book is a collection of my blog posts over the past 10 years I've been writing. It's a mix of "most popular" and "shit either Victoria (the book's producer) or I felt like putting in here."

The entries are, for the most part, in chronological order. As I read through them while compiling them, I noticed something I never really intended started to show, which is my development as a writer.

Wherever possible, I've left the "quality" of the writing alone. The 2013 me wants badly to go back and slap the 2003 me for blatant abuses of literary brevity, punctuation, dashes, commas and whatnot. But in the interest of rounding out the picture of "Joe Peacock as a writer the past 10 years" I'm leaving them alone for the most part.

Additionally, my life situaiton changed in early 2013. I am no longer married. References to "we" or my ex-wife are mostly left intact for the same reason.

What you're holding is pretty much a portrait of me, in words. It's not just my sense of humor or my opinoins or my perspective, it's also a bit of a road map of how those things have changed the past ten years.

Here's hoping it doesn't suck.

Introduction:
I'M SCARED SHITLESS.

No, seriously.

The act of releasing a new book is indeed scary, but that's not why I'm scared. I've released books before. Two, in fact. Both of them named the same thing (Mentally Incontinent), even though they were completely different books. I thought it was clever when Seal did it with his records in the 90's, so I figured I'd try it. It wasn't clever, it was just obnoxious. Oh well. Live and learn.

I'm scared because this book is the first book I've ever released while not working at some other job, or running a small company, or otherwise deriving income from another source somehow. This is my first book as a Full Time Writer™ and it's Freaking. Me. OUT.

What if it doesn't sell? What if no one cares? What if, what if, what if... These questions, I've asked myself before. Each time I released the other two books, I had my fair share of ulcers and doubt. But this time, it's not so much "What if it doesn't sell?"

It's "What if I can't make it as a writer?"

Much, much scarier question. Because it's all I've ever wanted to be. And the truth is, it's all I'm really good at. And if I can't...

I mean, I've spent the last, oh, 18 years of my life climbing various ladders, corporate and not. And with every rung, I kept asking myself two things:
1) What will this raise in pay or status get me in terms of more freedom to write, and
2) How much can I write while I should be doing the thing I was hired to do?

It sounds immature. After all, "Buckle up your big boy pants and get your ass to work" is some of the best advice any father could give to any son, because in certain situations, it's the ONLY way you'll get anywhere. And sometimes, you've got to take a crap job somewhere and do whatever you can to rub two nickels together to make a dime.

That's not a problem for me. I can work just about anywhere and do just about anything when it comes down to it. And I will, should I have to. But right now, as I sit here in September of 2013, I've found myself in a position I've not only never been in, but I never actually conceived I'd ever be.

In the past 12 months, I've experienced more cataclysmic change than any one person I've ever met experiences in a lifetime. I've:

- Divorced my wife of 10 years and 364 days, whom I dated for over 14 years,
- Lost my house
- Lost my company, a boutique animation and video game studio that was my only source of income,
- Lost three of my pets,
- Sold nearly everything I own (literally) to pay out debts and keep from going hungry,
- Had my identity stolen,
- Lost four people I know or am connected to to suicide

And yet...

And yet, I still have my health. I can still walk with both legs with no impediment. I can still see. I can still hear. I can still speak. I have a vast network of some of the most amazing friends anyone could EVER ask for. And most importantly, I can still write.

I have nothing. And yet, I have EVERYTHING.

So I'm starting over.

I'm at the bottom. The very, very bottom. And I stare up at the ladder I once climbed and I know, I could climb that very same ladder very similarly to the way I climbed it before. I could call my friends in the tech sector and score a job. I could work my way into any number of web or social media or video projects. I could be right back on top of the same mountains I've climbed before.

And in short order, I'd be back here, at the bottom. Because that's what got me here in the first place.

I've been chasing either dollars or prestige since I was 18 years old, when the dot com bubble started rising. I quit college after six months because it was possible back then to make an insane salary building websites. I didn't necessarily love the work, but man, the paycheck was fantastic, and I was pretty good at it.

But like anything you do just for the money, it got old. So I started diversifying. I got into design. I got into Information Architecture. I got into Social Media. I got into video production. I got into animation production. I got into all sorts of things that seemed very interesting, but only because they kept the pay scale where I felt it needed to be to keep the lifestyle I'd built floating merrily along.

And oh, what a shitty fucking lifestyle it was. I start a project with all sorts of grandeur and glee, and within months, I'm bored. So to compensate for the drudgery of the grind all week, I order presents for myself on Amazon or go shoe shopping or take trips or otherwise try my best to buy happiness with the money I earned being unhappy. I had a big TV that I used to play video games that I'd distract myself with to forget how miserable I was going to be when I went to work the next day.

And somewhere along the way, I started writing. And boy did I write.

My first book project, the first Mentally Incontinent, saw nearly 80 stories written to fill out 12 chapters of a book. My readers voted on their favorites, which went into the book, while the others just sat in the archives. Then, I did it all again, only there were another 120 stories for the 2nd book. And all the while, I wrote articles and posts on my blog. I freelanced for magazines. I wrote for CNN and Huffington Post (and before them, AOL News) and newspapers.

I was writing constantly. For the past 10 years, it's been the only thing I can say has consistently made me happy.

So here I am, at the bottom, starting up at the ladders before me. I didn't ask to be here. It wasn't planned. It's like every single strut holding up the platforms that built my life rotted out at once, and down I tumbled.

But now that I'm down here, I look around and realize... It wasn't the struts. It wasn't the platforms. It was the foundation that was faulty. I've built an entire life on the wrong premise that somehow, I'd make enough money being what I thought I should be, that one day I'd be able to be what I want to be.

It doesn't work that way. Period, end of story. The more money you make doing anything you're not happy doing, the more you'll spend trying to make yourself happy. It's a zero sum game.

So it's time to try something new. And by that, I mean fundamentally different. I'm changing not just what I'm doing, but who I am. And for that reason, I'm embarking on a new career. I want to be a full-time writer.

This book is the first book of my new writing career. It's being released in October of 2013, and covers the best material from my blog since I started writing it in 2003. I have another I'm working on currently that I plan to release in December of 2013 called The Book I Wish Someone Had Written When I Was Your Age, and another that I've started planning for March of 2014 that I've actually been working on for nearly three years.

After that, I want to release a new book every three months. Some of them will be shorter, some longer, but all of them will be on time. Because this is my new life, and this is all I want to do with it. And there's nothing else keeping me from doing the one thing I want to do:

Write.

And that scares me shitless. We all dream of doing the thing we wish we could do, because in our dreams, the wish is safe. There's no way to prove that you can't, or that you're not good enough, or that no one will care. It's nestled safely in your brain and your heart, kept away from the harsh realities of actually trying it out.

But there are worse fates than figuring out the one thing you always wished you could do, isn't what you are meant to do... Like doing everything you thought you should do, and never once trying to make it at the one thing you wished you could do.

I'M NOT SORRY.
POSTED JULY 9, 2013

When I care about something, I engulf myself in it. I pay full attention. I soak it all in. I want to study every single corner, seam, side and stitch. I want to know it, fully and wholly.

When I love, I love with my whole heart. I don't have room for embarrassment or regret, because my heart is 100% dedicated to love.

When I trust, I trust fully. I subscribe to the theory that the best way to figure out if you can trust someone is to trust them.

I get hurt. A lot. Sometimes, very badly.

And yes, I get sad. I have to face memories and pain and periods of time being alone and broken. And I'm not sorry. I don't regret it one bit. I don't have time for it. Regret is distraction. Wishing something never happened is basically saying I wish I hadn't lived. And having actually been clinically dead before, I'm not about to wish that. I'm going to live as hard as I fucking can.

When I die, I don't want a perfect shiny heart, protected in plastic and encased in a safe box. I want my heart to have scars and stretch marks and all the signs that show it was well used.

MY FIRST EVER BLOG POST

POSTED FEBRUARY 21, 2003

Yes, indeed, it's a beautiful day for doing nothing.

If it weren't for the fact that I love showers too much to forsake my job responsibilities and become a street person, nothing is exactly what I would do.

And I would be so damn good at it, I would get regular merit promotions. In no time at all, I would move from Street Person to Lead Street Person, eventually moving to VP of Street Living and Integration. Of course, this title would demand a lot of my time and responsibility, which would then preclude me from doing nothing.

Paradox!

I'm gonna go get a cup of coffee.

THE DAY I HIT A TURKEY IN MY CAR

POSTED APRIL 5, 2003

I was driving along, merrily minding my own business, when I came to a stop sign. Right before I came to a complete stop, I noticed a blur out of the passenger side window and heard a "Thump" against the front panel of my car.

Not sure what the hell just happened, I exited my vehicle and went around to check on it.

The beleaguered bird was startled by my appearance, gobbled loudly, and kinda leapt and flapped down the road for quite a while. I just stood there, dumbfounded by the fact that I just hit a turkey, watching this goofy bird run down the street.

I shook my head, got back in my car, and went to work.

In other words, my life is fucking dull.

HOW GOD (APPARENTLY) CREATED ME

POSTED APRIL 14, 2003

If you have ever played tabletop roleplaying games, you will know what I am talking about here.

In RPG's, when you "roll up" a character, you roll dice to determine the character points you put into various attributes, i.e. strength, wisdom, charisma, etc.

Once that happens, you can select character "attributes" or "defects". Attributes, such as keen hearing or super smell, cost points because they benefit your character, while defects like "weak eyes" or "addicted to cocaine" give you more points since they add harmful qualities to your character.

There is one defect you can choose called "Weirdness Magnet" which causes all kinds of weird things to happen to a character at random times, such as a dolphin puking on the character, or bipedal cows destroying a once fantastic meal, or even a person attempting to hold up a grocery store at 4:00 am while the character is trying to buy cat food and Pantene.

I think when God rolled my character up, he took that defect.

The only thing is, I don't think he used the points he got back on attributes, because I don't seem to have any.

MALL DAZE
POSTED OCTOBER 14, 2003

This is an entry from one of my old journals when I worked in the mall. The original date on this entry is 4.12.1996. I worked at a kiosk which sold movie and television memorabilia (It was actually a pretty cool job, as I was a pretty big collector of the crap this store sold).

The series - 55 entries in all - are called "Mall Daze". Here's Mall Daze #5:

Is this a new trend?
Booth Writing?

Today is "Fuck Up Day" at the mall. Every single gene pool reject ever created has come up to good ol' Southlake Mall to visit me. I want to scream. The barrage of mindless questions never ceases.

"Which way is Macy's?"
"Head toward the sign that says 'Macy's'."

"Where's the nearest bathroom?"
"Open your mouth, I'll show you."

Talked to Mandy last night, hard to do that when Michael keeps making jokes at her expense. She is really stupid. I have no clue why I am with her.

GODDAMMIT I WORK AT THE MALL MALL MALL
MALL MALL MALL MALL MALL MALL MALL MALL
MALL MALL MALL MALL MALL MALL MALL MALL
MALL MALL MALL MALL MALL MALL MALL MALL
MALL MALL MALL MALL MALL MALL MALL MALL
MALL MALL MALL MALL MALL MALL MALL MALL
MALL MALL MALL

God, the most depressing figure of all time just walked past me. Eyes droopy, slouched posture. Short gait, shuffling past like Quasimodo.

Slay the children now, spare them the tortures of shopping at the Gap.

I want a good body. One that I can travel the world unclothed with and no one would want to arrest me, for they love my body so much and are touched by its beauty.

The past is a freight train that allows you a moment's head start then barrels toward you and runs you right over. The only way to avoid it is to step off the track and onto the road beside, where a Yugo full of depression and decaffeinated coffee slams into you at its top speed of 40 miles an hour.

* * *

Yah. I know. Awful.

Anyway, In this "Mall Daze" series are 4 entries over 7 days, all of them detailing a new girl who had started working at The Limited store across from the kiosk I ran. In each entry, I went into detail about how beautiful she was, how her hair flowed like silk in an autumn breeze, how gracefully she seemed to move as she walked, her poise and posture, all that great stuff. I would go into insane missives about how I longed to learn everything about her - her greatest fears, her most cherished achievements, etc. and so forth.

Then, there's a 5th entry. It says:

"I met the girl from The Limited today. Her name is Megan, and she is a bitch."

And that's it. That's all it says.

GRAPE NUTS

POSTED APRIL 12, 2004

When I was a teenager living at my parents' house, I used to eat massive, heaping bowls of cereal in the morning. If you've ever watched The Beverly Hillbillies and seen the size of Jethro's bowl, that's what I'm talking about. I'd pour the bowl 3/4ths of the way to the top with cereal, top it with milk, and wolf it down. Captain Crunch, Cookie Crisp, Fruity Pebbles - all of my victims disappeared nearly instantly in a vortex of my inhalation of my part of a complete breakfast.

One day, my dad came home with a box of Grape Nuts he had purchased during that day's grocery shopping extravaganza. Up until that time, I had never tried Grape Nuts and had seen the marketing propaganda claiming its nutty goodness and wholesomeness and yatta yatta - I knew I had to try them.

My father tried to warn me. "Don't pour too big a bowl, because I WILL make you eat all that you take." Having been raised during the Great Depression, my father had a great amount of disdain for wasting food, and would not allow anyone to leave the table unless they cleaned their plates. Being that I was a young buck, foolhardy and hungry, I ignored my father's sage advice and went ahead with the pouring of a standard Joe-sized bowl. I sat down to eat my Grape Nuts at 6:00 AM that morning.

At 7:00 AM, I was STILL eating that same bowl of Grape Nuts.

I begged my father to let me go dump them out. He refused.

At 8:00 AM, I had barely made a dent into the bowl full of brick mortar sitting before me. I PLEADED with my father - "Dad, this is disgusting, PLEASE let me throw it out."

"Not a chance," he replied, sitting in his place at the head of the table. He explained to me that we were both going to sit at that table as long as it took for me to eat every single spoonful of Grape Nuts.

10:00 AM rolled on by. The bowl had grown in size, no kidding. "Dad!" I exclaimed. "Look - I'll BUY a new box of Grape Nuts to replace this one. A whole box - NO! TWO whole boxes! Just PLEASE, for the love of God, let me throw this crap out!"

He just sat there and read his funnies.

By the time noon had arrived, my face was pressed into the crook of my elbow, resting on the table. My stomach felt as if it would explode violently, sending the substance that was neither Grapes nor Nuts all over the place. The bowl stood at 75% of its original volume.

I sat at that table until 9 PM. No shit - NINE O' FUCKING CLOCK AT NIGHT.

I spooned the last spongy glop into my mouth. I had already vomited twice and was well on my way to my third trip to the Isle of Bile when my father chimed up, "Ok, I hope you've learned your lesson."

"Oh, yes," I replied, a note of sickness hanging on my syllables. "I will listen to your advice from now on."

"Oh, I'm not talking about that," He replied plainly. "I was talking about eating Grape Nuts. They're disgusting."

My face conveyed shock and amazement. "Then why the HELL did you buy them?"

He shrugged. "Your sister is making a macaroni collage. She needed something to be 'sand' so I picked up some Grape Nuts."
He shook his head, ruffled my hair, and marched out of the room. "Time for bed. See you in the morning."

YES, I'M OBSESSIVE

POSTED JULY 25, 2004

I was introduced to the music of Jeff Buckley around 1993, just after a very short show here in Atlanta had blown every single attendee away. Unfortunately, I wasn't able to attend that show (or any other he played here, which is just sad. Each time he came into town, some ridiculous tragedy befell me). A guy I went to school with had taped the show and brought it for me to hear, and I simply fell in love.

Immediately, I went in search of music by this Buckley guy, and all I could find was the Live at Sinè EP - 4 songs, performed acoustically, that absolutely haunted me. I couldn't BELIEVE that there wasn't more work by this guy out there! Fortunately for me, 1994 came around and Grace was released, and the whole world began to clue in to a fact that I'd learned a year previous: this Buckley guy was 100% amazing. It was also in 1994 that I began attending collectable record / CD shows with Mike, looking for things you couldn't find in the stores - most notably, rare Smashing Pumpkins and Jeff Buckley stuff. I'd happen upon the random Last Goodbye single or Eternal Life CD-5, and my existence would have meaning for a while.

Hearing rare and unreleased material by Jeff elated me in a way that is still to this day unrivaled in any other artist I collect. I picked up EVERYTHING that I could find with his name on it - bootlegs, show recordings, radio broadcasts - anything that had the word Buckley on it, I bought it, regardless of price (once I had a job and could afford it, that is).

11

Then, tragically, Jeff Buckley departed this world.

In 1997, Jeff Buckley drowned in the Mississippi River just outside of Memphis. This was a devastating blow for me. To say that he was my favorite artist at the time (and still now) is an understatement. Unfortunately, the market for his rare / unreleased stuff went haywire after he died, so anything and everything that was coming to light - the early releases of "Sketches for My Sweetheart The Drunk" (Then simply called (Untitled - New Buckley Demos, Memphis 97), The Mystery White Boy sources, the Peyote Road Theater tracks - they quadrupled in price almost overnight - a fact reflected at the next CD show I attended after he died.

Now, there's something that every comic book nerd, record collector, toy enthusiast, etc. knows about shows - there are customers, and then there are regulars. Customers breeze into a show, look around, point and say "ooh, looky there." They might even spend some money at a dealer's table - and in some cases, a good bit of money, especially for that one item from their past that they coveted as a child or if you have a huge deal on recent release stuff (10 cd's for 30 bucks, 10 comics for a dollar, whatever). In fact, the majority of a dealer's take at any given show / convention will be from these passers-by.

But then, there are the obsessed people who are at every single show, every month / season / year (whenever they have them). These people started off as normal customers, looking at the odd rare Mint "White Album" (Beatles) or the super old Amazing Fantasy #15 (First appearance of Spiderman) or the first release of the Invisible Woman action figure (easily the rarest action figure to ever be produced) - and while they did this, something scampered down from the table, crawled across the floor and up their pant leg and bit them. They got infected - and they fell in deep. These people will be at every show, every time. If they come by a dealer's table and see something they didn't see the last show that they want, they will pull out a huge wad of cash and say "here." They won't shuffle or contemplate or hem and haw. They will simply buy it from you. You may have to come down on the price a bit for that ultra-rare UK-only release of "Halo eleventeen - broken, fixed and broken again" by Nine Inch Nails, but doing so for these people is WELL worth it. They are the mouths of your industry. Everyone who collects whatever it is you're there to sell probably knows these people, because they're at EVERY show. They're experts on the collector market. If you make them happy by giving them the final piece they need for their shrine to Treznor, they will make sure to tell every one of their fandom friends about you.

It's safe to say that, if you know what's good for you, you will NOT piss these people off.

So there I was at yon CD show. I was standing in front of a dealer table that I'd never seen at this show before. He was what we call an opportunist. He had no real motif - most dealers deal exclusively in one thing or another. Some do live videos of shows, some do singles and imports, some do 60's material. This guy, however, simply sniffed the air and found out what was hot, and then picked up items he could resell to capitalize on whatever was the popular wave of the time. He had Tori Amos's "Y Kant Tori Read," the sole reason I can't respect that ridiculous excuse for an "artist". He also had, sitting on the back shelf, a white box with 4 white paper sleeves. The box was marked "Jeff Buckley Sinè Set - 93".

"HOLY SHIT!" I yelled, drawing his attention immediately. Mike looked over from a box of Helmet singles he already owned every copy of.

"What?" he asked. I responded by letting my mouth gape open, my eyes pop out of my skull and my index finger point to the box. "Wow," he replied. "You gonna get it?"

"I... Uh... well, YEAH!" I enthusiastically replied, drawing a wide smile from the dealer. He reached around behind him, grabbed the box, and plunked it in front of me.

"Great set," he casually said. "Very hot item right now."

"Yeah, I bet!" I replied. "I've heard rumors... but man, I can't believe I'm staring at it!"

"Yep!" he said. "Ever since he died, people's been askin' for his rare stuff. I got my hands on these and I'm hopin' to move 'em."

"Oh, I'll definitely take them off your hands!" I replied. "How much are you asking?"

He replied with an answer that really shouldn't be repeated here, as it was so grossly offensive that, should I repeat it, might bring about fines from the FCC.

"What!?!" I replied. "Dude, that's a CAR. I'm not paying you a car for that set."

"Fine," he replied, placing his hands around the box in preparation to remove it. Reflexively, my hands shot out and grabbed hold of the set.

"Hold on!" I said. "Can't we work something out?"

"Hmm... 'Fraid not, if you ain't willin' to pay me what I'm askin'."

"Look, I have some stuff I can give you in trade," I replied, whipping my bag up on the table and removing several ultra-rare recordings that I had duplicates of. "Look, here's an original pressing of Matthew Sweet's Goodfriend, and... let's see... OH! How about the 1963 Blue Note session with Ellington, Coltrane, Davis and Roach?"

"Sorry, not interested. Cash only."

"Come on, man!" I demanded. "There's got to be something I can do to make you part with the set."

"No, thanks." He said, tugging the box away from me forcefully and placing it back on the shelf. I shuffled away with a giant pout on my face, saddened that there were Buckley recordings that I couldn't possess simply because I was unwilling to pay a small Ford for them. I slowly arrived to a dealer named Keith's table.

"Dude, why the sad look?" He said in lieu of a greeting.

"Man, this dick over there wouldn't make a trade with me," I replied with a frown. "What a jerk."

"What were you trading for?" Keith asked. "More Matthew Sweet stuff? OH - Speaking of that, I have the new demos for... What is it... Mars, something?"

"Blue Sky on Mars, and thanks, but I already have it," I replied, patting my bag. "Have a few extra, if you think you can move 'em..."

"Nah, I think you're the only person on Earth who likes that guy," he replied. "So what was it you were trying to get?"

"Oh, the Buckley Sinè soundboards. That guy wants $2,000 for them."

"HOLY..." Keith shouted. "That's INSANE!"

"YEAH, I know!"

"Fuck...." Keith said, shaking his head. "That's just too much. I don't see how he can command that price. Just because the guy died a few weeks ago..."

"Yeah, I know," I said. "It makes real fans suffer, you know?"

"Yeah..." Keith said, looking away and scratching the 5 o'clock shadow that was coming in on his face 4 hours early. "Wait... You know who has those? Jim Bileux, down the row here. I just saw him talking to some guy about them. Have you seen him yet?"

"Nah, haven't been to that side yet," I replied. "But if Jim's got 'em..."

"Yeah, check with him," Keith replied. "If he doesn't have 'em, I'm SURE he can locate 'em for you."

"Alright!" I replied over my left shoulder, my body long since heading in that direction. I arrived at Jim's table where he was haggling with some newbie over the price of Prince's Black Album, a once rare CD pressing that, at one point, commanded over $1,000 at shows.

"Joe!" Jim said. "How ya been?"

"Not bad, Jim," I replied. "I got something to ask you for."

"Sure! Whatcha got--"

"Hey!" The customer said. "I was talking here!"

"Yeah," Jim said to him, cutting him a look that would carve a pumpkin. "You're talking nonsense. I'm not parting with this disc for less than $700, and that's that."

"Whatever," the angry customer replied. "I saw a guy over there (points in a random direction) who had it for $300!"

"And what did this guy look like?" Jim asked without batting an eye.

"Um... Tall guy? With a beard? And glasses?"

"Ah, that's Mark. And yeah, he has it, but he sure as hell doesn't have it for no $300. I'm sure he has it marked at $1000 just like I do, because I'm the one who sold it to him for $600 earlier today."

The guy pouted. Defeated, he marched off and allowed Jim and I to continue our business. "So, Joe, what can I sell you today?"

"Well, I'm looking for that Buckley Sinè box. You have it?"

"Nah," he said shaking his head, "But I can get it for ya. What's your budget?"

"I dunno," I said. "I saw some guy over there that had it for two grand."

"TWO GRAND???" Jim said. "Preposterous."

"Yeah, I know," I agreed. "That's just sick, Jim."

"Look, let me talk to Grahame at Marshall's Records. I'm sure he can do way better than two grand." And with that, he marched off and left his son to watch the table. I smiled wide as I followed in tow, hopeful that I might secure this elusive and very expensive set of recordings. Grahame Marshall is literally the patriarch of the CD collecting business. He's routinely the man who sets the going rate for just about everything in the market. Quite literally, if it exists, Grahame Marshall has either two copies or knows someone who does - and you can count on the fact that he's going to give you whatever it is you're looking for at a fair price. Once we arrived at the Marshall's Records table, Jim jumped right on Grahame and set to business.

"Grahame!" Jim said loudly as Grahame turned to look. "You got that Sinè set?"

"What's that?" Grahame replied.

"That Jeff Buckley set. The one from... what year was it, Joe?"

"'93," I replied.

"1993," Jim said. "White box."

"Lemme look..." Grahame answered, and then dove under the table. Right then, his assistant (I don't know his name. Consequently, you don't, either) spoke up.

"I saw it at a table earlier," Random Assistant Guy said. "Over there, I think. Near the wall."

"Yeah," I replied, "And he's charging 2,000 bucks for it, too."

We heard a resounding clunk as Grahame's head hit the underside of the table. He emerged, rubbing the crown of his skull and holding a white box with some CD's in it. "TWO GRAND, you said? Did I hear you right?"

"Yeah," I said.

"Who was it? Who was he with?"

"I dunno," I replied. "Never seen him at these shows before."

"Hmm... Let's go see him," Grahame said, carrying both me and the object of my desire over to the new dealer's table. Jim followed, and on the way, we picked up Mike. All four of us landed at the new buck's table and proceeded to watch our fearless leader ask to see the box on the shelf with the Buckley in it.

"Here ya go," the asshole said as he handed it to Mr. Marshall.

"How much you have on this?" Grahame asked calmly.

"$2,000," The man replied plainly.

Grahame scoffed. He looked hard at the man, then scoffed again. He fingered one of the CD sleeves and began to extract the disc from inside.

"Woah!" the dealer said. "What do you think you're doing?"

"Examining the disc," Mr. Marshall said. "If I'm going to pay 2 grand for some CD's, I want to make sure they're pristine."

"Oh, I assure you, they're top quality," The dealer said, snatching the sleeve from Grahame's hands. "Absolutely flawless, never been played. Now, you buying or what?"

"Let me see the disc," Grahame said forcefully.

"I can't risk you damaging the set," The dealer replied. "Now, are you serious or not?"

Grahame stared at him hard. Quickly, he snatched another disc out of the box and quickly pulled it from the sleeve before the dealer could react. Grahame Marshall nearly choked on his bile as he looked at the CD, and then showed it to us. "LOOK AT THIS!" He shouted. "What a forgery!"

"Sir," the dealer said harshly, "I assure you, those are genuine! How dare you accuse me of selling a forgery?!?"

Grahame smiled wide as he plunked his set upon the table. He opened the top of the box - much brighter white with much clearer printing - and pulled out a disc. The top was bright white with inlaid silver writing, whereas the newbie dealer's disc was a dull grey with silver writing formed by the lack of printing.

The dealer knew that the gig was up.

Grahame Marshall turned to me and said, "Now, if you are interested in the GENUINE article, I will sell it to you for... oh... Five Hundred."

Without even hesitating, I reached into my pocket, pulled out a wad of cash, and handed it to him.

I'M NOT A BAD PERSON

POSTED AUGUST 22, 2004

I swear to God I'm not.

But dammit... sometimes, Jehovah's Witnesses just plain NEED the hose turned on them.

Especially when they've been standing there for the past hour watching you prune your flowerbed, all the while preaching and talking and refusing to take your subtle hints (then later, out and out demands) for them to leave.

Now, I feel bad for having done it. I do, I really do. But really, you would have done the same thing. I mean, think about it - you're out in your own yard in a cul-de-sac that you have to cross a bridge to get to. You see two Jehovah's Witnesses approach. You nod and smile and know that there's no way they're there to visit someone else, because you are one of only two houses in that cul-de-sac. They engage you in conversation and you politely tell them that you're not interested and quite busy.

"Oh, that's alright, we can talk to ya while you work."

Anger Meter - 30%.

You dig and you weed and you plant bulbs, wiping sweat from your brow with a grimy glove, smearing the resulting mud all over your face. You huff and pant as you slam the post-hole-digger into the rocky ground. The sun is relentless as it beats down on you; large damp spots form under your armpits and in the small of your back.

And still, these people continue a one-sided conversation about... Oh, I dunno. Jesus coming over here in a canoe and taking 144,000 people back with him to Disneyworld. Whatever the hell they believe. You say "Listen, as much as you want to tell me these things, I really don't have time to hear them. As you can see, I'm quite busy."

"Well," they say, "It doesn't seem like we've been much of a hindrance on your workflow so far, so we can stick around. It'll be alright."

Anger Meter: 70%.

You stare right into their eyes, making sure to pay equal attention and equal time to both of them. You turn around, walk inside, and fix yourself a cold drink of water. You retrieve a rake and a garden trowel from your garage and head back outside, and they're still there. They now have their bible open to some page and begin quoting scripture at you. You say "Ok, honestly, this is ridiculous. You're trespassing at this point, and I don't want to be a dick, but this is, after all, my property and I've politely asked you to leave. So I really need you to just skedaddle on outta here."

"And deny yourself the glory of God's word? You'd ask messengers of God to leave? Wow, you must really want to go to hell."

Yes, he said that.

Anger Meter: 90%.

"Well, sir," you say, "The way I figure it, I've got another 50 years before I need to make things right with God. You, however, have about 10 seconds to make things right with me, and the only way to do that is to GO."

"Well, I think I'm going to have to exercise my First Amendment Rights here," he says to you.

"The First Amendment is null and void here," You say. "You'll have to go someplace that I don't own, and the nearest spot for that is either over THERE, past the cow pasture, or back the way you came, across that bridge. I'd recommend the bridge, though. Less cow shit."

"You can't revoke my First Amendment rights," he said. "This is America - one country under God - that's Jehovah, mind you - and I'm free to.."

At this point, you cannot hear him anymore, because you've marched over to the spigot and turned it on full-force. You have the sprayer nozzle in your hand; the fine mist escaping from where the threads of the nozzle don't exactly match up cooling the hot blood pumping through your right arm. You have the nozzle aimed squarely at the Jehovah's Witnesses, and one says, "You wouldn't DARE."

Would you?

Yeah, me too. So I did.

And God - er, Jehovah - was it wonderful.

INSTANT MESSENGER TAG

POSTED NOVEMBER 14, 2004

Joe The Peacock: *tag*
Joe The Peacock: *hide*
Sarah: oh i LOVE this game!
Sarah: *runs around to find joe*
Sarah: jooooeeee come out come out whereever you aaaarrreeee
Joe The Peacock: *runs to home base*
Joe The Peacock: *trips*
Joe The Peacock: *skins knee*
Joe The Peacock: *breaks tooth on pavement*
Joe The Peacock: *gets hit by bus*
Joe The Peacock: *has piano fall from sky and land on corpse*
Joe The Peacock: *has squished bits picked at by crows*
Joe The Peacock: *decomposes*
Sarah: *wins!*

THE RULES OF THE GYM
POSTED JANUARY 5, 2005

I have come up with some fairly simple and OH SO necessary guidelines for those of you who have decided to pay your membership dues and head to the mecca for pretention, the local gym. These rules are NOT hard to follow, and I think that anyone and everyone who's ever stepped inside a gym, even to deliver a newspaper, would agree with me on all of them.

First, **For The Guys:**

1. Stop ogling the girls. It is human nature to look at beautiful things, and the more beautiful they are, the more you want to look. But come on - show some respect. Get a look, go back to whatever it is you were doing.

2. Stop ogling the girls. Yes, it's THAT bad a problem that I have to say it again. Seriously. Stop. I know you're a beast and have only six brain cells, every one of them tasked with thinking about boobies. But for chrissake, have some decency, you dipthong. You're making them uncomfortable.

3. You're not in the UFC. I know you love buying Tapout and Affliction shirts at Target, but just because you can afford them doesn't mean you're now rollin' with their crew or whatever. There's no need to stare anyone down or act like a badass. You're not. And we're not in competition. You can nod and smile, it's okay - no one will think any less of you, I promise.

4. Flex in the mirror at home. Sure, you need the mirror to watch your performance as you lift. And yeah, it's really cool to see yourself as you are all pumped and stuff... but must you do a full pose-down in the presence of everyone there?

5. If you sweat a lot, carry a towel. Wipe down the equipment you use. It's just respectful. No one wants to lay in your salty perspiration - if we did, we'd just walk up to you, turn around, and rub our backs on you like a bear would a tree.

6. Wash your clothes once in a while. Please.

7. If you cannot bench 315 pounds, don't get your buddy to sit there and "spot" you while the ladies pass by just so you can rattle the plates. Really, this one isn't too huge a deal - you want to damage yourself, fine by me - you're an idiot and deserve the pain. It's just frustrating to sit there and watch you trying to showboat for a crowd what doesn't give a rat's posterior.

8. If you don't know how to use a machine or do a certain exercise - ask a staff member or someone doing the exercise to teach you a bit about the equipment and routine.

9. However, don't go asking in the middle of a set. It's called "lane courtesy" and it's a term borrowed from bowling. While someone is concentrating on working out, don't go bugging them.

10. Unless your name is Lee Haney, Arnold Schwarzenegger or Joe Weider, don't give unsolicited lifting advice - Unless you see someone who's risking SERIOUSLY hurting themselves. And even then, be polite about it.

11. Just because she's female does NOT mean she needs or wants you to spot her. Leave her alone and go back to your machine, Randy Pan.

12. The treadmill is NOT the place for a race. Eyes down or straight forward - let other people have what little privacy is afforded them by line-of-sight displays.

13. A Hypothetical situation: let's say there are 5 exercise machines in a group. For the purposes of this discussion, assume the leftmost is #1 and the rightmost is #5, with #2, #3 and #4 falling where you'd logically assume they would. If I am on machine #1 and there is NO ONE ELSE ON ANY OTHER MACHINE, do NOT get on machine #2. Especially if you haven't been following rule #6.

14. Wear a shirt, you puffed-up prima donna.

15. To clarify: Shirts consist of a torso and sleeves. If you've cut off half the torso to show your abs, you've failed at rule 14. Same if you've cut off the sleeves. And sure, sleeveless shirts are okay, but if you've EVER spent money on a spaghetti-thin single strip of cloth that goes over each shoulder and meets a 2" wide piece of fabric around your waist, you're a disgrace to humanity and should IMMEDIATELY proceed to the vasectomy clinic to save the human race from your spawn.

16. SHUT THE FUCK UP. No one cares what you bench, used to bench, will be benching, etc. and so forth. Write it in a journal at the gym, and if you really need to talk about it, read it aloud to yourself when you get home.

17. Grunting is understandable and ok - yelling is not. Quit trying to draw attention to your Herculean efforts by screaming like a banshee.

Now, because I am not one, I don't really know much about the rules for women as they apply to other women. But I do have a few guidelines for you gals.

So, **For the Girls:**

1. QUIT ENCOURAGING THE GUYS. Christ... this is the GYM. It's not a single's bar, quit treating it like one. I'm ESPECIALLY talking to those of you who laugh and flirt and flip your hair all over the place and blatantly poke your ass out when there's a guy present, and then get all pissy and angry when his eyes become glued to it. Wonder why the guys break rules # 1 and 2 in their list, making you feel so gosh darned uncomfortable? It's in part because you broke this rule. And while I'm at it,

2. NO MAKEUP. Now, I understand going to the gym after work or hanging with friends, and you have makeup on from that activity. That makes sense. I'm referring more to those who get all dolled up just to come to the gym - you come here specifically to get sweaty, and the last I checked, Maybelline has not a single product geared toward gym use.

3. Closed-toed shoes only, please. I know you're a girl, and as such, you're not supposed to stink, but your toes sweat just like mine do. Plus, just seeing your open toes in a gym makes me want to drop a weight on them.

4. Wear appropriately fitting workout clothing. Before you leave the house / locker room, look in the mirror. And again. Ask your friends. Ask them again. It's one thing to wear close-fitting workout-specific clothing and spandex. It's another thing entirely to wear those clothes one size too small because you think they tighten your flab and make you look like J-Lo from the back. They don't - if your ass and legs look like a chewed wad of bubblegum out of spandex, they look that way IN spandex.

And then, there are a few things that really apply to everyone in general.

1. Stop comparing yourself to everyone in the building. You are there for YOU. Who cares if you lift more or less than anyone else, if you run slower or faster, if you can swim farther and faster, etc.? If you're an athlete, relish in your own performance and quit grandstanding for those smaller / weaker / less fit than you. If you're a beginner or are just starting out, quit giving a shit about what other people may or may not be thinking about you right now - get in there and work your hardest.

2. Don't laugh at the fat guy / girl. They're there just like you, they're working just as hard as you. In almost every way possible, they're 10 times the athlete you are - not only did they show up to the gym to get better, they did it amidst snickering and comments from assholes like you - and that takes more guts than you'll EVER have.

3. Don't spit in the water fountain - spit in the sink in the locker room or in the trashcan.

4. Passing wind is a natural occurrence, especially if you are exerting yourself. If someone lets one or 2 fly, or burps a little while running, just grow up and let it slide. That said,

5. Don't go farting all over the place. If you ate something last night that didn't agree with you and your intestines are blowing like the foghorn of an icecutter, STAY HOME AND RUN AROUND THE BLOCK. If one's coming up and you can at all help it, sneak off to the corner or in the locker room and do it there.

6. Wipe down the equipment when you're done with it. And YES, you need to wipe off the bridge of the bike / cross training machine, you need to wipe off the display of the treadmill, you need to wipe off the handle grips, and you need to wipe off the bench / seat of whatever you were sitting on. All of these things are entailed in WIPING DOWN THE DAMN EQUIPMENT.

7. Be courteous with "working in". There are quite a few unspoken rules of the gym, and this used to be one of them until now. It goes like this:

- If you are alone and you see another solo person working out on equipment you need to use, wait until they are done with the set and ask nicely if they mind if you work in.
- If you are alone and there are 2 people on your needed equipment, it's a bit less kosher to work in. If you can help it, wait.
- If you are alone and there's 3 or more folks, just wait or use something else.
- If you are not alone, you don't work in unless invited. Do not ask. Not even if it's just one guy and every other piece of equipment is taken. It's one thing to be by yourself and work into a team's routine, but it's just wrong to impose a 2-person waiting period into someone's workout.

8. When you need to wait on equipment - do so at a close enough distance to indicate you're waiting on that machine but a far enough distance that you are not crowding whoever's currently on it. And don't stare at the person on it currently - it's uncomfortable enough knowing you're holding someone up, so don't make them feel like more of a jerk by making them think you mind.

9. When someone else is waiting on your machine - cut down on the lollygagging. If you're with a buddy, don't clown around between sets and make the person / people wait on your goofy ass. It's just rude.

10. Eat somewhere else. Don't eat your energy bar / granola nut cluster / peanut-butter-coated-pinecone-rolled-in-birdseed when you're on the equipment. Not only is it unsanitary for you to eat around other peoples' excretions, but whether you realize it or not, you're leaving crumbs and sticky crap everywhere. Stop.

11. Don't sing along with your walkman. If you're singing along with whatever shitty music they're piping over the speakers in the club, that's kinda annoying. But there's NOTHING more annoying than some dipshit trying to be the next Ashlee Simpson while listening to the song over their headphones. It's not karaoke, and you're liable to get a 5lb plate hurled at you.

I think everyone will agree that these rules are not out of line. In fact, I think everyone would agree that they are really very simple and direct. AND NECESSARY. Please share them with anyone you know that attends a gym or otherwise works out.

Thank you.

HOW TO ACTUALLY TALK TO ATHEISTS IF YOU'RE CHRISTIAN

POSTED MARCH 27, 2008

You know what's great?

Unicorns.

In fact, unicorns are freakin' AWESOME. And you know why? Because once you accept one into your life, they provide you with a lifetime membership into the Beer, Massage, Chocolate and Steak club. Have you not heard about the beer, massage and steak club? Well, let me tell you all about it - it doesn't matter if you don't like beer, or steak, or chocolate, or massages - whichever one you like, you get 24 hours a day for the rest of your life. And if you like all four or any combination of them, well... You're in luck! Because That's what the rest of your eternity will be - massages (happy ending or not, your choice), steak cooked just the way you want it, chocolate of any sort coated in any topping (or as a topping on anything you want), and any beer ever made or ever conceptualized, always on tap and never flat. And to get all of this, all you have to do is accept a unicorn into your life.

What? You don't believe in unicorns? Well, I assure you that they are very real! And I know this because I've accepted a unicorn into my life, and I trust that it will one day gain me admittance into the BMCS Club. How could I have accepted it into my life? Well, I just believe in them. And I trust they exist, because there are texts available to me that discuss them, as well as people available to teach me all about them. I mean, after all, with such great eternal rewards, why wouldn't you believe?

Okay, fine, don't believe in them - you're going to end up in the Pushups for Eternity club. That's where you have to do knuckle pushups on mounds of broken glass with Rush Limbaugh sitting on your back for all eternity. All because you won't accept a unicorn into your life.

Pretty silly, right? Well, my dear Christian friends, that's exactly how you sound to an Atheist.

Now, I know that the message of Christ's death and resurrection sin so that humans can spend eternity in Heaven isn't being sold by (most) Christians as steak and chocolate and unicorns. That's not my point. I do not want or intend to discuss the actual merits (or lack thereof) of the Christian faith. My point is simply that you're asking a group of people to believe in something they do not believe exists, for a reward they cannot prove they'll ever obtain.

And I'm sure that the first reaction that you, as a Christian, felt toward my example was distinctly negative. I'm sure your feelings ranged anywhere from marginal discomfort to outright repulsion; given the notion that your chosen religion - the belief system that you've based everything you know and do around - could be compared to unicorns, steak clubs and push-ups in hell, well... I think I'd be offended myself. But I assure you, it is not my intention to offend you. I have but one goal, and that is to illustrate a single fact:

What you're currently doing - cold-call witnessing and talking to strangers at the mall about your faith and standing on street corners holding signs that read "REPENT"? Well...

It's not working.

It's at this point that you're probably ready to just write me off as yet another heretic. And that's your right, and I certainly can't stop you. However, you need to understand that I didn't intend to upset you. If I did, however, I will not apologize. Instead, I'd ask that you give me a chance to explain my case by pointing out that your reaction to my comparison actually proves my point:

Confronting a person by attempting to convince them that everything they believe and know is wrong and that you are right is quite possibly the worst way on Earth to persuade them.

But I'm getting a bit ahead of myself. Before I illustrate how your current arsenal of witnessing tactics are not only ineffective, but are actively harming your religion and its' stance in an ever-growing public consisting of non-believers, I need to give you a bit of background information. And it's very important that, no matter how much you THINK you know these points, you pay attention to what I'm about to say, because the rapid swelling of the ranks of the Neo-Atheist movement have proven that what you think you know about them is absolutely, unequivocally, 100% WRONG.

First (and most important):

Atheists do not believe there is a God.

Yep, I'm using the definition of Atheism as my first point. And I do this not because I think you don't know what the word means, but because I'm fairly certain you've not yet realized the concept. When you witness to an Atheist, the person whom you are addressing does not believe there is a God - therefore, any information about God, Jesus, the holy trinity, the parting of oceans, great floods, and the creation of man falls on deaf ears.

To put this in more universal terms, you're attempting to sell a concept for which there is no proof other than the beliefs of men who have spread the word before it.

Whether you like it or not; whether you accept it or not, the fact remains - you're attempting to convince someone that something they cannot see, feel, hear, or otherwise partake of any empirical evidence of its existence, exists. Regardless of how much you believe in the story and how much it has affected your life and the lives of those around you, they do not.

This is important to understand. Until you do, you're arguing with a stop sign.

Atheists do not *need* to believe in a God.

We've established that you're communicating with a person who does not believe what you are sharing with them exists. You're asking them to buy on faith the fact that spending time in church, telling other people about this belief and living a life based on it may one day reward them. That's difficult enough. When you add to this the fact that you are not only selling them something you can't prove exists, but that they don't even want, things turn from difficult to impossible.

Atheists assert that the foundation for their actions and deeds lie in proven methods related to science and the establishment of undeniable fact. In this, they believe that they have everything they need to live a healthy, rewarding life.

They're not wrong - no more than you are in asserting that your faith in the tenets of Christianity are all you need to live your life. And that's the point. It's hard to convince a man with two working legs that he needs to buy a third, or worse, get rid of his and try the ones you have on. And when he looks for your version and cannot see, feel, touch or otherwise prove that they actually exist, he's going to completely dismiss you. It's not personal, it's just how we work as people.

You're no different. Think about the last time you heard about a confidence scheme on the news - twenty or thirty elderly couples were duped out of their life savings by a man promising investment returns or selling a product which did not exist. If you are honest with yourself, you'll admit that your very first reaction - the one you had before you caught yourself and realized that these poor people are victims - was "Holy cow, why didn't they research it before they invested?"

It's crazy to buy something you can't prove exists, isn't it?

Witnessing is interruption marketing.

It's unfortunate but true - just about every method of "witnessing" to non-believers equates to human spam. To start, I'll list just a few of the methods we all know about:

- Knocking on doors and talking to strangers about your new church / Christ / a church-related event designed to get new members
- Cold-calling people from the phone book / phone lists to invite them to your church / discuss Christ and his teachings
- Direct mail campaigns
- Holding up signs on street corners
- Walking up to strangers at Starbucks / the mall / anywhere besides your church
- Handing out literature (i.e. "Chick Tracts")

It's really easy to point these out as interruption marketing because... Well, they are. Honestly, they're low-hanging fruit. Easy targets, right? Probably unfair of me to just pick those and use them to illustrate the tactics all Christians use to witness. So let's talk about some techniques you may have employed that, to you, probably didn't come across as brazen as the above mentioned tactics:

- Have you ever asked a co-worker to attend church with you?
- Have you ever asked a stranger to attend church with you?
- Have you ever asked either of the above about their faith in God or Jesus Christ?
- Have you ever shifted a conversation that had nothing to do with church, Christ, or God into a conversation about any of the above?

When you did any of those things, did you notice an eye roll? Did the person groan? Did they shift in their seat and, at the very least, say they would go (or research what you just said, or give the matter some thought) and then never got back to you?

These techniques probably feel natural to you. They feel like you're sharing the good news of your faith and the joy it brings to your life, and it probably feels great to share that joy with others.

There's another organization / concept that those involved are equally as glad to share, because it's changed their life and they can't wait to spread that good news. This organization thrives on new members. Each individual collection of people works diligently to get more folks into the stable, because the larger they grow, the more they thrive and the farther they can spread the word of this great, life-changing group.

Surely, you know who I'm talking about. It's called Amway.

Now, before you get up in arms, I did NOT just compare your belief in God and Jesus to selling cleaners and credit cards and pre-paid cellphones. But I did, however, compare your technique of spreading the word about your belief to the technique of spreading the word about Amway.

Again, try to put yourself outside of your own perspective and into the shoes of your intended audience. You're interrupting their time and space to bring them a message you feel is important. And sure, you have the right to choose your faith and the right to free speech, but as G. K. Chesterton said, to have a right to do a thing is not at all the same as to be right in doing it. And ultimately, "You need to hear this because I need to say it" is the ultimate in self-serving causes... And if you're serving yourself, you certainly aren't serving God.

So. You're dealing with an audience that doesn't believe that what you want to share with them even exists. They don't need it. They don't want to hear about it. Your attempts to share it with them are seen largely as annoying or, at the very least, an interruption in their day. And the result of these tactics is a massive swelling of the ranks of the "New Atheist Movement" (Neo-Atheism) in America and abroad; a movement that has been covered in great detail and has caused great concern within all denominations of the Christian church.

What to do, what to do...

Well, considering the facts, you've really only got two choices. The first is to just keep doing what you're doing. After all, it worked in the past. Your church regularly asks you to do it. It feels good to witness, and at the very end of the day, you can justify a few "lost sheep" if you gave it your best effort, right?

Well... If you're fine with that - if screaming your message through a megaphone and praying (literally) that someone hears you - is okay with you, well... Look forward to staying as frustrated as you are now (if not more so). Stay persistent, right?

To quote Seth Godin, quite possibly the most brilliant modern marketing guru alive today:

> Persistence isn't using the same tactics over and over. That's just annoying. Persistence is having the same goal over and over.

And the goal is to get people to follow the teachings of Christ and live a Christ-like life, right? Well, telling them to do so over and over again in ways that disrespect their time and personal space is nothing more than simple badgering. It might FEEL like you're doing the right thing, but as we all know, feeling like you're doing work, and actually getting work done are two different things. But there's something you can do that will bring you far closer to your goal than just talking and hoping:

Become the prototype.
Live the example, and let your actions spread the message. Get people to see the merit in the life you live and adopt your practices. Let's follow two scenarios - one for each path you can take.

Using the traditional, human-spam model of witnessing, you use interruption-marketing techniques to spread the word about your faith. Because you are Christian, and because you are employing techniques that are unwelcome and unwanted, you communicate the following through your actions:

- Christians would rather be correct than listen to differing opinion.
- Christians do not respect the personal space (mentally and physically) of non-believers.
- Christians feel they are superior to non-believers because they have salvation.
- Christians would rather rely on faith as evidence than rely on fact.

All of these are going to lose your audience. Period.

And as I said before, if you're fine with that - if you're okay with the notion that saying the words and annoying or inconveniencing people with your methods of spreading what is supposed to be a message of brotherhood, unity, respect and love... Well, let's just say that you might need to evaluate the motives behind your actions, for they couldn't possibly be borne of love, respect or brotherhood.

Did Jesus ever hand out a pamphlet about himself? Did he ever tap people on the shoulder and say "Hey, have you heard the good news about me?" No... Not according to any of the literature I've ever read... And I've read a lot of it.

No one pays attention to magazine ads and billboards. People use TiVo to skip commercials on television. There are any number of email spam filters available to prevent just that sort of communication from inflicting itself on you digitally. In every segment - including yours - interruption techniques fail.

Considering your audience's opinion that you are infringing on their freedom to choose not to follow your faith, and their personal space with selling tales of what they consider to be mythical tales and arguments based on belief, you've lost before you've begun... And to go ahead with that program anyway implies a selfishness that only further harms your cause.

It's time for a new tack.

If I am the target for your message, I'm going to be far more receptive to one that incorporates respect for my time and my belief (or lack thereof). I will probably dismiss, as you do, the one which interrupts my routine and infringes on my time to tell me you're right and that everything I have spent years figuring out and pondering and basing my life and views around is wrong.

The second scenario, using my proposed example of witnessing by example, you employ the exact methods that Christ himself used to bring people in line with a respect and love based lifestyle. Live the teachings of your faith and sway action by your deeds. It may not feel like it's as effective as talking and handing out literature - but the rational being will concede that that stuff has already failed everywhere it's being employed. And ultimately, living the example may not SEEM like it's as much work as hitting the street to hold posters or cold-call people to invite them to your church... But it's far less intrusive and far more effective in the long run.

Make no mistake - this is NOT giving up on saving souls or witnessing. It's a changing of tactics, one which requires diligence in action, commitment to the lifestyle, and confidence that those around you are taking notice.

Spreading the 'good news' is fine... But it's hardly news at this point, and there's nothing good about not respecting my right to be who I am. And I can't guarantee or even suggest you'll convert everyone you meet with this new tact. But obviously, judging by the level of concern within all denominations of the rapidly spreading New Atheism, what you're doing isn't working the way you think it should. In fact, it's doing more to push people toward the movement you're fighting so hard against. That doesn't seem like a good plan to me.

Eventually, living the example will entice someone who is paying attention to ask you your motives, or at the very least, inquire about the specific actions you're undertaking (such as volunteering for community service, feeding the hungry at a shelter, working with Habitat for Humanity, etcetera). And when they do, you'll have to engage them in conversation about your faith.

When you do, you should know that electing to enter into conversation with an Atheist equipped with your faith and scripture as tools is akin to electing to explore the ocean with a torch. The equipment you've chosen simply will not work in that environment. You can't blame the environment - after all, it is what it is, and you chose to go there.

So, here are a few pointers:

- Don't bring it up first.
- If you do bring it up first, and the other person is disinterested or reacts negatively, just let it go.
- If the conversation does continue, remember that respect is paramount. You're not right, and I'm not wrong - you simply have faith in something I do not. That's not a weakness on my part, even when you consider it a strength on your part.
- The faith you have? It's belief in the absence of proof or fact. That's the definition of faith. So, don't offer belief as evidence. You can, however, offer it as motive. "I believe in God" does not prove that God exists. "I volunteer at hunger shelters because I believe in God" does prove that you have a motive for your actions.
- You will not sway an Atheist with promises of eternal reward or threat of eternal damnation. You can't point to heaven or hell on a map, so there's no evidence of their existence. Furthermore, bribery and intimidation are the tools of those who seek power, not those who seek redemption.
- The Bible is not regarded as the word of God to an Atheist. It's a book written by men. Using it as evidence or proof of anything more than your motives for doing what you do is going to be dismissed.

Even if the conversation never ensues, it's a universal truth that action speaks louder than words. People DO take notice of those who act in accordance with a respect and love based lifestyle. They feel good when they see a person helping another person - and in fact, it makes them want to help out themselves. One need only look at the total figures of collected donations for the victims of Hurricane Katrina and the World Trade Center attacks to see this in action. Deed follows deed. Tell a person what to do, and you may get them to do it... Make them want to do it, and it'll get done, no matter what.

Ultimately, salvation has very little to do with saying the words "I believe Jesus Christ is the son of God and died for my sins." There are many, many people - some of whom hold the highest offices in the American government - who say this, and then go on to live lives that, by any account, are not at all Christ-like. How many people in your church have spent a week engaging in debauchery and other 'sinful' behaviors, only to appear in church on Sunday, ready to ask forgiveness for what they've done? And how many go right back out and do it again? How are these people better than those who live good lives and help their neighbor and further advance brotherhood and unity... But don't believe in God?

Which of these two types of people would you rather point to and say, "I taught them that?"

If you're more interested in lip service than in actually influencing people to live better lives, I'd say you need to revisit that book you proclaim to live by and, you know...

...Actually read it.

TEN ARGUMENTS AGAINST SAME-SEX MARRIAGES (AND HOW STUPID THEY ARE)

POSTED JUNE 17, 2008

So, California has joined Massachusetts in granting marriage licenses for same sex couples.

Surely, this is the end of the world as we straight folks know it. And thank God, because I'm really getting tired of the one we've been living in.

It makes NO SENSE to me - a heterosexual male married to a heterosexual female - why two people of any gender who decide they trust one another enough to share assets and benefits can't form a legal union in order to do so. But wait, the bible says... And what about the kids... And, if we allow this, won't men be marrying their dogs in five years...

Come on. This is nonsense.

Recently, I've been getting a TON of emails marked with the tell-tale "FW:" from right-wing acquaintances and family members that quote wholesale the Ten Arguments Against Gay Marriage website. I've been deluged by these zealots who, rather than discuss things intelligently, find it easier to just forward via email the concepts and ideas of people who think just like them... That is, not at all.

It is my intention to rip asunder these ridiculous arguments.

Note: this article doesn't cover the arguments against homosexuality, because frankly, no one's going to change someone's mind regarding love and monogamy if they can't already see that two people loving one another is two people loving one another, regardless of the number of penises involved. Zero, one, or two, it's just love.

So here you go, my dissection of those ridiculous ten arguments:

* * *

Argument #1: *The implications for children in a world of decaying families are profound.*

Oh you are so right. Two men raising a child in a home where rules are obeyed and respect for all people is taught is SO MUCH WORSE for the structure of family-based society than a husband who cheats on his wife, or who beats the kids, or who simply doesn't care about them.

Saying that the "family" is a cohesive unit solely on the merit that the union of a man and a woman resulted in offspring is somewhat akin to saying that a baseball team is solid based on the fact that there are nine guys on the field.

It's not the structure that counts... It's the contents of the framework. If there were a woman batting .400 against fast-pitching males, don't even pretend that the Yankees wouldn't pay her 22 million over five years to wear the pinstripes - regardless of the all-male history and composition of Major League Baseball.

If two men or two women can provide a stable, loving home for a child, WHO THE HELL ARE YOU to forbid them from being able to do so? You'd rather the child languish in the hellhole that most orphanages and shelters have become?

You'd rather they work their way through the hit-or-miss foster system in this country, only to become unstable, distrustful adults who are far more likely to commit crimes involving violence against another person?

Just ask yourself one question - if you knew a child was being battered by a mother and father, and you knew a same-sex couple who would be willing to take that child in and raise it and give it a loving home, would you rather it stay with the "family" based on the fact that it's a union between a man and a woman?

If the answer is anything other than "hell no," you honestly need to reevaluate your faith and why you proclaim to have it.

Argument #2: *The introduction of legalized gay marriages will lead inexorably to polygamy and other alternatives to one-man, one-woman unions.*

Boy, this sounds familiar... What do they call this? You know, in Philosophy 101 in college, they have this list of logical fallacies... This one is, like, a greased incline or---

No wait - slippery slope. That's it.

I cannot think of a more ridiculous argument against allowing two people to share the benefits and title of marriage than this. If we amend the current state of thinking to include the union between to people to be simply that - a union between TWO PEOPLE - then the next thing you know, we're going to amend it to be between THREE people, and then FOUR, and then a goat might enter the picture...
Come on. Wake up. Just because a concept evolves to the societal standards does not mean that suddenly the standards will change to force the concept to adhere to the new standard. It doesn't work that way - in fact, it works the OTHER way. The second you open the door for a group of people to finally enjoy the benefits they're rightfully entitled

to, they tend to become quite guarded and protective of those benefits. They actually become defenders of that which they have earned.

Argument #3: *An even greater objective of the homosexual movement is to end the state's compelling interest in marital relationships altogether.*

Is that so... There's an objective of the homosexual movement to earn a right to benefits and tax incentives by forming a union between consenting adults, and then they're going to just about-face on the whole concept altogether and get rid of it?

Is that how that works?

I bet they don't even love each other. All those videos and pictures of two women or two men standing hand-in-hand on the courtyard steps of the counties and states which now allow same-sex unions, crying their eyes out with joy that they now get to have a legally-recognized union... Those are actors. Gay actors. They're just fucking with us.

Why would anyone do this? I mean, honestly... If you want to get right down to it, marriage as a legal (not religious, LEGAL) union is designed to incorporate tax breaks and asset protection to encourage procreation.

That's right. God and the government want to save you money so you can have some babies.

From AmericanCatholic.org:
The very purpose of marriage is to develop union between husband and wife and to bear and raise children. In more technical language, we call those two purposes unitive and procreative.

God does not will that all married couples have children, as we know, and we don't understand why. But our tradition of listening to God, revealed in Scripture, in the experience of the Church and all creation, tells us that married couples need to be open to bearing and raising children.

But somehow, childless couples are getting the same protection and rights as couples WITH children! THIS IS BLASPHEMY! HOLY FUCKING SHIT!

SO why the hell aren't Christians everywhere going apeshit over childless man/woman marriages? Could it be... Like... Uh...

Seriously. I have no snarky comment for this one. No joke, no witticism. I just don't get it.

Argument #4: *With the legalization of homosexual marriage, every public school in the nation will be required to teach that this perversion is the moral equivalent of traditional marriage between a man and a woman.*

It IS the moral equivalent of traditional marriage between a man and a woman, because morals enter into marriage about the same amount as they enter into making a peanut butter and jelly sandwich.

There is no moral reason for marriage in the eyes of the LAW.

There is only a contractual business agreement between two consenting adults (who, currently, have to be male and female equally).

Same as speeding tickets, copyright law, and curfews. No morals. Just bounds and requirements. Like it or not, Christians, when a justice of the peace can perform a ceremony that results in the same contractual bounds as a

48

priest, it's no longer a religious ceremony. It's just your preference that a man (or woman, for you more progressive types) of the cloth say the words.

And, rather than compel schools across the nation to teach morality, how about we just ask them to knock off the moral lessons altogether and stick to science, maths and humanities? Don't morals start in the home?

If they don't for you, you're part of the reason most teachers hate their jobs.

Argument #5: *From that point forward, courts will not be able to favor a traditional family involving one man and one woman over a homosexual couple in matters of adoption.*

Good.

From my response to #1, repeated here for the lazy:

Just ask yourself one question - if you knew a child was being battered by a mother and father, and you knew a same-sex couple who would be willing to take that child in and raise it and give it a loving home, would you rather it stay with the "family" based on the fact that it's a union between a man and a woman?

And again, If the answer is anything other than "hell no," you honestly need to reevaluate your faith in this Jesus guy and why you proclaim to have it.

Argument #6: *Foster-care parents will be required to undergo "sensitivity training" to rid them of bias in favor of traditional marriage, and will have to affirm homosexuality in children and teens.*

Right, just like they have to undergo "sensitivity training" to rid themselves of racial or gender bias, and have to affirm equality on both counts in children they take in.

You've obviously not run into many foster-care parents. It just so happens, however, that my wife and I have done all the groundwork to become foster-care parents (because we never intend to procreate - which makes us blasphemers per argument #3). We feel that procreation in light of the fact that there's a ton of children at the pound waiting for someone to just take a damn interest in them is pretty fucking selfish.

There, my hat's been thrown into that little ring.

Anyway, at no point during the application process were we required to undergo any sort of sensitivity training whatsoever. At no point were we required to prove that we don't harbor any sort of gender or racial bias. At no point were my college credentials (or lack thereof) called into question. All they really cared about was criminal record and salary. Did we seem stable? Yup.

That's all it took.

So, supposing my little ruse works, all I need now is for the state to give me a little black kid so I can burn him with cigarettes. Or, a little girl, so I can constantly scream at her and remind her how inferior she is to the superior male gender. I can now totally fuck up any kids under my care and unleash them onto society, because my wife and I are a male/female couple and SEEM stable.

Guess what folks? That shit happens EVERY SINGLE DAY. And I know it does, first hand. I won't go into how or why, but what you need to take from this is that the foster care system in America is fundamentally broken - the very last thing we should give a shit about is the concept of same-gender unions and how they impact the psyche of a foster kid.

Argument #7: *How about the impact on Social Security if there are millions of new dependents that will be entitled to survivor benefits?*

Ah, there it is... The first "G" in the three tenets of Christianity - Gold (the other two are God and Glory).

"What's going to happen to MY MONEY when them faggots is allowed to marry?" Well, you yokel, how about you take a good look at what's happening to it RIGHT NOW?

This is precisely the kind of argument that cripples America, and as a consequence, our progress toward getting off this planet and out into the solar system so we can fly cool starships. It's not the interest-free loans that the past four administrations (including Clinton's, so don't go thinking I'm picking on Republicans) have given themselves based on the Social Security reserves. It's not the complete mismanagement of the actual fund itself, with payouts going to undeserving early pullers who are drawing more than they put in.

No. It's the gays.

Gay people are going to be the death of Social Security when they're allowed the same rights as us straights! Just you watch! Actually, Social Security is doomed, regardless of whom we allow to get married.

Argument #8: *Marriage among homosexuals will spread throughout the world, just as pornography did after the Nixon Commission declared obscene material "beneficial" to mankind.*

"The point is that numerous leaders in other nations are watching to see how we will handle the issue of homosexuality and marriage."

You're right, there'll be a worldwide epidemic of governments opening the concept of marriage to include same-sex marriages. Gee... How horrible.

So what would fix this one? If America allowed same-sex marriage, but no other country on earth did? Would that fix it? Of course not... All this argument is doing is saying "one will lead to another!" And it's entirely right - if America can open its' collective mind to allow for two consenting adults who intend to remain monogamous, regardless of gender, then why shouldn't Britain, or France, or any other nation? Why would this be a bad thing in and of itself?

Simply the number of marriages on record worldwide? Is 2 million gay marriages worse than one million? It's not like the fact that homosexuals can now form a legal union is going to go turning otherwise straight people gay... It's just going to allow individuals of the same sex who want to enter into that agreement to be able to do so. Nothing more.

Don't worry, it's not a gay virus. It's just a new idea entering a closed mind. I know it feels the same to you, but give it a chance.

Argument #9: *"Perhaps most important, the spread of the Gospel of Jesus Christ will be severely curtailed. The family has been God's primary vehicle for evangelism since the beginning."*

This is basically saying "My belief system doesn't allow for homosexual marriage, and if homosexual marriage is allowed, then my belief system loses a foothold in societal control."

If your belief system doesn't allow for the possibility that a) two people of the same gender can't have an unyielding love for one another and b) that they want to form a union based on that love such that one can provide for the other, share health benefits, and have their property and assets protected under the same laws that protect male/female unions... Well, your belief system isn't really based on love and logic, now is it? And if it lacks those two cornerstones of the human condition, it's not much of a belief system.

Additionally, I challenge you to find one - JUST ONE - verse in the bible (or any religious text) where Jesus Christ speaks out against the union or bond between people of the same gender.

Just one.

I'll save you the trouble: you won't find it. What you will find are overly general sentiments advocating and supporting the existing laws of God, which, previous to the New Testament included human-interpreted (or human-invented-with-God's-name-attached) laws which spoke against homosexuals.

Borrowing from ReligiousTolerance.org (which is a fantastic site, by the way):

> In Matthew 19:3-12 and Mark 10:2-12, Jesus supports the concept that God made a man and a woman so that they could marry. He is quoted as saying in both Gospels: "What therefore God hath joined together, let not man put asunder." Also, in Matthew 5:17-18, after the Sermon on the Mount, Jesus said: "Think not that I am come to destroy the law, or the prophets: I am not come to destroy, but to fulfill. For verily I say unto you, Till heaven and earth pass, one jot or one tittle shall in no wise pass from the law, till all be fulfilled."

That's pretty much it - Jesus supported and advocated the laws of God. But in this, Jesus would then be advocating that no man partake of swine (read: no bacon! OH THE HORROR) or other dirty animals; that we humans only eat fish on Friday; and that a man who steals from another man should have his hand cut off (yep, the Old Testament put God's seal of approval on Hammurabi's Code).

But wait, didn't Jesus cleanse the animals? And didn't Jesus advocate a code of morality into the code of laws (love thy neighbor and all that yakkity-yak)? In fact, didn't Jesus Christ FUNDAMENTALLY alter the core of theological law as professed by scribes recording the word of God?

As good a question as that might be, the real question is: if your lord and savior, Jesus Christ - the son of God - were here on this Earth today, would he speak out against homosexual unions? Would he even have an opinion on the sanctity of court-approved business relationships between consenting adults for tax and insurance benefit?

Probably not.

Argument #10: *"The culture war will be over, and I fear, the world may soon become 'as it was in the days of Noah' (Matthew 24:37, NIV)."*

I don't get this argument. Not just this one line, but the whole damn thing. I think it was put here just to round the list out to ten and serve the author's selfish need to proclaim just how into God he and his wife are. Honestly, this whole notion of a "culture war" between Christians and non-Christians bothers me. Why is it that the majority of the non-religious culture is content to just be themselves and let others be themselves, while the Christian side insists on "winning" this "culture war" by inflicting themselves upon those who are not them?

And more so, why do they think they - regardless of denomination - are going to win any points with a non-Christian when they can't even settle some of the most basic arguments of Christianity amongst themselves? Methodists arguing with Baptists, Lutherans yelling at Presbyterians, Catholics yelling at... Well, everyone... Why would I want to actively join an internal war amongst Christians? Can't I just let you guys bicker about it amongst yourselves while I sit at home and watch some football on Sunday?

At the very least, if you're going to insist on interrupting me with your religious marketing, do so respectfully, go back and read the chapter "How To Actually Talk To Atheists If You're Christian".

* * *

Let's just be honest here - people are against same-sex marriage for the same reasons they were against the right for women to vote, or for black men to own land, or for colonists to exercise their rights to bear arms and free themselves from unjust taxation... It upsets the status quo. It doesn't jive with the way they know the world. It forces logic into a head full of belief.

Basically, it forces them to look directly into the bright light of social progress... And when your eyes have been shut for so long, it's uncomfortable.

I have my own personal predilections that some would call closed-minded - and they are. I'm not perfect. None of us are. And that's precisely why we're not qualified to go passing judgment on and imposing our will upon the lives of others.

What's it to you that two dudes or two chicks want to make sure their partners are covered under the healthcare benefits they work hard to keep? You get to put your wife or husband on your policies... Can't they?

Or is your love for one another somehow more valid than theirs?

All I know is that I know several homosexual couples who have told me they plan to make the trek to California this summer to get hitched, and I've read quite a few articles on the subject. Not once have I heard statements like "she rooked me into getting hitched" or "I guess I'll marry her because I knocked her up and, like, it's just right, you know?"

These people I see on TV lining up - LINING UP!!!! - to get married after five, ten, twenty years of being together... They're crying with joy. They're so damn happy that, finally, all the years of knowing what they know about one another - that they love one another - are finally going to be legally sanctioned.

Meanwhile, you've got men going out for one last hot night filled with strippers and booze before they "latch on the ol' ball and chain." You've got women acting like complete whores the night before a wedding, throwing themselves all over men at bars at bachelorette parties because "This is their last night of freedom." You've got married governors hiring sex workers on the taxpayer's dime to fulfill dirty fantasies, or tapping their foot in restroom stalls for a little man-on-man play. I personally know fourteen married men - FOURTEEN - who go to strip clubs on Saturdays and then to church on Sunday to repent.

And that's the much-cherished sanctity of marriage that gets bandied about in the halls of state congress?

The day every single Christian on this planet begins honoring and cherishing their mate, I might listen to ill-founded belief-based arguments against legal unions for same-sex couples.

Mind you, I said "might." I can't promise anything... It's not like I can just turn off logic.

ONLY YOU CAN PREVENT BULLSHIT EMAIL FORWARDS, "SWIFFER-WILL-KILL-YOUR-PUPPY" EDITION

POSTED DECEMBER 16, 2008

Folks, let me share with you a little bit of information that, until this morning, I thought everyone knew:

It's 2008. *[note: it's 2013 now, and not much has changed...]*

I know, right? There's a lot of stupid people out there, but even the most functionally retarded among them knows by December 16 that they've been living almost an entire year in 2008. That's 19 years after Tim Berners-Lee invented the world wide web, 39 years after the invention of the internet in general, and a whopping 172 years after Charles Babbage invented the first computer, the analytical engine. In 2008, there are more computers than there are people in this nation, and almost all of them are connected to the internet - as are cell phones, music players, wrist watches... There are even toasters and alarm clocks that are connected to the internet.

So why the FUCK don't people use these miracles of modern ingenuity to check Snopes.com whenever a hyperbolic, exclamation-mark filled email warns them about complete bullshit instead of just hitting the stupid "Forward" button?

The latest one to hit my inbox? The "Swiffer Wetjet Will Kill Your Puppy In The Liver!" email:

Subject: FW: SWIFFER WETJET WARNING
From: [Name Withheld]

-------Original Message-------

I checked with snoopes [sic] this one is true.
Take care of your pets
HV
[note from me - whoever "HV" was on the original chain, he or she is a FUCKING LIAR.]

-----Inline Message Follows-----

Subject: SWIFFER WETJET

Recently someone had to have their 5-year old German Shepherd dog put down due

To liver failure. The dog was completely healthy until

A few weeks ago, so they

Had a necropsy done to see what the cause was. The
Liver levels were
Unbelievable, as if the d og had ingested poison of
Some kind. The dog is kept
Inside, and when he's outside, someone's with him, so
The idea of him
Getting into something unknown was hard to believe..

My neighbor started going through all the items in the
House. When he got to
The Swiffer Wetjet, he noticed, in very tiny print, a
Warning which stated
'may be harmful to small children and animals.' He

Called the company to
Ask what the contents of the cleaning agent are and
Was astounded to find out
That antifreeze is one of the ingredients (actually,
He was told it's a
Compound which is one molecule away from antifreeze).
Therefore , just by the
Dog walking on the floor cleaned with the solution,
Then lickin g its=2 0own paws,
It ingested enough of the solution to destroy its
Liver..
Soon after his dog's death, his housekeepers' two cats
Also died of
Liver failure. They both used the Swiffer Wetjet for
Quick cleanups on their
Floors. Necropsies weren't done on the cats, so they
Couldn't file a
Lawsuit, but he asked that we spread the word to as
Many people as possible so
They don't lose
Their animals.

This is equally harmful to babies and small children
That play on the floor a
Lot and put their fingers in their mouths a lot.

PLEASE, EVEN IF YOU DO NOT HAVE BABIES,
SMALL CHILDREN
OR OWN A PET;
PLEASE FORWARD THIS ON! YOU MAY NOT HAVE
ANY
CHILDREN
OR PETS BUT SOME OF YOU
HAVE FRIENDS OR FAMILY WITH PETS AND ALSO
FAMILIES
WITH GRANDCHILDREN AND GREAT
GRANDCHILDREN

(Sorry for the word wrapping. It came to me that way, and I'm not about to go copy-edit this hunk of filth.)

Now, Snopes has done a fine job of dissecting this email's validity based on their proven methods (anecdotal evidence, no hard facts, no case records, statements from Proctor & Gamble and the ASPCA, etc.). But there's one aspect they didn't go into (probably because they're nice) that I would like to explore a bit (probably because I'm not nice).

Basic high school chemistry teaches us that "one molecule away from [x]" is completely meaningless. It's purely semantic how closely related one molecule is to another, and it's only worrisome based on your brain's comprehension of English and what words mean. IT HAS NOTHING TO DO WITH ACTUAL SCIENCE

Saying that Swiffer WetJet cleaning solution is "one molecule away from anti-freeze - so it'll kill your pet like anti-freeze" is like saying that table salt is one atom away from chlorine, so if you spill it on your shirt, it'll bleach it white. It's not just borderline retarded, it's full-blown stupid. Only in a nation full of dummies could a statement like that even remotely bother anyone.

Think I'm being too hard on the poor animal lovers who fell for this? Think that I am insisting that any level of understanding in a specialized field for the general populace is unfair? Well, you're a dummy too.

Look, I write stupid books about myself for a living. I don't know jack fucking shit about chemistry. But I do understand what atoms are, what molecules are and how, when a mommy atom and a daddy atom love each other very much, they bond and form a substance, and that some substances in the world share similar building agents as others. Which means that me, an untrained non-expert who sat through high school chemistry class, understands that just because substances share root atoms doesn't make them the same (or even nearly the same... The same atom which makes a Hydrogen bomb go "BOOM" is found in your drinking water).

A basic level of understanding of how things work is not too much to ask of people. If you know how to press the "forward" button in your email client, you should also know how to Google shit. You don't even have to know the name Snopes to find it with a basic search for "Swiffer WetJet pets".

I sent out an email to the 300 or so people whose email addresses appeared in the chain of the conversation. It was worded civilly and explained the points I made above, but nicely. It also requested that everyone in the chain pass the information backward to everyone they've sent the email to. I stopped short of asking whoever "HV" was to go choke on a cock and die for lying to everyone the way they did.

What I'd ask of you, kind reader, is that you begin doing the same. Begin emailing anyone and everyone who forwards you nonsense. Let them know that, with the wildfire of email misinformation spreading as it does, that you've decided to become the fire marshal. Give them sources to check, call them on their bullshit if they say they checked them, and politely embarrass them into knocking this shit off (feel free to use letmegooglethatforyou.com's embarrassing Google forwarder. I love it and use it often).

I don't mind the email. I like contact with people. I don't consider it "spam." I do, however, consider it insulting and lazy that people claiming to care enough to pass this shit along, but don't ACTUALLY care enough to research the material and find out if, at the VERY least, they've been exposing their pet to danger all this time so maybe if something does crop up, they can let the vet know.

GARBAGE IN, GARBAGE OUT

POSTED JULY 13, 2009

I had a conversation this weekend with a friend of mine who just can't seem to turn the corner in terms of his career. He too wants to be a designer of things, specifically on the web. And since I do that, he was talking to me about his path and the things he is doing to advance along it.

I'll save you the two-hour transcript: the answer is "absolutely nothing."

He doesn't read Smashing Magazine, Ajaxian, 486 Berea Street, A List Apart, PSDTuts, or even PhotoshopDisasters to see how things SHOULDN'T be done. He owns a book on Photoshop and one on Flash - no design books (or even books with pretty pictures), no catalogs from photography houses or design shops. No magazine subscriptions to HOW or Communication Arts. I asked him if he knew what font Apple used before switching to Myriad, and his answer was a question: "Where would I even find that out?" He couldn't even determine the difference between a typeface and a logo with some text illustrated in.

His pedigree? Atlanta Art Institute. He took classes in illustration. He has taken no classes in design or layout and doesn't know the difference between the two. His "studio" is his living room in his apartment - lots of illustrations he's done on the wall, but nothing regarding layout or design, just character sketches and some paintings of flowers.

There's an old programming axiom: GIGO. Garbage In, Garbage Out.

The basic premise is you get out of things what you put into them. Just like making a cake (chocolate, even): If you start with high quality ingredients, you end with a high quality cake. If, instead, you substitute shit for sugar, you get a cake that tastes... Well, pretty bad, I'm sure. I'm not willing to test it.

This is true everywhere, in all aspects of life. Surround yourself with confrontational people, you'll be confrontational. Eat unhealthy food, you'll be unhealthy. Hate breeds hate, ignorance breeds ignorance, etcetera. And where my friend is concerned, I feel he's worse than the person who experiments by replacing sugar with shit in his cake... He doesn't even know where to find recipes for cakes to experiment with.

This is inexcusable. I don't hate the guy, and I don't think less of him as a person... But I absolutely feel no pity whatsoever. Somehow, I found the resources I needed to find to learn the things I needed to learn to do the things I've done, and there's not a day that goes by that I don't find a brand new one.

It's simple: wanting to do or be something is not the same as doing or being it. You can want all you want - in fact, it's the one thing humans can do to an unlimited degree, as there's no fatigue associated with desire. But I'd argue that there's a clear difference between wanting to *be called* a designer and *being* a designer, and it all begins with the actions you take to reach your goal.

The same goes with being a writer, or being a football player, or getting in shape, or anything else. If your path is paved with effort, you'll get where you want to go. If it's paved with words, you're just going to end up stuck on the side of the road with a continual string of flat tires.

Reading a book on Photoshop and thinking it'll make you a great designer is no different than reading the instruction manual for a hammer and thinking that'll make you a great carpenter, or watching a video on how to sharpen a pencil and thinking you're now ready to be the next Stephen King. The art is not the tool.

Ingest healthy food and be healthy. Research successful designers and good design, and be a good designer and make good designs. Study great writing and produce great writing. Or, keep talking about how much you wish you were what you think you want to be and get unflatteringly honest blog posts written about you.

FOR THE LADIES: GETTING KICKED IN THE BALLS

POSTED OCTOBER 26, 2009

This post is primarily for the ladies out there.

The reason it's for the ladies is because men already know all of this stuff. They've known it since the age of six of so. It's a constant part of our consciousness. It never leaves our minds, ever. It's pervasive to the point of being an immediate physical reaction that precludes thought and logic... Anytime anything approaches any area even remotely near our twig and berries, we immediately go into "guard" position.

But women just don't get it. They don't quite understand why the pain of being racked is such that it deserves this sort of attention. And the hard part of this is that it's several reasons packed into one, all of which aren't very easily described. But I'm going to try.

Of course, there's the **embarrassment factor**. Contact was just made with our unmentionables. A violation has just taken place. Aside from the immediate and lasting impact of the actual pain, there's been an emasculation, and we don't like it. That's our BOYS. You don't touch our boys... Unless it's a mutually agreed-upon exchange involving intimate contact, and even then, you do it GENTLY.

Then, there's **the generational impact**. It's instinctive to men to protect the progenitor of future generations, and when we get racked, there's a base animal rage that flows through us in reaction to the possibility that we may have just lost our "go juice," so to speak. It's primal, and it's uncontrollable, and if we could, we'd immediately kill the individual who just attempted to kill the millions upon millions of unborn lives packaged in our danglies.

But we can't, because **it hurts in a way that nothing else has ever hurt, ever**. I won't go so far as to say it's the most excruciating pain I've ever felt... Breaking a limb (or several), or pulling a muscle / ligament from the bone, or yes, childbirth, might have higher pain thresholds. But the worst part of the pain from being racked isn't the physical sensation of pain, it's the complete shutdown of the rest of our entire bodies.

The sensation is akin to being punched in the stomach... But coupled with the inability to breathe and the black hole that just formed in the area of impact, there is a dull, throbbing pain deep within our bodies. If you asked any man to point directly to where it hurt, and they were capable of moving and/or speaking at that moment, you'd get a pointer to somewhere between the nads and the small of the back. And the pain actually varies based on the type of impact. The following guide assumes no puncture or laceration, with a force insufficient to permanently incapacitate the area:

The full-blown nutshot: This is full contact, full force on both orbs. The pain is severe, but distributed. The body shuts down. The lungs lose air. The throat can only groan. The mind concentrates immediately on the affected area.
- **Pain index:** 8
- **Time of incapacity:** 45-60 seconds
- **Lasting pain:** 5-7 minutes for immediate tenderness, dull aches for an hour

The single-nut slammer: This is full contact, full force on one orb. The pain is severe, concentrated to a single roundy.

As with the full-blown nutshot, the body shuts down, you can't breathe or talk. But the pain is actually more severe, being in just the single bobbly.

- **Pain index:** 9
- **Time of incapacity:** 60-120 seconds, depending on force
- **Lasting pain:** an hour or more for immediate tenderness, dull aches for 2 hours after

The glancing blow: BY FAR the worst of the three. You'd think hitting both boys would be the worst, but no. The slight clipping of a buckeye is, without a doubt, the worst pain a man can feel. It's crippling, and for reasons you'd never expect - we can still move; we're not completely incapacitated like the full-blown nutshot or single-nut slammer. But I'm fucked if I know why I'd want to, because every single muscle and nerve ending is now tied directly to that ball. If I so much as flex my index finger, I feel pain in the area. It's not dull, it's VERY sharp and piercing. It's almost like being stabbed. A completely different sensation, and it destroys the rest of your day.

- **Pain index:** It goes to 11
- **Time of incapacity:** hard to articulate. Not incapacitated like the other two injuries... But you sure as hell think you are.
- **Lasting pain:** The whole day. Maybe even the next afternoon. In case I haven't been clear, it's BAD.

And so, combining all of this into one morsel of knowledge, you now know why, if you asked a man which he'd rather have injured - [any body part here] or his best buddies, he'd pick [any body part] 9 times out of 8. It's not just the pain (although, that has a lot to do with it). It's the combination of evolutionary imperative, pride and excruciating pain.

And you now also know why you guys can't go comparing this pain with childbirth. Yes, you win - childbirth is more painful. But the buildup to it is 9 months, and you know it's coming and can opt for a cocktail of awesome drugs to cope. But with dudes, you get the double whammy on the double baggy of unexpected pain with loss of pride, topped with the cherry of knowledge that it could happen again almost immediately, and without warning.

And as always, ladies, you're welcome for yet another look into the world of men.

LA LA LA

POSTED DECEMBER 17, 2009

You know, of all the musical notes, I feel most sorry for "La."

I mean, think about it. Do is a deer - a female one, at that.

Re is a drop of golden sun. What note wouldn't want to be a drop of golden sun? I mean, golden suns put raisins into bran and make it tasty. They also make babies laugh while sexually ambiguous creatures in primary colors coo at the camera.

Mi, I call myself. And hey, let's face it, I'm a pretty big deal.

Fa is a long, LONG way to run. That's impressive shit right there.

So is a needle pulling thread. Functional. Useful. A blue-collar everyman. Does its job and is proud to do so.

And then we get to La. It's just a note to follow So. It does NOTHING ELSE but follows So around. And yes, while I respect the work ethic and can-do attitude of our worker note, I can't help but feel that anyone who followed it around would be at the very least misguided, and at worst completely retarded for sidekicking for a working stiff. It's boring.

I mean, La could at the very least hang out with Ti, which is a drink with jam and bread. Tasty, right? I mean, why the hell hang around with a seamstress all day when you could at least enjoy a tasty snack?

And sure, La rose to prominence in the mid-2000's when one of the Simpson girls (the one with the fucking massive nose which became the fucking hideously obvious plastic surgery mistake) made a song all about it. But really, what else does La have going for it?

Even if it did have other successes, it wouldn't actually make any use of them. It'd just follow So around and be its do-boy.

Pathetic.

ON CHANGE (SHORT VERSION: SHUT UP AND DO IT)

POSTED APRIL 19, 2009

I'm sitting in the food court at Indianapolis International Airport right now. I'm telling you this because I have to start writing this thing somewhere, and after the conversation I just had, I have no idea where to start -- so I figure I'll just start going with what I know and see how it works from there. So far, so good.

When I got here, I figured I'd kill a bit of time by getting a bite to eat. I went to Qdoba and ordered a naked pork burrito, and while I was ordering, I noted that there was once a time when I would have not only ordered the burrito with a shell, but also with shredded cheese, extra cheese sauce, double meat, extra beans, and chips on the side. I noted this because, for the past, oh, year or so, I've become aware of just how much I used to eat. Much like a recovering alcoholic marks every single day they've been sober, recovering fat asses can't help but think back to how little they thought about what they ate.

While sitting here eating my naked pork burrito with lettuce and salsa, a rather rotund gentleman sat down a few seats away from me with a large sack emblazoned with the trademark red square and yellow "M" of a McDonald's bag - but long before he even sat near me, I could smell that oh-so savory smell of The Fries.

Now, I could get all expository and go on and on about how fucking GOOD McDonald's fries are. And you know why? Because they're fucking GOOD. But I won't, except to say that if I have one weakness in this new dietary whatever I've discovered, it's those damn fries. They smell good. They taste good. They even sound good. See if you can sit near a batch of them and not succumb to the siren's song they sing. You can't. I can't. No one can.

After he pulled out his fries, he pulled out two cardboard flip-top containers that mentioned something about a double cheeseburger. This used to be a typical meal for me when I ate fast food. Two burgers, a batch of fries, and a soda. Really, no big deal in the grand scheme of things. And as glanced at his meal, I didn't do what you probably thought I did, which was note "OH MAN THAT WOULD BE SO TASTY RIGHT NOW WHY AM I EATING THIS NAKED BURRITO WHATEVER."

No. I just thought "Man, those fries smell good." I didn't WANT them. I just thought they smelled good. That's a big change for me.

He looked over at me a few times, and I could tell he was checking out the big Akira tattoo. He asked me who did my work, which broke the ice a bit. I told him about Todo and how amazing he is, and he went on to say how much he admired the work, and how when he lost some more weight, he was going to get his tattoo done.

I mentioned the fact (and this is a big thing for me) that one of the reasons I work out every day is because I never want this amazing piece of art to look all bent out of whack. And I immediately felt bad, because I know that, at that very moment, what was going through his head.

I know, because it used to go through mine, and the things he said right afterward confirmed it.

He talked about how he used to play football in high school and college. He talked about how he just hasn't been hitting the gym lately, but that he feels that, if he really dedicated himself, he could probably get back in shape pretty quickly. He talked about how much he used to bench, and that one of the things he hates about going back is how he can't bench that. He talked about knowing "this stuff isn't all that helpful" (pointing to the McDonalds), but really it's not that bad in the grand scheme of things. He then said he'd probably get back into "it" this summer.

This was, almost verbatim, the exact dialogue I'd have with guys who were in shape when I was at my most out of shape. And like I used to be, this guy wasn't absolutely blubbery and fat - He was just a "big guy."

And I was SO close to starting to talk to him about how I used to be, and why I decided to try out for the AFL, and the work it took to get to where I'm at now (which is still a long ways off from where I'd like to be). I wanted to tell him that, like him, all of us ex-athlete adult males think "Oh, man, three months of dedicated training and I'll be right back where I was." And I wanted to tell him why I know that he keeps putting off the gym because he actually HAS gotten close to three months of dedicated training in the past, and the weight didn't just fall off, and how he blamed it on the fact that he probably didn't train as hard as he used to, and how he had a job, and no time, and so on and so forth.

And I didn't. Because, like me a few years ago, it would have fallen on deaf ears.

You can't want something for someone. And to lose twenty to thirty percent body fat, you have to REALLY want it. No amount of encyclopedic knowledge or research will drop the weight. No amount of money spent on gym equipment will drop the weight. Walking through the doors of your local gym won't drop the weight.

It takes a long, long time. A year. Two years, even. Constant maintenance on the diet. Constant exercise. Constant attention to energy expenditure vs. caloric intake. Constant desire to want to be better. Constant affirmation (and reaffirmation) that what you're doing is positive, and not just a waste of your time.

And some guy with cartoons on his arm and a little bit of muscle sitting in the Indianapolis International Airport isn't going to give you that, no matter how badly he wants to.

I could tell that he had a mental process going on in the back of his head that was saying "you know, now that I'm talking about this, I really SHOULD join that gym. I really think it's time. And maybe my reward will be the tattoo I've always wanted." And in-between bites of Double Cheeseburger, he asked me how much I bench, and how often I work out. He even said "Yeah, maybe today will be my last day of eating this crap." And he kept eating the crap.

The cognitive dissonance was astounding - and only because I realized I used to be the exact same way.

And now that he's left, I can't stop thinking about him. I wish him luck. What he wants is what he used to be, and he's so far from it, he's giving up before he even starts. I was that way for years. "It's not going to happen, so why bother?" Right? In the case of this guy, I know that, unless he has a reckoning that shocks him into finally deciding to stop trying or talking about trying, and actually get to work on changing his lifestyle, he'll likely go another round or two of this cycle. And I hate that for him, because it's the worst form of failure there is - knowing that you just didn't try hard enough.

But I don't pity him. And I also don't think any less of him. If he wants it, he'll get it. But he doesn't want it.

You don't change because you want to change. You just wake up one day and do it, and no matter how hard it is, you never go back to what you used to be. This goes for everything, not just weight loss. Stopping smoking. Stopping drinking. Starting on writing a book.

Everything and anything - you just fucking DO IT.

And the big secret is that, no, you won't stop wanting what you used to have, and you don't stop thinking about how nice it would be to just go back to the easy stuff - the laziness, the addictions, the whatever-it-is. And you just made a decision every day to not be that person. Eventually, you don't think about it every day, you think about it a few times a week. And then once or twice a month, you'll remember how nice it was when you did whatever it was that gave you comfort and made you fat (or lazy or addicted to something). And eventually, you just don't have the taste or the craving or the desire to be whatever you were - because now, you're someone else.

That's change. And it sucks, and it's hard, and it's work. And that's why it is so rewarding - because once you've done it, no one can take it from you. It's yours forever. And conversely, you can't give it to anyone else. They have to go make their own change.

So, change. Cast off the comfortable blankets of whatever it is that keeps you in the bed you've decided to lie in, put your feet on the floor, stand up, and move forward. And no matter how tired you get, don't go back to that bed. There is no snooze alarm for change. There's just daylight being burnt, and when the sun goes down and they day is done, that's it. The opportunity is gone, and you quite literally die being something other than what you wanted to be.

So change.

I'D RATHER

POSTED APRIL 22, 2009

Some things I do, people react in public, on the comments and by submitting to link sites and whatnot. Some things, I guess, invoke a more personal and private type of response. Those things are the ones that tend to "hit home" or really make a point that readers would rather not drag out into the streets, but they feel like they should talk to me about it. It's also those things that I put the absolute least amount of thought into and just start blabbering about.

I got a LOT of email on the "On Change" thing I wrote. I didn't even think about the words as they came out of my fingertips when I wrote it. I just did. And I guess some people liked it or needed to hear it. And one common thread came out from a LOT of you who wrote me back -- The "I'd Rather" thread.

As in, "I start doing x (like, write a book), and the entire time I'm doing it, all I can think is "I'd rather be doing y (like playing video games)." And that's what makes change so hard.

I know exactly what you mean. And here's the bad news first: it never actually goes away. You will ALWAYS prefer to do something comfortable and fun to something you perceive as work.

But here's the good news -- Eventually, it DOES become fun. It becomes something you enjoy doing. It's not work. It's relaxing, and enjoyable. Working out becomes your catharsis for the day's stress. Writing becomes your escape into worlds you invent and control. Building bookshelves becomes a silent protest to Ikea as you build shelves at 3x the quality for half the price.

It does. I promise. And that's part of the change. You become someone new, someone who sees that the "old fun" of playing video games was temporary and fleeting moments of enjoyment, and the time spent doing the "new fun" of working out is a long-lasting investment that pays dividends your entire life.

Not that video games are bad or evil - I still play them as often as I can. It's just that I quit preferring them over the other stuff in my life that I also enjoy doing, like writing books and working out, because no one ever walks up to me and squeezes your bicep and says "Wow, Joe... Have you been playing video games?" And they NEVER say "I was just browsing Amazon and randomly found your video recording of how you beat the boss on level 4-3, and I have to say, I was HOOKED! I watched all your video game replays!"

Anyway. I just wanted to follow up with that, and from there, I'm done. Look for strange observances on the packaging of chewing gum and reminiscing over old 90's bands starting again next post. Who knows, I may even upload another picture of my cat.

AUTHORS, WRITERS AND WANNABES (WHO ARE ALSO DOUCHEBAGS)

POSTED DECEMBER 30, 2009

Hi, I'm Joe Peacock. I've had a book published by a major publisher, and before that I self-published a book. And before that, I wrote short stories and blog posts on the internet. And before that, I kept journals.

So, I guess I'm qualified to talk about the differences between Authors, Writers, Working Writers and Wannabes (AKA: Douchebags). And if I'm not... Who's going to stop me? So fuck it.

Authors: have constructed a body of work (book, article, paper) and published it. Self-published or through a publishing house, either way. Not necessarily a working writer, and not necessarily concerned with the art and craft of the written word. Mathematicians can be authors. So can painters.

Writers: The short version: Writers write. They're never not writing. They are students of the written word; always looking for new ways to express ideas through the act of writing. They keep journals, or they blog, or they write articles or they write novels... It can't be stopped. The words pour out. And Writers don't necessarily have to be read to be Writers. In fact, Writers may or may not want to be read, but they MUST write.

Working Writers (AKA: Those who have the right to, when asked "What do you do?", answer "I'm a writer"): Take the above definition of Writer. Add the fact that this person received a check for an amount of money for a piece of writing, deposited it or cashed it at the bank, and the check cleared. You have a Working Writer. Now, Authors may have done the same thing - but remember that Authors aren't really students of writing, they just compose works which include written words. Writers are not necessarily Authors. Authors aren't necessarily Writers. But a Working Writer is an Author. Make sense? No? Too bad, I'm kinda bored with this point, because I now want to talk about:

Wannabes (AKA: Douchebags): Blah. Blah blah blah blah. This is what you hear out of the mouth of a Wannabe - first they disparage the unfair bias of The Industry because they can't get published and are too lazy (or weak) to self-publish. Then, they won't shut the fuck up about their work... Regardless of whatever else you may have been talking about beforehand. They mention their "short fiction" while giving directions to the interstate. They bring up their book during discussions on the weather (usually on Dark and Stormy Nights). They've participated in and failed to finish NaNoWriMo, usually only once, and usually a few years ago, but it STILL HURTS. They go on and on about how tedious and tiring and laborious the job of writing is, forgetting that every job on Earth can (and probably should) be that if it's worth doing - but unlike actual Writers, they can't see past that stuff to realize the good parts, because they're too busy focusing on the lifestyle of the tortured artist.

Now, the point of all of this isn't just to vent (okay, maybe that's part of it, but not the whole point). It's to illustrate for you and everyone else that, if you've found yourself walking through a Starbucks with a pencil behind your ear mentioning your book or writing to strangers - WITHOUT BEING ASKED - in the hopes that maybe they'll be interested in hearing your ego-feeding tale of artistry and pain... You might want to try shutting up, sitting down, and writing it out.

It may or may not result in your becoming an Author or Working Writer, but at the very least, it'll keep me from crushing a cup of hot coffee out of frustration, burning my hand and wrist and wasting two dollars and ten cents... You fucking douchebag.

ANGER AS MOTIVATION

POSTED JANUARY 17, 2010

I think all creative types have something they'd consider a motivation. And in my experience, many - if not all - of them can point to some art teacher or writing instructor or parent or other force in their life that was an influence of one sort or another.

It's at that point that you begin seeing a division - those who had positive influences and those who had negative influences. And the ones who had negative influences - people who said "no" or "you can't" or "get real" or "whatever, go get a real job" will probably lie about it when asked, but if you could read their minds and dig deep into their souls, you'd find out that a lot of their motivation to succeed and be creative and produce comes from proving wrong the ghosts of their pasts.

It was for me. Maybe it still is. But something I learned very recently has caused me to begin changing my perspective and draw motivation and energy from the positive repositories in my life:

Spending your life proving everyone wrong is a complete waste of a life, because ultimately they don't actually *care*.

Insults are easy. They take no work whatsoever. You just hurl one and move on. Insults are heat-seeking - they'll find the target and explode, sure enough.

But what you have to understand when someone takes this easy path is that they weren't negative and derogatory because they actively wanted you to fail - that takes a form of concern, and anyone who is truly concerned with another person doesn't actually do things that take effort. No, these folks just cast off your dreams and insult your passions because they're too weak to understand passion and drive. If they actually did understand it, they'd have an empathy borne only of going through the trials of pass and failure.

People who get it will take time to give you a critique - an honest assessment of what they see and where they think you stand based on it. And that critique may FEEL uncomfortable... Sometimes, it even feels insulting. But it's not the same as being insulted. It's not dismissive and it's not easy, it takes time and effort to offer. And there's the difference - no one spends time doing something they don't care about.

And, while anyone who honestly cares about you won't blow candy-flavored smoke up your ass and fill you with false hope, they will be supportive and proud as you climb each rung of your own ladder of success. And the ones who hurl insults and try to drag you down actually don't care if you fail or make it - they're not invested. They just want to dig and stab and wile away a few hours or minutes entertaining themselves with your misery.

Teachers, parents, aunts, uncles, friends and complete strangers are all OTHER PEOPLE. And to hate them - to let them be the reason you keep pushing forward - is giving them WAY too much of yourself. The problem with being fueled by the fires of anger is that they tend to consume all of the oxygen around whatever you're doing, and you can't actually sustain the life of that project. Not to any meaningful degree, anyway. It'll die.

And don't make the mistake of thinking that, because you put the final stroke of paint on your canvas, the work is done. It's not. Art doesn't exist in forms and materials, it's the spirit of the work that speaks to the world. It's communication, and if what you just built or made is comprised of bitterness, anger, hostility or jealousy, it'll show. The art can still die after you've constructed it, especially if you've built it on such a weak foundation.

The same goes for trying to impress someone with your art. It's not an honest motivation, and that will show. And ultimately... They won't care about it nearly as much as you care about them caring about it (I had to re-read that last sentence 4 times to make sure I got it right, and I'm still not sure, but I think it is, so...). So why waste your time?

THE TOP 1 REASON YOU SHOULDN'T FLUSH KITTY LITTER

POSTED FEBRUARY 3, 2010

So, my parents' cat died a few weeks ago. Yes, sad, I know. But as much as I liked Ms. Kitty, that's not the tragedy here. It's merely the precursor to that which is.

My parents, not wanting anything to go to waste, decided I needed very much to take home the auto-scooping cat box they bought for Ms. Kitty. I protested and insisted that the box doesn't really fit into the current dichotomy in our home - we are perfectly fine replacing the litter every 3 days, and the auto cat box thing requires clumping litter to work right. But they insisted, invoking the memory of their dearly departed cat.

So, I caved, and made the best of it by installing this automatic scooping cat box - along with a fucking cat water fountain I was also forced to take, I shit you not - in my office for Mofo, my office cat. Mofo is a bit standoffish, hence her name - so she lives alone in my office, separate from the other cats. And some weeks, I might go four or five days without cleaning her box, because after all, she's just one cat and she doesn't really stink so bad.

The auto scooping cat box has been fine all week, doing its little job with nary a concern - until today, when the little bucket that holds the poos and pees got full, and the auto scooping cat box began whirring and whining and crying because it couldn't fit any more offal into the container, causing it to jam. So I took the little bin out and considered it.

I've never used scoopable cat litter before. Thus, I've never really considered the proper disposal of individual poos and pees - I've always just hauled out a litter box liner full of waste litter and filled the box back up. But that's not how this automatic scooping cat box thing works. It works with clumping litter. Says so right on the warning label.

Because I was in a bit of a hurry to return to my work, I did the first thing one does when one considers what to do with poos and pees as they sit festering in a small bin in your hands - I dumped the whole lot into the toilet and flushed it.

Big, big, BIG mistake. With a capital F-U-C-K-I-N-G. You see, clumping cat litter clumps when wet.

I think you know the rest of the story from here.

Needless to say, I spent the next two and a half hours learning the fine arts of using a plumber's snake and removing a commode, and the reason they make and sell latex gloves. I had to scrape and pry out what had essentially become concrete from the crooks in the flush tube of the commode, meanwhile snaking about 25 feet of drainage.

As an aside, if you've got a toilet in your home that hasn't been removed and cleaned in a while... Just leave it there. You do NOT want to see what happens to the back lip of the drain as all those years of Wendy's value meals brushed past the lip and left small amounts of themselves which built up over time.

Trust me on this.

SO, LIKE, WHAT THE HELL, JOE? (AKA LET'S TALK DEPRESSION)

POSTED MAY 18, 2010

All three of you who read this blog might have noticed, I've been kinda gone for a while. And before I was gone, I was very irregular with posts.

There's a very good reason for this. The reason is that I didn't post anything.

Now of course, there's a good reason for the reason. And it's one I'm reluctant to talk about, even now, a week after I decided I was going to talk about it. I've agonized over this one, wondering where the lines are between writing to entertain you fine people and spilling my guts. I've opted for something in the middle - an open and frank discussion about the issue without revealing too many personal details.

I have been depressed. And I will give you a second to scoff, chuckle, and shake your head over reading that line, because I know that I've done the exact same thing in the past when I read or hear or see someone saying they're depressed. I think the word has been abused (much like the word "literally" has been - SERIOUSLY PEOPLE, it means "actually; without exaggeration or inaccuracy" - if you're literally blue in the face, YOUR FACE IS ACTUALLY BLUE, not just frustrated).

But this depression was not just the inability to find happiness or the loss of joy. What I went through is another thing entirely. The only way I can explain it is that I felt coated in it. I couldn't wrestle my way out of it. No matter how hard I worked out or fast I ran, it was on me and wouldn't go away. Every movement I made was done so out of sheer will - getting out of bed, fixing breakfast, running that marathon back in January... My mind was locked on one very real, very inescapable thought: my life was not worth living.

Those are heavy words, and it's the first time in my life I've ever felt that way. And this wasn't just a few days of bad juju - this was MONTHS. From about October until literally last week (SEE! That's how you use it, folks). To say I lost my perspective is to say the very least. I was joyless. I was an actor. If you saw me at a book signing, you saw a performance, not me. You saw smiles that were well-timed and scripted. I knew when to nod, when to laugh, when to smile, when to shake your hand, when to hug you, when to say "It's so great you came!" - and every single action was a forced act. I was miserable.

The reasons I ended up in this state are many, but can be summed up by saying just about every single irrational fear I have manifested themselves all at once, over a week in October. I'm sorry to tell you that I won't be going into detail - but what you need to know is that I suffer from two irrational fears, neither of which involves spiders or the dark. They're very deep, personal scars received from a childhood spent in fear of nearly everyone I met or knew.

And they both manifested themselves just in time for my house to fall apart (a roof leak flooded our upstairs bath, and a toilet leak from a stupidly-repaired toilet the previous owners left us with rotted out the floor in the downstairs bath). Two of our cats fell ill and I had to manage that. I was coordinating all of the touring, release party crap for the book, some very annoying clients who I couldn't make happy to save my life, and to make matters far worse, my wife was experiencing a fantastic career boon which took her on the road the entire time, leaving me to deal with all of this by myself.

Note: none of this is her fault, and she didn't even know about half of it. That's the thing - she's never, ever even once seen me not be "the strong one." And here I was, learning day by day just how weak I really was, and I couldn't even tell her. It was miserable. And once I revealed to her exactly how deep this all ran, she was pretty much flabbergasted. She had no idea. That was the worst part... Not being able to share any of this with her.

So yeah, I slipped into a depression - one which got worse and worse every single day, because unlike any other time in my entire life, I wasn't able to just wake up the next day and everything would be alright. My creative anxiety, abandonment issues, and inability to be self-reliant stacked on themselves every single day. It was the perfect storm of pain. And once it took hold, it was like a cloak that was coated in that glue they use in rat traps. I couldn't take it off.

The real issue is that I never dealt with any of my childhood issues - ever. I buried them. Every time I'd see a crack forming in the road, I'd just pave over it all over again with Rollins songs and simplistic "rely on yourself! Be your own hero!" punk rock manifestos. Meanwhile, a sinkhole was growing and was never honestly dealt with. It's a shame that I let it go for 33 years, because when that sucker opened, it swallowed me whole. I felt like the entire foundation of my life gave way and the structures that made up who I am collapsed under their own weight.

I don't think anything I write can do the feeling justice for anyone who's never felt it. I know nothing I've ever read did it justice until it finally happened to me. All I can say is imagine the worst feeling you ever felt, coupled with the worst self-doubt you've ever experienced. Multiply this times 100 (yes, 100 - this is not hyperbole, it's the most intense sadness and doubt you've ever experienced). Then, stretch it across a period of six months.

Intense is not the word. It's more like... Oppressive.

So how did I get out of it? In a few ways, I'm still not. But in all the ways that count, I am. I am smiling honestly now. I'm happy. I find joy in things. I see the future as bright and full of hope again. I can say that the Art of Akira Exhibit did wonders for this - it's the first ever "creative" project I've undertaken that had nothing to do with me, so I was able to fully throw myself into it and love it. I've found a new strength in confronting all of this. I'm working on a new book project (details soon) and I'm actually not anxious about it at all.

I have learned to let go of certain people in my life who were damaging and hurtful. I learned to be truly honest with my wife and tell her when it hurts, how it hurts, and why it hurts - and trust her to understand it. And the only way any of that happened was a forced march across the murkiest, darkest swamps I've ever traversed. It was slow, almost torturous... And I made it out. Alive.

I tell you this stuff not because I need an excuse for the lack of writing, or for the absences, or for any perceived reduction in quality of what I do. I tell you these things because I truly, sincerely love you. Not that I necessarily want to come to your house and hang out with you and trade notes or whatever... But in the sense that you are human and you care enough to read what I write, I love you. And if you never, ever go through this in your life, I will be happy, for I want you to be happy. It's an honest, sincere desire of mine - be happy.

And if you are going through this right now, I want you to know it WILL end. It will stop, and you will make it out alive - despite how badly you might not want to. I know that I had a moment - the first and only in my entire life - when I considered that option. I'm not proud to say it. In fact, it's taking everything I have not to delete this entire paragraph... Hell, this entire post. But it's too important. I think that the ONLY thing that pushed me past the dip and began my journey up the other side of the pit was a long, very heartfelt series of conversations with a very close friend who is the only other person I know to have gone through something like this. It could be said that she saved my life.

I'm not out to save yours. I'm just here to let you know that there is always a tomorrow, and every tomorrow leads to the future. And you can steer that series of tomorrows to bring you wherever you want - and while it's hard (damn, damn hard) to steer it toward a brighter day when you're honestly depressed, trust me - it will happen.

"The only way out is through" - Robert Frost (and, if you're into them, Nine Inch Nails)

It's now one of my favorite passages. It's the most honest and brutal truth I've ever faced. There are no escapes, short of a final one - and that's just cheating. You have to push forward. You have to work harder than you've ever worked. You have to find one - JUST ONE - instance of joy and cling to it. The memories and pain and doubt will quickly begin to wash back over the shore of your happiness... You can't stop it. There's no trite or simple way to say it - you will get sad, over and over... But find that joy. Know where it is. Mark it down; plant a flag. And come back to it every chance you get. Much like shells on the beach, more will show up - plant flags there too. Plant so many flags, you can begin stringing up netting and placing sandbags to keep the tide from rushing over it again. Eventually, the wall will be built, and you will have found your path across the ocean.

[After I posted about depression, I received a TON of email, messages, tweets and posts about it. I wanted to clarify and explain to people what was going on with me:]

Some Clarity On The Depression Post Thing Whatever

I've gotten a ton of email (well, not really a ton - email doesn't actually weigh anything... But I bet if I printed it all out and weighed it, it still wouldn't be a ton. At least a pound, but that doesn't sound great, does it? A pound of email? Whatever) about the depression post from last week. And to my surprise, not a single one of them was negative. In fact, I'm overwhelmed by the kind words and support you guys expressed.

But I'm also dismayed by just how many of you wrote to say something on the order of "Thank you for putting into words what I've been feeling." I'm dismayed because of how many of you are actually feeling that way. It's a horrible, sick feeling. Literally a disease. And it hurts to know that so many people in my proximity are experiencing it.

I was also inundated with curiosity from people who couldn't quite relate to how things were, or why I never asked for help, or how I could let things get that way. So I've decided to do a little bit of a follow-up on that post, explaining a bit of how I felt, why it went the way it did, and how I got the hell out of it. Those of you who wrote to tell me how your experience was will be able to relate to some of this. Those who wrote who are experiencing it now, hopefully this helps. And those who've never felt it and were genuinely curious about it all... Well, here you go.

How I felt:

Sad. Not "death of a relative" sad... Worse, actually. The death of someone meaningful to you has a clear and concrete cause. They died. This lacked such a luxury. In fact, I found myself wishing for a reason. If there's one thing that can send sadness into a perpetual spin, it's a clear lack of reason for it. Because now you're feeling unjustified feelings, which if you're not menstruating at the time, means you're probably crazy. Real crazy, not the insane wacky Wile E. Coyote crazy. Brad Pitt in 12 Monkeys crazy.

There were days where I lamented the fact that my body couldn't sleep 24 hours at a stretch. I cursed the sun. I cursed the alarm clock. But in truth, I needed neither. I didn't sleep. Not restfully, anyway. My mind never stopped grinding on what I perceived was the problem.

The problem was a variable, susceptible to change at any moment. It was like taking on a nest of hornets with a fly swatter. You kill one, another is right there waiting to sting you. I drove myself mad day after day isolating on each and every feeling, trying to figure out what caused it. I was looking for answers to riddles written in dead languages. Every time I'd address what I thought the problem was, I'd argue it out with whomever I felt was able to fix it... Usually Andrea. We'd talk for hours about it, and at the end, the problem that was being discussed was solved. But my feelings were still there.

The metaphors are infinite. An itch I couldn't scratch. A splinter in my soul. I could bore you for months with the crap I wrote in my journals about how I was feeling. But looking back on it, I know that the worst part of the worst moment in my life was that I had no idea why I was feeling what I was feeling. I only knew that it was sad and it was real and I was absolutely unable to handle it.

It never left me. At the movies, on a run, during workouts, while writing and working. Airplane rides were awful, because you aren't allowed distraction before takeoff or landing. The moments between when I decided to turn off the TV or

Xbox or computer and actually attempt sleep, and the moments just after I awoke began to terrorize me every single day. I'd dread either of those times, like dreading recess due to the bullies.

Pulling out of it was hard. When you hit rock bottom, you don't just go "splat" - you bounce a few times. I hit rock bottom on December 19, 2009 on an 18 degree night in Indianapolis, IN. I remember the night clearly, even now. Every single second of it. I found myself crying on the shoulder of a parking attendant while sitting on a curbside at a garage in the Indianapolis "square." The reasons why are many. As I explained in my first post, this was The Perfect Storm of events in my life that triggered every irrational fear I have. Every single time one problem would look like it could be solved, two more showed up which dragged me away from the first. And that night, everything peaked.

How it got so bad (or, the difference between feeling depressed and Depression):

First, a lot of "like I said's" and a bunch of metaphors:

Like I said, I had no idea why I was REALLY feeling this feeling. I saw every symptom as the cause, like seeing a runny nose as the cause of your flu. I lacked adequate understanding to actually discover the virus, and even once I found it, I lacked the ability to kill it.

Like I said, I tried addressing every single issue that happened, as it happened... But everyone has a point of exhaustion. In boxing, they teach you to find that point and exploit it - it doesn't matter how strong or big or powerful your opponent is, if you can outlast his need to breathe, you're going to beat him. This outlasted my ability to fight it. I ran out of steam - and that's when the piling on began.

Like I said, you don't just hit bottom and then boom, decide to start climbing again. You bounce. It hit me in waves for days afterward. You get a gulp of air, and then brace yourself for the next one. You can finally see the shore off in the distance and you want nothing more than to swim toward it... But these damn waves, they keep coming.

Eventually they stop. Eventually, you float in the middle of your ocean and you realize you're either going to have to start swimming back to shore or just sink into oblivion. So I swam. And this is where the REALLY weird stuff starts - the echoes. Every time I began to think about other things, I remembered suddenly "Hey, I just took my mind off of feeling bad." And just like telling you you're not thinking of a pink elephant covered in peanut butter right now, you can't help but suddenly do so.

How I got out of it:

Friends and therapy. Period.

I talked things out as often as my friends would let me. Eventually, they got to the point where they realized that what I was saying was making me sad or angry or nervous wasn't actually what was affecting me, because unlike every other time in my past, I didn't immediately perk up when I found the "solution" - I just kept finding more problems.

So I finally went to a therapist. I talked with him about everything that was hurting me. He listened over multiple sessions, until he also realized I was just flinging things at the wall without figuring out why. Eventually, he seized on my irrational fears and helped me to deal with them.

Now, it's not magic - I knew about both of my irrational fears. I've known about them since I was first lead to Jung and Foucault and Nietzsche as a teenager. It's not hard to understand that a boy who was abandoned by his father and bullied his entire young life because he drew and wrote has issues with abandonment and creative anxiety. Duh. But dealing with that stuff? That's an entirely different matter. And I never did. And just like any callous, the layers get deeper and harder the longer it's allowed to form. And when it's finally scraped off or peeled back, the skin underneath is VERY tender.

Therapy is vital. While I won't ever pretend that my therapist "really knows me" - he doesn't, and we both admit that directly (how can he? He's not me) - I will state with impunity that he helped guide me to and through the forest of my emotions to figure out what was really at the core. From there, he gave me tools to help deal with it.

It's very important to realize that NO ONE CAN TAKE YOUR PAIN AWAY. If you feel like they do, you're simply masking what's wrong. Only you can fix you, period, end of story. It's every bit the same as losing weight or running a marathon or writing a book. No one can do it for you. You must do it yourself, or else you haven't done it.

But what they can do in all of those instances is support you, coach you, and give you the understanding and knowledge to deal with the problem. Anyone who's had a successful encounter with a personal trainer will tell you that they probably started thinking a trainer would fix them, but they ended realizing that the trainers themselves aren't responsible for the success. They were simply coaches.

It's the same here. And I fixed myself by realizing a few things: 1) I wanted to get better, honest and genuinely, 2) I had no idea how to do that myself, 3) I sought help and found it, and 4) I rewrote every single piece of programming I'd recently put in place that caused certain stimuli to cause certain responses.

Every time a negative thought came into my head, I smiled. Seriously. It helps. Every time I'd start remembering that I felt bad a few minutes/hours/days ago, I'd simply say "STOP." I'd actually say it aloud. I'd backtrack to the beginning of whatever train of thought led me there, rethink it very deliberately, and where I veered into self-loathing and sadness before, I'd steer off in another much more productive direction. I looked at myself in the mirror, right in my own eyes, and remind myself that I love myself, and regardless of who else loved me - as nice as it was - loving myself is all I really need in life. Everything else is ultimately just luxury.

Eventually, you stop being sad every single second. You go entire minutes thinking other thoughts. The minutes turn into days, and now you're remembering you were sad instead of feeling sad right then and there. Then it's weeks between feelings or remembrances, and then at some point, you're looking back and saying "Jesus, I'm so glad I'm done with that."

To broaden the time periods between "flutters" of depression, I got very, very busy. I worked my ass off, in fact. I started doing a column for AOLNews. I finally launched The Art of Akira Exhibit. I started pounding away at new ideas for books and projects. I designed a whole bunch of stuff. I read a lot of books.

And it wasn't easy, either. I had to force myself to stay focused nearly every minute I was doing something besides feeling sorry for myself. Every. Single. Minute. But I couldn't blog or write stories about myself during that time, because every single thing I wrote, no matter what it was, began devolving into some sort of breakdown of feeling sad or why this thing sucks or that thing blows or why everyone hates me or why do I even have a career, I should just give this up and go back to software development. So that's why the very inconsistent posting on the blog. But here I am again, writing things that aren't so mopey -- and actually loving it.

That's not to say I haven't been sad or down since I pulled out of the Depression. I have. But those moments have actual reasons, and I can deal with them and move on immediately. And I'm not "Good Ol' Joe" - I'll never be the man I was before last October, when all this started. And I'm glad for that. I've dealt with some pretty severe emotions, events and issues, and I'm forever changed for that. For one thing, a very real truth was revealed - that a lot of people in my life did a lot of damage when it came to my self-image and my confidence in my ability to create. They still do. So I've taken steps to either distance myself from them or remove them from my life outright. Life's too short to spend it wishing the people you love loved you back, and anyone who tells you you can't be who you are doesn't actually love you.

I only have one regret in the entire experience: that my wife felt helpless for a brief period. I don't regret sharing any of this with her. She now knows me more completely than before, and our love is stronger than ever. We conquered another mountain together. There's something incredible in that. I just wish that I didn't have to put her in a position where, for the first time since we met, she had to wonder what was wrong with me because what I was saying was wrong wasn't actually the problem.

Anyway, there it is, all the questions you guys have been asking, piled into one big follow-up post. Thanks for reading this.

I SO SO SO HATE THE DENTIST

POSTED MAY 20, 2010

Today, I sat through a ton of drilling, filling, and capping due to a tooth I broke a few days ago.

I hate drilling. I hate filling. And I hate capping. I hate the dentist, period. I can't stand even talking someone to one, much less go in myself. But I couldn't deal with the pain or the sharp edges on the tooth for long, and went ahead through with it.

It brought to mind the story of what happened the last time I went to the dentist. It was such a horrific experience, it spawned a 12-part story on Mentally Incontinent circa 2004 or so. And I thought, given how long it's been, I'd share here with you guys. I hope you enjoy it.

Tales of Dental Woe (in 12 parts)

PART ONE

Whereupon Joe cracks a filling, which leads to cracking a tooth (which leads to a root canal that you will read about in part 2)

Now, there is something you must know about me right from the very, very start:

I HATE THE DENTIST.

I cannot stand anything even remotely relating to dentists or dental work. I've done enough in my life to practically guarantee that I will be going to hell, and knowing hell as it has been described to me by every Baptist I've ever met, I know that I have an eternity of unpleasantness to look forward to. I fully expect my little corner of hell to be a dentist's chair with a speaker piping in the "All 'American Idol Losers' Radio Network" directly overhead (although, to be fair, I'm not so sure that the "All 'American Idol Winners' Radio Network would be any better).

My hatred for the dentist started way back when I was just a little tyke. I can remember doing everything within my power to avoid going to the dentist - which usually meant misbehaving so badly that the dentist du jour would forbid my mother ever bring me back into his / her office. I'd squirt the water pik at the dental assistant, I'd spit on the lamps to watch the bulb steam and eventually break, I'd mess with the chair to the point of the adjustment motors grinding to a halt - I was TERRIBLE.

That is, until I met Dr. Bob.

Dr. Bob wasn't like the other dentists. He actually understood kids. He knew what made them tick and what made them respond -- and that was putting the fear of Almighty God into them so they'd stop screwing around with his stuff. He'd routinely tell me that God was watching and "Jesus didn't die in agonizing pain on the cross to forgive sins like playing with my dental tools, so you'd better just stop right now, young man." Yeah, I guess it was probably a horrible thing to do; convincing a child that Jesus was selective in the sins he forgave, but hey - it made me sit still. And when I sat still enough that he could poke whatever needles he needed to into my mouth without gashing my cheeks or impaling my tongue, it actually wasn't THAT bad.

As a result, Dr. Bob was the only dentist I would visit for the next 20 years. Literally - from age 6 until age 26, he was the only person I'd ever go to. It didn't matter where in the country I was working or how far away from him I lived - if I had an issue with teeth, I flew home and drove to Decatur to see Dr. Bob. He was the ONLY dentist I trusted. So, imagine my dismay when, one night about a year and a half ago, I discovered that I had a cracked filling by way of biting into a piece of steak (yes, a piece of steak - and not a tough piece, either, just a nice juicy piece of steak) and breaking a tooth right in half. Immediately, I hopped on Yellowpages.com and looked up Dr. Klein's number and found out - *GASP* that there was none listed.

I immediately called my mom who, between inquiries as to why I was moaning in agonizing pain, found the only number we knew of that he had. I called it up and got the worst news of my life:

"Dr. Klein passed about six months ago, sir. I'm... I'm terribly sorry."

Well, crap.

PART TWO

Whereupon Joe is a whiny brat (which leads to the root canal I said you'd read about in this part, but to teach you a lesson, I will make you wait until part 3 to meet)

"Docthor Bobh Kleinh ish deadh," I told my wife with my palm held to my mouth.

"Who's that?" She asked.

I gave her an irritated look. "My denthisth," I stated. "Wait - Well, noh anymorth..."

She gasped and smacked my arm. "God, you're terrible," She replied. "The poor man passed away, and you're making jokes."

"Well it's noh fair!" I lisped. "He can't be deah! My tooh hurs!"

"Uh... What?" She asked.

"My tooh hurs!"

"Your WHAT?" She said, smirking.

"Tooh! TOOH!" I said, gesturing toward my cheek.

"Ohhh, your TOOTH," She said. "Yes. Indeed. He simply CAN'T be dead, because your tooth hurts. It all makes sense."

I glared at her. "Shuh Uh," I tried to yell. "Thih isn'h funneh! My tooh! It HURS!!!!! Goh... Whah will I do now?"

"I dunno," she said. "Call the dentist, maybe?"

"He's deah," I replied plainly. "It's terribullhy inconveinhenh."

She sighed. "Not him, you jerk. ANOTHER dentist... A LIVE dentist."

"Noh Noh Noh," I insisted. "No fuhhin' wayh."

"Why NOT?" She inquired.

"I don't goh to anyhonh elsh buh Docthor Bobh," I answered. "Fuh THAH shiih!"

"Oh, you big baby!" She answered, remembering my long diatribe about dentists and my hatred for them. "So what are you going to do, go around with a broken tooth for the rest of your life? Just grow up and call another dentist."

And you know what? I actually considered it for a moment. For just a brief point in time, I entertained the thought of just foregoing the dentist and dealing with the pain of the broken tooth... And then I inhaled once more and the rush of wind against the exposed nerve convinced me otherwise. She was right. I would have to see another dentist.

I say again... Well, crap.

PART THREE

Whereupon Joe's dead dentist forces him to visit another (which is where that stupid root canal you've been promised for 2 parts finally happens, but not in this part, you now have to wait until part 4)

There's something else you should know about me: I'm EXTREMELY lazy.

For instance, I have to choose a new dentist, right? I've been going to the same one for 20 years simply because I HATE going to the dentist and he's the only one who'd actually make me comfortable enough to go. So you'd think that, after his death, I'd spend days, weeks... Months, even, researching every dentist in the tri-county area to find one that might meet with my approval.

You know how long I spent? Ten seconds. Yep, just long enough to type three w's, the words "yellow" and "pages", and a period with a "com" following it into my browser window (which, incidentally, was Firefox, because Internet Explorer is dumb. I just thought I'd mention that). I picked my state, chose "Dentists" from the dropdown and clicked

"Go". Oh, look, there's one 2.4 miles from my house. Guess what that means? New dentist found, mission accomplished, all that jazz.

It's like I said - I'm lazy. Once I've resigned myself to the fact that I have no choice but to do something, I look for the absolute quickest way to get it done... Damn the consequences.

So I called, told them it was an emergency, and secured an appointment for the following morning with Dr. Lucile Fur. And that, ladies and germs, is how Satan became my new dentist (get it? Lucile Fur? LuciFur? It's funny! And it's also TRUE because she was the DEVIL).

As you'd probably expect, Satan's dental office was hot as... Wait. No. You know what? I'm not going to pun there. Nope, not gonna do it, no matter how much you might want me to. You can just imagine it yourself, you pun-lover, because I refuse to grab at such low-hanging fruit. But yes, it was very, very hot in there. They made me wait for nearly an hour, during which time I was forced to read three-month old copies of People and Sports Illustrated to keep my mind from getting SO bored, it would lift the lid to my skull and scamper giddily out the window, daring me to chase it (which of course would go horribly, not having a brain and all. I'd just fall over, and really, what kind of game is THAT??). Finally, Satan's assistant poked her little horned head from behind the portal into the torture rooms.

"Mr. Peacock?"

"Yuh," I said, still holding my palm to my jaw.

"Dr. Fur will see you now. Come with me."

PART FOUR

Whereupon Joe FINALLY tells about the stupid root canal (but not before he gets into trouble, which is what happens in this part, leaving the actual root canal for part 5)

I followed Satan's little minion down the hall and into a stark white room with a horribly-situated beige dental chair in the rear corner, facing the doorway. She curtly bade me sit and, having read my bible, I knew better than to cross a demon -- especially one which had easy access to those little scythe-like dental pick things that they shove under your gums and laugh while they make you cry for your mommy. So, I took my place in the one-size-too-small-for-Joe dental chair and awaited what was coming for me here in the sixth-and-a-half level of hell.

And I waited.

And I waited some more.

And I grew bored (much like you are with this story... Only there's no Novocain for you). So I began doing what I always do in the dentist's office when I get bored -- I began playing with the little "toys" littering the office. I flipped on the suction thingy and began squirting water from the water pik directly into it, causing it to go "Gurgle Gurrsh Gurahhallla Gurg" -- and boy, was it fun! I don't know if you've ever done that, the whole "mess with the expensive equipment" bit, but man, you should try sometime! It's nearly hypnotic, the sounds that come from the suction straw when you squirt the water into it. OH! OH! And also, you can blow little bits of paper or lift the cover on magazines from across the room with the little air blower thingy on the other side of the water pik! It's SO COOL! You can make a game out of it - rip off a corner of your dental bib, roll it into a ball, and place it in your open and flat palm. Then, blow it across the room with the blower thingy! For added fun, squirt it first so it becomes a super-cool makeshift spitball. See how many you can get to stick on the wall opposite you before the dentist walks --

"Mr. Peacock!" the stout woman stated from behind a light blue mask and safety goggles, her latex-clad hands on her hips.

"Uh... Yuh..." I responded, a still wet wad of apron in my hand.

"Entertaining ourselves, are we?" Dr. Fur asked rhetorically.

Embarrassed, I dropped the wet ball and attempted to replace the water pik / blower thingy to its proper place on the tray, but failed miserably and accidentally let it fall where it was pulled taught at the end of its cord. "Uh... Sorruh..." I said, replacing my hand to my cheek in some sort of physical sign of pain.

"Oh, it's okay," She responded. And then she said six words (see? SIX! She is the devil!) that sent a chill down my spine:

"You're about to get your punishment."

I yelped -- literally yelped, out loud - as she laughed and took her place on the stool beside me.

PART FIVE

Whereupon Joe-Joe suffers for his sins (and learns a valuable lesson about root canals performed on dead teeth, which he will relate in part 6)

She was just joking about the punishment, she said.

Right. Whatever. That's why the next two hours were filled with a special kind of agony reserved for only super, super, super bad kids.

First, Satan scraped and poked and prodded the dead area of my broken tooth. She shoved a spikey thing in there, she blew air on the exposed nerve, she wiggled the hunk of remaining tooth -- honestly, the only thing there was left for her to do to cause me unimaginable pain was kick me swiftly in the balls. One of those giant, WWE-style axe kicks where she waves her hand to the crowd who chants her name – "SATAN! SATAN!" – as she winds her leg up and then brings it right down on my round-and-tenders.

After doing all of her initial digging around, she administered a few shots of Novocain to deaden the area. When I asked, she assured me that there would be no feeling and all I'd really be aware of is some "light pressure."

SHE WAS LYING. Oh, not about the pressure -- I felt pressure, alright. I felt pressure like you wouldn't believe when she pulled out her industrial-sized angle grinder and sawed my tooth apart. But I also felt sharp, stabbing pain. She told me that it was psychosomatic. She assured me I shouldn't be feeling any pain whatsoever.

"BUH I AHH! I SWEAHH!" I screamed through the mouth-holdy-opener thingy.

"But you shouldn't," She replied, and kept right on drilling. I tried to focus on other things to take my mind off of the oil prospecting taking place in my poor molar -- like the smell of burning bone matter as she drilled, or the taste of my own tooth dust mixed with blood and small hints of Novocain that escaped the needle as it was inserted and landed on my tongue.

As you can imagine, it didn't help.

Eventually, it all came to an end. My jaw felt like it'd been held open by a tire jack for a month. My upper-left gum felt like there was some sort of latin dance of love performed on it by a hot-blooded woman wearing spiked stiletto heels. But it was over -- all of the pulpy decay, along with the nerve of the tooth, were excavated and I was left with a temporary crown on top of a hollow shell of what was once a molar. The suffering was finally over.

Or so I wished.

PART SIX

Whereupon Joe is in much pain - both from the root canal in Part 5 AND from something else (which you will discover in Part 7 and must be dealt with in Parts 9, 10 and 11)

"So, how was it?" My darling wife asked as I groggily opened the door and stumbled inside.

"It SHUCKED," I replied, my lips numb with Novocain.

"Well, it was a root canal," She answered. "They don't tickle."

"Yesh, buh thish dhenshih... She wush th' DEBIL," I stated.

She laughed. "Well, at least you got the crown put on the same day, so you don't have to go back," she replied. "Why don't you go on upstairs and get some rest... I'll be up there shortly."

And that's exactly what I did. It didn't take much time at all for the heavy anvil of sleep to fly through the air as if launched from one of Wile E. Coyote's slingshots and land on my head, and in no time at all, I was drooling blood and blowing spit bubbles all over my pillow. When I woke up a few hours later, I stirred through the haze and immediately clamped on with both hands to one thought pounding in my head:

"OW."

I got up and took some ibuprofen, attempted to drink a little water, and went back to sleep, where I slept for another six hours or so. Sometime around 4:00AM, I woke back up and was once again greeted by the same thought as before.

"OWW."

This pattern repeated itself throughout the entire next day, as well as the day after and the day after that. In fact, the pain - in varying degrees of assorted levels - persisted for a little over a year. Yes, a year. Of tooth pain. That's 365 days of pain in the tooth. That's no good. But there's this interesting phenomenon that takes place when something hurts in a place where you've pretty much sworn off allowing anyone to poke or prod in again forever: You just grow used to it. You allow it to persist, because the alternative is just THAT much worse. So even though I had this pain in my tooth, I could handle it because there was no way in hell I was going back to the dentist unless some particularly skilled necromancer could raise Dr. Bob from the dead.

But somewhere around a year into this exercise in futility, my attention on my canalled molar began to grow - as did a particularly large abscess.

PART SEVEN

Whereupon Joe sees nasty white goo seep from under his crowned tooth, forcing him to go back to a dentist (whom you don't have to wait until part 8 to meet, thankfully)

"NO," I insisted. "There is NO WAY I'm going back to a dentist."

Andrea sighed. "Joe, there is pus oozing from a tooth. I'd say you really have no choice."

"Oh, I have a choice alright," I replied. "Why don't you go to the garage and get the ball-peen hammer... I'll get started hitting myself in the head with a brick to deaden the pain."

"Don't be ridiculous," she answered. "I've seen enough Animal Planet to know an abscess when I see it, and if you let it go too long, you're going to end up with a huge hole in your gum."

"What?" I asked, shocked. "What the heck do you mean?"

"Well, when an abscess ruptures, it leaves a pretty gigantic hole in the spot where it popped," She answered.

I cringed. "God... are you serious?"

"Go to the dentist and find out yourself," She answered.

Well, crappity crap.

So once again, I hit yellowpages.com and did a quick search. I scanned the list for a dentist near me, skipping immediately over Dr. Fur's Infernal House of Mouth Pain and hitting the next dentist on the list -- which, ironically, was less than .10 of a mile down the road from the House O' Dental Hell. So I called, explained my situation, and made an appointment for the next day.

I knew the second I walked into this new dental office that I was going to like it, because situated in the corner of the waiting area was a free internet terminal. There were TV's in each corner, each one playing a different channel. The magazines were from THIS MONTH. And the best part:

There was air conditioning.

But really, I didn't get to enjoy any of these things, since it took less than 10 minutes before I was taken back into Dr. Tom's office and seated in a very cushy and comfortable "oversized" dental chair made specifically for gigantic dudes my size. The room had its own TV hanging from the ceiling that was playing CNN, although I didn't get to watch much of it because Dr. Tom was in to see me almost immediately.

"Hey there, Mr. Peacock," he said in greeting. "My name is Dr. Williams. What seems to be the problem?"

"Well," I said, full of trepidation, "I have this crown, and... Wait. First, you need to know something."

"What's that?" he asked.

"I HATE going to the dentist," I answered.

"Oh," He said casually. "Well, you're in luck. I specialize in people who hate me."

I looked at him quizzically, like he just solved an algebraic equation using an abacus. "Well," I said, and continued to explain my situation.

"Well, let's take a look-see," He said softly as he flipped down what looked like the scope on a pair of night-vision goggles that rested on his head and changed the channel on the TV to what shortly became The Joe's Mouth Network.

PART EIGHT

Whereupon Joe finds out that there's something wrong in toothville (that will be rectified in parts 10 and 11, but only after he finds out even worse news in part 9)

"Oh, my," Dr. Tom said in such a manner as to leave no doubt that this was most definitely not a good "oh my".

"Whuh?" I asked, feeling my lips and tongue slightly wrap around his latex-clad thumb.

"This is definitely no good," he replied, confirming my suspicions. "I'm going to have to remove this crown to see what's going on in here."

"Whaih!" I cried as he removed his thumb. "Thih... *cough* This crown cost nearly a thousand bucks to put in the first time!"

"Yes. It's definitely a nice crown... very well done," he answered from behind his dental mask, reaching for some sort of weird device that looked like a cross between a pair of pliers and something you'd see in a Vietnamese POW camp. "It's too bad I have to pulverize it."

"PULVERIZE?!?" I said with a gulp. "But... But... Pulverize sounds like it hurts!"

"Well, if you're small, made of porcelain and glued to the molar slot of a nervous young man's mouth, then yes, it'll probably hurt. Otherwise, all you'll feel is a bit of pressure."

"Pressure? Pulverize?" I asked. "What is it with you and 'P' words that don't sound like 'Pain' but essentially mean the same thing?"

"Calm down," he responded in a calm and soothing tone. "I assure you, this won't hurt. Just watch the procedure on the monitor above us."

And so I did. I calmed down. I watched. I felt some pressure. But to my absolute disbelief, I felt no pain. I did, however, nearly choke to death on a tiny piece of porcelain that fell down my throat. I also nearly bit off Dr. Tom's index finger when he went after it to retrieve it. And I nearly punched the dental assistant when Dr. Tom couldn't get the porcelain chip with his fingers and asked her to retrieve it with the suction tube, only she didn't so much retrieve it as she performed invasive suction surgery on my sinus cavity from jabbing that damn tube into my mouth too fast. But overall, it ended alright.

"Okay, now that that's done," he said, and leaned in close to get a better look. "Yep, just as I feared."

"Oh, God..." I half prayed.

PART NINE

Whereupon Joe gets the worse news, along with some instructions (which make things hell until part 10)

"This tooth is cracked vertically, nearly all the way up the root. It's going to have to come out," Dr. Tom said.

Gnar.

"Fine," I replied, quite confident in Dr. Tom's abilities. "Whatever it takes to get rid of this pain. Let's do it."
"Alrighty," he answered. "I'll go prepare the referral—"

"REFERRAL?" I barked. "No… Let's do it. Here. Now."

"Oh, I'm not the guy for that," He answered with a slight chuckle. "I'm going to send you to an oral surgeon who can do it a LOT faster than I can."

"ANOTHER Dentist?!?" I cried. "I can't stand this!"

"Look," he said, taking off his gloves. "Dr. Paul is an old friend of mine. He's going to take good care of you. You'll barely feel a thing. Just relax for a moment and I'll write up that referral." He stood to exit the room as I sighed and accepted my fate. Just then, he turned back around and added, "And keep your tongue out of the socket. You'll just make it worse."

God, I wish he hadn't said that.

I left his office with a slip of paper that bore his signature and an insatiable desire to slide my tongue into the shelled socket left by the removal of the crown. It was 5 days before I could make it to Dr. Paul's office, and every single minute of every single hour was spent mentally forcing my tongue to stay on the right side of my mouth, far away from the gap in my teeth. I'd put my tongue on the far rear molar and inch near the hole, I'd place it on the bicuspid just to the other side of it, ever so nearly tempting fate and exploring the hole. But one thing kept me from actually doing it:

"You'll just make it worse." The final words of Dr. Tom.

Finally, the day of my appointment came. The sun shone hard through my car windows, intensifying the heat of the brutal Georgia summer. Luckily, I had a tasty, ice cold sweet ice tea from Quiznos and a freshly serviced air conditioner in my car to help keep me cool. I drove deep into the southland to Griffin, GA, the home of the stereotype of your typical Georgian as well as Dr. Paul's office. I referred to my printout from Google Maps constantly, hoping I wouldn't fly past it and end up being terribly late for my appointment.

Right.

I was 45 minutes late for it. And it's not because I couldn't find the place... It's because I simply couldn't believe that the building I was led to was a dentist's office. This was a tiny house situated between a gas station and a "Fish Supreme" restaurant with absolutely no signage in front of it to designate that this was where you got your teeth cut out of your mouth. It was only after I eliminated every other possibility on the block that I finally got out of my car and headed up the sidewalk. There, on the door approximately 100 feet from the road was a tiny plaque reading "Dr. Paul D.D.S."

I sighed and walked in.

PART TEN

Whereupon Joe very nearly says "Fuck This Shit" and walks out, allowing his mouth to rupture and bleed everywhere (which, of course, he doesn't, which leads to the drama in part 11)

"Uh... Fuck this shit," I whispered to myself as I walked into the overcrowded front waiting room of Dr. Paul's office. There were 25 people all waiting for their turn under the knife sharing 6 chairs and a small wooden bench in the front of this repurposed house that was VERY similar to the one my grandfather lived in when I was a kid. Hardwood flooring with steel grate registers for heat, radiators as air conditioning, closets with small painted knob-latches in just about every room... I half expected my aunt to be drunk in her bedroom and my cousin Buffy to rush out, greet me and suggest one of 2,000 things to do that day that would get us out of that house.

"Can I help you, honey?" I heard from my right. Behind a half-opened frosted glass window was an older woman with an abnormally white smile and way too much makeup.

"Yeah, uh..." I stammered, deciding whether or not I should bring my other foot past the threshold of the doorway or simply turn tail and run. "I... I'm late."

"Ah, Mr. Peacock," She said in a thick southern accent. "We was wonderin' what happened to you. Come on in, fill these out." I saw a clipboard with a stack of documents jut from the other side of the window; a small silver chain holding a pen tailing behind. I bit my bottom lip, walked all the way into the room, grabbed the clipboard, and popped a squat over in the corner of the room that was least populated by nervous sweaty folks.

It was nearly an hour after I finished my paperwork before I was called back to see the butch... er, Um.. Dentist. I was soaked in sweat as a result of my wait in the room that some engineering genius decided it was a great idea to install water radiators as cooling in ANY building in Georgia, much less one where a person is predisposed to be overly anxious. My bet? He probably graduated from Georgia Tech.

I followed the dental assistant down the ancient hardwood hallway to a room that looked more like a laundry room than a dentist's office (and for good reason... It was also the laundry room).

"You can sit there," the assistant said curtly, pointing to a small dental chair. "Dr. Paul will be back here in a moment."

As she left, a door slid open at the back of the room revealing another dental assistant with a basket full of bloody aprons and towels. I stood there frozen as she separated the two types of garments into individual baskets and began another load of wash, complete with a heavy dose of bleach and a scoop of unscented Gain.

The smell of the laundry made me sweat even more as the bleach fumes rolled across the room and entered my nostrils and eyes.

"Yeah, okay, I'm outta here," I said aloud as I turned around to make my exit. I nearly collided with a midsize man with a mask and thick-rimmed glasses covering his face.

PART ELEVEN

Whereupon Joe gets crazy high and bleeds a lot (which plays a major part in part 12)

"Hi there!" He exclaimed as he extended his right hand. "I'm Dr. Paul. And you're Mr. Peacock, right?"

"Uh... Yeah," I said, contemplating just how easily I could execute a quick Shock-Lock-Rip maneuver from the glory days of my linebacker career in high school football and shoot past this man and out the door. I thought better of it, realizing that nothing could be worse than the throbbing pain in my gum, and the sooner I just shut up and sit down and got this over with, the better off I'd be.

"Why don't you go ahead and take a seat and we'll get you all prepped and ready," he stated.

I took a seat and he got me all prepped and ready, which involved applying some sweet-tasting local anesthetic to my gum before injecting liberal amounts of Novocain in and around the area where he was going to chop my mouth to bits. He also put a nitrous oxide mask on my face, which was probably the greatest mistake any man could make with me. I am a total and utter lightweight, and it didn't take much from the mask to get me nice and lucid.

"Alrighty, Mr. Peacock," Dr. Paul said as he returned from whatever the hell it was he was doing while I was getting stoned. "Are you ready?"

"He he he he he he," I replied.

He began work on digging my molar out of my mouth. According to him, he had to split the tooth into three sections and remove each one individually, which was nothing short of absolutely horrendous. The smell of burning tooth rose into my nostrils as he sawed bilaterally up the bone and burned away a lot of core material.

And all I could do was laugh.

Between the bleach and the burning molar flying into my nose, I began to develop quite a stream of mucus oozing from my nostril. The dental assistant did her best to keep it clean, but I could taste in and amongst the flecks of broken tooth and blood and bleach and my sweat the salty, disgusting flavor of snot.

And all I could do was giggle.

As he began removing hunks of tooth, I became keenly aware of the limits of Novocain as an anesthetic. The deep infection of the roots of my tooth were largely unaffected by the deadening agent and immense flashes of pain flew up my jaw and into my brain, setting it alight and causing tears to stream down my face. I wanted to cry out; I wanted to yell "Get your goddamn hands out of my mouth before I beat you to death with your own golf shoes, you fucking sadistic son of a bitch!"

But all I could do was snicker.

"Okay, last piece," Dr. Paul said as he clamped down on the third slab of tooth. "Ready?" he asked.

"Hehehe! Ha! HAHAHA!" I replied.

He yanked and I sobered up REALLY quickly.

"HOLY FRAGGLE ROCK!" I cried out as the flames shot from the empty socket in my gum and I began to swallow heat and blood and bone.

"Yeah, I'm sorry about that," Dr. Paul replied. "Your tooth was incredibly infected and, unfortunately, there's just no way to deaden the inside of a tooth."

Sorry's fine and all, but I still wanted to Shock-Lock-Rip his ass.

The assistant cleaned me up and stuffed wads of gauze into my mouth. I peeled myself from the chair I'd soaked in my sweat and headed to the front desk, where I paid for the privilege of being cut and broken and stabbed and drugged. I left my grandfather's house and got into my incredibly hot car, cranking up the engine and feeling an intense gust of stale, hot air fly from the vents and hit me in the face. I had the worst headache I'd ever had in my entire life and was thirsty beyond belief, so I took a sip of the tea I'd left in the cup holder of my warm car. I couldn't muster the power to spit the liquid back into the cup due to the numbness in my mouth, so it just dribbled down my chin and all over my shirt.

Sticky, hot, bloody and feeling like crap, all I wanted to do was go home.

PART TWELVE

Whereupon Joe doesn't get to go home (not right away, anyway, but you'll see why in this part because there are no other parts)

Things were beginning to get better – if only slightly. The air had just started to turn cold and De La Soul's "Pass tha' Plugs" had popped on the randomized MP3 player, a song which always makes me feel better. I was just settling into my seat for the 20 minute drive home when I became aware of a small tint of blue light in my rearview mirror. It only glimmered in my peripheral vision for a second before it went away. But then it came back again.

"Wha?" I asked myself as I looked up to see what was going on behind me. Just as my eyes met the mirror, I heard a small "WHOOP!" scream loudly behind me.

"FUCHHHHH!" I screamed through my gauze as I pounded the steering wheel with one hand and turned it slightly with the other, heeding the request from the Griffin police officer behind me to pull over. I sighed as I placed my car into park and turned down the stereo so as to avoid further pissing off the officer from the notoriously hard-nosed police force of Griffin.

He took his time waddling up to my driver's side window, which I rolled down just as he arrived. "Driver's License, proof of insurance and Registration," he demanded. I pulled my wallet out from my back pocket and produced the information he requested, heeding the advice from my father to always wait until it's requested before digging around to get it, so as to let the officer see you move and not spook him (really good advice, by the way. It's part of the reason I've gotten out of so many tickets).

He examined the documents and ducked down to look at me. "Mr. Peacock, the reason I pulled you over is because you are driving erratically. Have you had anything to drink this afternoon?" He asked from behind his mirrored sunglasses.

"Noh," I replied, releasing a small pocket of blood-laced drool that began tumbling down my chin.

He tilted his head with curiosity, much the way a dog does when you attempt to explain string theory to it. "You alright there, son?"

"Noh," I replied. "I juh goh donh ah uh denhuh."

"You what?" He asked.

I reached into my mouth and removed the bloody wad of soaked gauze. "The dentist," I said, my mouth still numb. "I just had a tooth removed."

"Oh, my," he said. "I bet you feel like hell... You sure look like it." He looked me over for a second. "Did he put the gas on you?" He asked.

"Yeah," I replied with a bubble of spit forming between my lips.

"Hmm..." He muttered. "Wait here for a second." He took my information back to his car and did... Something... With it for about 15 minutes. All the while, I was mopping up drool and blood from the bottom of my lip, occasionally wiping down my goatee which began to look like a paintbrush dipped in some sick artist's idea of a statement against social norms. The cop finally exited his car and returned to my driver's side window with a small metal clipboard.

"Alright, here's the deal," he said as my stomach began to knot up. "I'm SUPPOSED to ticket you with DWI, but because I know what you've been through, I'm not gonna do that. But I DO gotta ticket you for something, so here's your citation for speeding five miles over the limit."

My stomach loosened, but thankfully not too much or else that'd have been a whole new mess. He bade me sign the ticket, which I did. "And if it's alright with you," he added, "I'm gonna follow you to your house, seeing as it's real close to the Speedway and I was headed that way myself." He was, of course, referring to the Atlanta Motor Speedway, the source of much gastric distress for me anytime there's a NASCAR or NOPI event.

"Thank you, officer," I said as nicely as I could.

"No problem at all," he answered. "I want to make sure you get home safely, but I'm mostly looking out for the other motorists on the road, to tell you the **tooth**."

He grinned a wide grin, proud beyond belief of his incredible pun. I laughed. Not because of the nitrous, but because it was the only choice between the two I had that wouldn't land me in prison for assaulting an officer.

It took about three days for the swelling and pain to subside, and when it did, I felt better than I had in over a year and a half. I got a call a few weeks later from Dr. Tom's office, following up on the surgery and asking about getting an implant installed in the empty socket.

"Will I have any issues in the future if I don't?" I asked him.

"Well… Your rear molar might move a bit. Otherwise, you'll just look like a hockey player."

I can live with that.

BOTH THE WORST AND THE BEST FLIGHT EXPERIENCE EVER

POSTED JULY 8, 2010

I'm on a plane from Atlanta to New York. I'm on this plane because the one I was supposed to be on an hour earlier left the gate without me. It left the gate without me because I arrived 4 minutes too late to get on board. I arrived 4 minutes too late because the TSA are staffed by inept power-hungry morons who can't cut it in legitimate law enforcement and need a job where they can subject people to their ridiculously needs to be in control of situations. And steal belts.

I arrived at the airport with about an hour to spare to get on my flight. It's a simple one day trip (I hope!) so I only brought my laptop bag. For this particular trip, I have to be dressed nicely, so I'm in slacks and a tie (for the second day in a row, actually - yesterday was a funeral).

I know the routine by now, so I took off my shoes and belt. I stuck the belt in an open back pocket on my bag, along with my phone (which I forgot to charge last night and is dead) and my wallet. I put everything on the belt and went through the detectors without issue.

The guy monitoring bags through the scanner decided my bag needed extra attention and called over a particularly obnoxious asshole to do a manual search of my bag. The guy started rummaging through my bag and after about five minutes, I asked if I could help him find whatever he was looking for. He immediately got all stalwart and said "Sir, I have to ask you to back away from the screening area." So I did, and the shouted "Okay, NOW can I help you find whatever you're looking for?"

He practically threw a narrowed-eyed stare at my head.

What followed was nothing short of ridiculous. He proceeded to question me about EVERY. SINGLE. THING. in my bag, including aspirin. I was getting fed up with his shit, but a) needed to hurry to make my flight and b) didn't want to end up like Jason Bourne in the Bourne Supremacy, receiving questions from a puffed-up fruit loop in a locked room somewhere (I've done it before - it's no fun).

By the end of it, he took 32 minutes to clear my bag, and decided to confiscate - of all things - my fucking belt. I didn't get a clear reason why either - he just said I could surrender it or exit security and ship it back to myself.

He was being a dick.

I said "Fuck it, keep it" and ran to the terminal tram. I was at gate B1, which is the last gate in a fairly large terminal (for those who don't know, ATL is HUGE). When I got off the tram, I ran - in dress shoes - to the gate. And from there, you know the rest.

I was rebooked on the 9:40 AM, and was feeling pretty frustrated and sweaty and wanted to beat someone and wished I had the power to shoot lasers from my mouth so I could kill people with my screams. Since my new seat was at the front of the plane, I knew I had a few minutes to waste. I took a short walk to get some water and generally just keep from yelling at people. I came back after getting a water and some yogurt and boarded to find a teenage brother and sister sitting on my row. The brother was screwing with an iPod, and the sister was - much to my surprise - reading a copy of my book.

I had to do a triple take, because it was just too weird. After a few minutes, I leaned over her brother in the middle seat and asked her what she was reading. She showed me the cover, and I smiled. "Ah," I said, " I read that one. How do you like it?"

She said it was pretty funny, that her brother insisted she read it after he finished it. The brother chimed in saying it was the funniest book he'd read in a long time.

"I actually know the author," I said. The boy, about 16 I'd wager, perked up. "He's a dick," I said with a grin.

He kinda frowned. "Really?" he asked. I proceeded to tell him all kinds of stuff about how awful I really was, that I treat people really horribly and added "He even interrupts people on planes who are trying to read a book."

They looked at me strangely. The boy then gave me a sly smile, indicating he got the joke. I smiled back.

"You don't really know him, do you!" he accused.

I grinned and said "Check the back cover."

Now, I was wearing a tie, NOT wearing a hat, and I've shaved my goatee and lost a little more weight since that photo was taken, so I can see why it took him a minute to put it together. Even after he did, he said "No way..."

I rolled up my left sleeve and showed him the tattoo. He pretty much flipped out.

We talked for a bit; I autographed the book and drew a pirate fighting a ninja. I was introduced to his parents and they said he was gaga over the book and insisted everyone read it. He got it with a gift card to Barnes and Noble he got for his birthday a few weeks ago. He gave me some critique on the Mentally Incontinent site, saying he only recently figured out how to find the rest of the stories (which gutted me - expect a redesign of that realllllly soon).

They're asleep right now.

It's been both the worst and best flight experience I've ever had.

YOU KNOW WHAT, IF A POLAR BEAR SHOWS UP IN MY DRIVEWAY I'M NOT GOING TO HUG IT

POSTED SEPTEMBER 12, 2010

I DON'T CARE what the marketing department at Coca Cola tries to tell me about polar bears. I'm not even playing about that, if a polar bear shows up in my driveway I'm not going to hug the damn thing. I'm probably going to shoot it, if I can get to a firearm. And if I'm not able to get to a firearm, I'm going to beat it with my steel Starbucks coffee mug, because that's usually what I leave the house with when I head out to my truck. Which is in my driveway. Which is where the polar bear might show up for hugs.

And I'm not hugging it. No. Not even if it's not in the driveway. If the polar bear shows up in, say, my kitchen, I'm not hugging it there, either. I'm grabbing two of the biggest knives out of my knife block and I'm yelling "<u>HAVE AT YOU!</u>" and I'm lunging at its eyes with the knives, because then if I connect it'll be blind and can't see me. And if it can't see me, it certainly can't hug me. Which is what I want - no hugs from a polar bear.

Because fuck polar bears. And fuck hugs. I don't want that shit. I'm telling you. If you're a polar bear and you're reading this and you're thinking "You know what I want is a hug" and then you think "You know who I want a hug from is Joe

Peacock" and then you think "You know where I want that hug from Joe Peacock is in his driveway" then FUCK YOU. And if you think kitchen instead of driveway, know that I'm going to stab your eyes.

I'm not even kidding.

[Among the dozens of comments on this post was this one, and it cracked me up so much I had to include it here:]

Comment by:
Sad Polar Bear in Need of a Hug *9/13/2010 12:37 AM*
hangs head and walks away

AN INTENTIONALLY VAGUE LETTER TO SOMEONE, FOR SOMEONE ELSE

POSTED SEPTEMBER 27, 2010

(A note: This isn't for me, per se. It certainly draws upon some feelings I've had, but it's actually a piece written for someone else; my small way of trying to empower this person to be okay with how they're feeling right now. I imagine we've all had to face something from our pasts that tears out our hearts and throws them against the wall. This is my answer to that; saying it's perfectly fine to not turn the other cheek. While I do believe that "anger is letting them win," sometimes, that anger changes into something far more powerful for you than it ever could be for them. Sometimes, it's okay to not let it go. Sometimes, it's okay to want to tear someone's heart out and show it to them so they can see how it feels. That's what this is about.)

You want to know why I can't forgive you?

Because you can never, ever take back what you did to me. You can't make it right; you can't fix the problem. You can't heal the damage. I had to do that. I had to fix myself; I had to make myself whole after you tore me in half. You didn't even have the decency to stick around and watch. And now, these years later, you want to make amends?

What, you get to act however you want, exacting your will against me, disappear while I figure it all out, and then show up again when your soul gets the best of you and ask me if I'll let you off the hook?

You're a terrorist. You're only happy when those around you are in discord. And the fact that I have to write this out for you is proof enough that you've not changed a bit... Your methods have. Why can't you just stay away? Why isn't one turn at screwing me up enough for you?

And you're not even brave enough to show up and ask me for permission to forgive yourself to my face (because that's what forgiveness is, after all... If you were even slightly human, you'd just forgive yourself without needing to involve me). Fuck you. I think you know how it'd turn out if you showed up here in person. I wouldn't be the only one who had to suffer through this. But you know that. You know enough to stay far enough away to keep safe, all the while lobbing your emotional ordinance at me.

The truth is, you shaped me. You shaped me through pain and torment. I scarred over in those places. I feel no pain there, but every time I see the mark, I remember how it all went down. And every time I do, I think about how I'd visit that pain upon you in a way I could be sure you felt it. Because I know you have no heart to break and no soul to trade away, it'd have to be physical. And that's why you stay far enough away.

Are you happy? Are you glad you had an effect on making me who I am? I hope so. I hope it was worth it. I hope it gives you some satisfaction; so that the entire exercise was not in vain.

But you didn't destroy me. Far from it. Yes, it felt that way at the time. It hurt so badly I wanted to end it all. I wanted to fall through the earth; I wanted to disappear. But as time passed and the distance between us grew, I pulled myself up and examined the rubble and rebuilt what I am... Only this time, I made myself stronger and more aware. I got to cut away the weak parts that you abused. I'm hardened. I'm reinforced. I will never allow anyone that kind of access again.

I'm as over it as I can be. Parts of me still ache when I hear your name. But it still hurts; as you knew it would when you left. And now you're back.

For your sake, stay away. For what's left of what I felt for you that was good, I hope you'll keep your distance. Don't write me. Don't call me. Don't show up at my door. I still have enough love for you that I don't want what would happen to you to go down. I don't want to hurt you, no matter how badly you hurt me. Be satisfied with the damage you've already done. Don't think for a second it's alright for you to do any more, regardless of your motivations.

You are poison. You are not welcomed. If you stay, YOU will be the one left hurt this time.

This is your only warning.

HOW NOT TO DO HOME MAINTENANCE, #72771: THE HEATER

POSTED NOVEMBER 18, 2010

Those of you who follow me on Twitter and Facebook saw a curious little post last night:

@joethepeacock: Good homeowner tip: every few years, apply some WD-40 to the fan on your heater's motor. Better tip: Turn the pilot light off first.

To understand what's going on here, I need to set the stage:

For your heater to blow hot air, two things have to happen: the air has to get hot (from the burner), and the air has to blow (from the blower). The blower has a motor. The motor has a fan, and in order for that fan to move, it sits on a spindle. All of this sits in a vented case.

A long time ago, whoever installed the air conditioning up in the attic was a genius and somehow set up a funnel made of the loose end of a zip tie where the condensation from the air conditioning would trickle right down it, through the venting, and onto the motor. After a few years of this, the whole thing began rusting up.

The HVAC guy said that, to save us a bit of money, he could just replace the fan and spindle for the blower, but every few years I'd want to get up there and throw a little WD-40 on the whole thing to keep it moving smoothly. I asked how I'd know when it was time, he said "When you turn on the heat and all you hear is humming or buzzing, it's time."

Well, that happened last night. So I went upstairs to check out the issue, and sure enough, the motor was "humming" (it had juice), but the fan wouldn't spin. It just sat there and buzzed, basically. So I took the cover off and moved the blades with my finger, and it chugged along with a good bit of resistance.

"QUICK!" I said to no one. "To the Garage!" I ran down, grabbed some WD-40, and headed back up to get the thing unfrozen. Thinking smartly, I also turned off the main blower motor via the switch near the assembly, lest the gas furnace blow up in my face.

Because I can't actually get at the blower motor spindle directly, I had to spray WD-40 through the vent slats and casing around the blower motor spindle and fan blades. This took a while (and a good bit of WD-40).

Having trouble imagining what this looks like? Just know this: A TON of WD-40 was being bandied about because I had no direct access to a fan spindle which was frozen up.

But one thing I didn't do: Turn off the pilot light. And when enough WD-40 collected on the blower spindle and fan to begin dripping down, it did so right on the open flame. And for bonus points, ignition took place just as I went to go spray the blower motor spindle again.

There was a huge "dripping" fire blowing all around my furnace assembly, and furthermore, I was holding an improvised blowtorch.

Without even thinking, I turned the spray of the WD-40 away from the furnace, but didn't think to let go of the nozzle, so now I was basically napalming all of my old toys and useless CDs in the attic. But only for a split second -- enough to scare the shit out of me. I am a safety freak (you wouldn't think so by how stupidly I behave), so anywhere there's fire, there's a fire extinguisher -- and in my attic, it sits right on top of the heater case. I grabbed it and put the fire out quickly, so there wasn't any damage. It just stunk to high heavens and left me shaking to the point that I had to sit in the frigid attic for about 15 minutes before I could brave the stairs down to the house.

So yeah, that was my night last night.

FOR A FRIEND

POSTED NOVEMBER 28, 2010

I hate to see you this way.

You have so much potential. You're smart, you're funny, and you're a damn fine human being. And you keep getting in your own way because you let someone else's damage stop you.

I know the drill all too well. You believe what you've been told -- that you're not good enough; that you're a loser. Those words weren't words. They were living things... Parasites, unleashed upon you which then burrowed deep into you and began to feed on your spirit. They live off you. They devour you.

Those who hurt you, they meant to hurt you. They're winning every single time you let what they say affect you. They couldn't have loved you; they couldn't have ever been your friend. They did this to you. Friends don't do that.

I wish I could have gotten to you first. I wish I could give you the weapons you needed to fight off the ticks and leeches who used you and then left you scarred. I wish the words I say could counteract all that damage and kill the parasites and help you see how wrong they were. I wish I could take it from you. Like I said, I know this all too well. I know the pain, I know the suffering, and I can handle it. I'm big and I'm strong and I've been there before; several times. I know how to fight them. I know how to beat them.

I wish I could teach you. I can tell you how I did it, I can give you the words to repeat in your mind and the methods to combat all that damage... But just showing you the moves is no different than teaching someone another language by constantly repeating it to them, only louder and more emphatic each time you don't get it. You have to immerse yourself in it. You have to live it.

Live like you love yourself. You don't right now -- I get that. But it's not real. It's because of them and what they said and the things they did to you. It's not that you loathe yourself; it's that you loathe what THEY convinced you you are.

It's not enough to say "don't let them win." They already have. The way to win is to draw a line in the sand right here, right now, and cross it. Treat that line as a whole new life, one where you're going to treat yourself right and love yourself. Cook good things for you to eat. Buy clothes you like. Exercise. Cut them off -- don't listen to them. Don't let them in. Treat them like dogs barking on the other side of a door you just closed.

And take it all one day at a time. Stop looking at the end of the tunnel and wishing you were on the other side of it. Just put one foot in front of the other. And know that those who really know you and love you know what you are. Not what you can be, but what you ARE. And all we want is for you to see it for yourself.

YOU WANT TO KNOW MY RELIGIOUS BELIEFS? OKAY, FINE, HERE YOU GO

POSTED JANUARY 5, 2011

You know, I can probably pull out an email a month for the past ten years where someone has either asked why I am an atheist, or called me an asshole because I am an atheist, or says that atheists can't possibly understand why Christians do what they do, etcetera.

I'm not an Atheist. It's almost comical the degree to which Christian people cannot understand that "Not Christian" ≠ "Atheist".

I'm also not a liberal, but conservatives can't seem to understand that people who don't agree with them ≠ Liberal. It's probably the same people. I need to write a script which compares all the hatemail I've received over the years to determine senders. I'll get on that, sometime around the time that I start caring about the opinions and feelings of people who start off their arguments with some sentiment which boils down to "You're wrong because you're an Atheist / Liberal."

You don't know me, apparently. And that's fine, you probably don't want to. I definitely don't know you if you're going to assume I'm wrong, wholesale -- on everything -- because you've deduced (incorrectly) that I believe in this or that.

First and foremost, I believe that my beliefs are exactly that -- the things I've chosen to accept in the absence of fact, guided by what evidence I've received, to help me put together strings of events or fill gaps left open by history (or my limited understanding of an infinite universe).

I do not care if you accept my beliefs. I do not care if you choose to believe them, or choose to think they're stupid, or choose to believe a different set of beliefs. Because they're just beliefs. Whether or not you understand this, beliefs are choices, and I'm not about to step on your right to make decisions which help you make it through the day, and I believe you owe me the same courtesy.

And that's where things start to fall apart -- the moment your personal beliefs extend any further than the immediate space beyond the tip of your nose (or, if you're a typical American, like I am, the space just beyond the area of your belly button, whichever is the furthest extended point of your body).

The reason I'm so hard on Christianity is really because, of all the religions I'm familiar with, it's the most hypocritical. Well, next to Hitchens Atheists. They're actually the most hypocritical religion, because they don't even think they're a religion. But I'll get to them in a minute.

And I'm not talking about hypocritical people. Christianity is rife with, for instance, men who go to strip clubs or cheat on their wives during the week, then show up on Sunday to ask for forgiveness. Or, people who sport many-thousand-dollars' coats or shoes or cars to a service where they're worshiping a man who gave freely to the poor. Every religion has their hypocrites, and in my experience, the ratio of horribly hypocritical Christians (or Fashion Christians, as I call them, who wear their spirituality on their sleeve for social benefit) versus honest, belief-led, good spirited, really damn great people who are Christians is about 1:1.

I'd argue that this is the same with any religion. In fact, I'd say is the same with any sampling of any group of people in any demographic for any purpose, because before I believe anything else, I accepted that the world is in balance and as it should be. For every bad there is a good, for every dark there is a light.

No, my biggest issue with Christianity is the hypocrisy found in the absolute basest tenet of the faith itself:

"For God so loved the world, that he gave his only son, so that whosoever believe in him shall not perish but will have everlasting life." --John 3.16

If you're like every other Christian I've ever tried to explain this to, you're probably shaking your head right now. That's a message of hope, you'll say. That's God's gift to the world.

Let's break it down:

God loves the world. Check.

God gave the world his only son. Fine, okay. I'll accept this aspect of the myth (not myth as in "lie" but as in "story", which is what every single religion is based on).

His only son died in a sacrifice made by God. This was the father putting the son to death. Why? So that I may be absolved from sin.

BUT! And here's where it sucks: I can only be absolved from sin if I choose to accept the sacrifice. If I do not, God will not extend the benefit of the gift given the world.

Putting it all together: GOD'S LOVE IS CONDITIONAL. The all-knowing, all-powerful creator of all things only loves those who love him back. God loves me so much, that I have to accept a sacrifice made to absolve me of sin. If I do not accept this sacrifice, I'm not absolved of sin, and thus spend eternity in hell.

Hell is described by the Bible and is generally accepted to be, well... Hell. It sucks. It's eternal damnation. It's difficult and punishing and really, really bad people go there to be forced for eternity to lay face-down on white hot plates of metal with one ton weights strapped to their back, or listen to The Barenaked Ladies, or other equally distasteful things for all of eternity.

Or, as it happens, even really good people who, by choice or by not being born to the right set of parents in the right country and not being indoctrinated with lessons from the "good" book, who might spend all of their lives helping others or even just smiling and generally spreading pleasantness around them. Because they didn't accept this sacrifice made by a loving God.

God loves me so much, he's going to punish me if I don't love him back. If that's not hypocritical, I don't know what is.

The way I understand love, it does not work this way. I've told my wife a few times in our lives that I love her so much, if it took being away from me to be happy, I'd have to let her go. Her happiness is the ultimate goal of my love for her. And if I make her unhappy, and I truly love her, I can't see any way to rectify keeping her around or holding her down just so I can have her. That is not love. That's ownership. That's coveting. That's dominion.

Love isn't force. It's not asking people to love you back, or else you are going to punish them. Love is a powerful thing that exists in absence of the promise of reward. When you love something with all your heart, the only thing you want is for it to be happy. Wanting it to be near you is a selfish thing, because you're holding it to yourself. If it chooses to be near you, you should feel honored and rewarded -- and if it chooses not to be, you stop loving it? You don't want the best for it? You will punish it?

And before you give me the whole "A loving parent punishes its child when it misbehaves" argument: **ETERNAL. DAMNATION.** That's not a spanking. It's not a guidance action made to teach a creation the finer points of social behavior patterns, its punishment and pain and torture forever. It's abandonment. Because of a choice not to accept the sacrifice made to protect me from making bad choices.

Whoever believes in him is not condemned, but whoever does not believe stands condemned already because he has not believed in the name of God's one and only Son. -- John 3:18

That's not only disgusting, it's also very typically human. And that, to me, sounds like a God made in our image, not the other way around. I will say it plainly, in print, so that God and all concerned can understand: I will not be the willing plaything or property of anyone or anything, no matter how powerful; no matter how severe the threat to my person or being. Ever.

If that means spending eternity doing knuckle push-ups on broken glass with that stupid "One Week" song playing over a loudspeaker, so be it. That's not foolish, it's utterly dogmatic and stubborn. It's choosing punishment over servitude.

I am as God made me. And if he finds fault with it, well now... He must not be a very perfect God. Do better with your next creation, sir.

Now, there are certainly aspects of Christianity which I like and have adopted for myself. I believe that Jesus Christ, who is Jesus of Nazareth, existed and was probably a really great guy. I believe he was a fine teacher and a shining example of the greater parts of our species. I believe him to be the son of

God insofar that I believe that Martin Luther King, Muhammad, Isaac Newton, Gandhi, Adolf Hitler and Justin Bieber to be sons of God. Or you. Or me.

Just because someone is charismatic and has the ability to lead does not make them in any way holy, beyond those who don't quite see it in them and choose not to follow them.

I believe in the teachings of Jesus Christ, and will give of my time and my material wealth to those who have less than I. I don't need to prove it to you -- if you've spent any time reading what I write, you know the amount of time Andrea and I spend involved with charities and social service. I understand the teachings of Jesus Christ. But I stop short of believing that he was any different than any other thoughtful and intelligent teacher.

I've also researched religions of the world beyond Jesus, and found far too many similarities to the "God - Mary - Jesus" and "God - Jesus - Holy Spirit" mythos for it to be an original story for me. For a little light reading, try reading a comparison of the lives of Jesus and Horus, whose myth existed nearly ten thousand years before Jesus's. And Christianity didn't borrow only from Egyptian mythology. Deitic sons have existed so long as deities have, which is to say as long as humans have been able to conceptualize them. It started with stories explaining why the sun was in the sky and went from there. Which is why I believe it's only that -- a story. A parable, even, if Jesus were a mouse and the world were an elephant with a thorn made of sin in its foot.

But I also understand that I'm making a choice to believe or not believe in the story. I've decided not to. I've decided instead to practice as much of the teachings of this teacher as I can, because he brought to the table some really valuable lessons. As did Carl Sagan, Henry Rollins and Douglas Adams, among several thousand others. I learn what I can from whom I can and try to apply it the best I can to my life.

But no matter how wise or thoughtful or deep I find any aspect of any passage, I am not about to go impose my will upon another person and force them to live life as I've decided it should be lived. Sure, I'll share my opinions on it... But here, in the context of a webpage with my name writ large atop it (and in the domain name), or in books with my name plastered on the cover. You know where you are when you get a dose o' Joe, and you're free to leave anytime you want. I'm not going to hold you down or force you to listen. Show up when you want. Listen to what you want. Take what you want from it. Live a good life. That's all I care about.

These throngs of bible-thumping neanderthal pieces of shit out there in there in the world, selectively enforcing only the laws from their religions' texts which happen to correspond with their personal prejudices... Well, let's just say that if I didn't subscribe to the philosophy in the previous paragraph, there'd be a pretty sizable dent in each and every one of their heads... As many as I could get to before I got arrested, anyway.

That they choose to read from the Bible and claim God -- the all powerful, all knowing creator -- wants life to be this way, and they are merely working through him to achieve it... It's disgusting. Just plain gross.

To pick just one example of several hundred I could choose, let's discuss the concept of gay marriage. Why? Because I have many gay friends, several of whom have committed themselves for the rest of their lives to another person who, if that person falls sick and dies, they can't legally make decisions for or manage their property the way I can with my wife. And the thought of not being able to be an actual husband to my wife makes me so sick in the heart, I can only imagine what my friends must feel each time they consider the fact that this huge group of supposedly loving, caring, wonderful people impose their beliefs on the whole of society to the point that these wonderful people, who I love very much, can't legally love one another.

That's why.

Gay people cannot choose to legally bind themselves to a legal contract which unites two people into one shared entity. Why? Because a book filled with chapters written across a span of several thousand years, many thousands of years ago, which people have chosen to believe is a rulebook for life has three archaic passages which say it's an abomination for people of the same sex to lay with one another. My favorite:

If a man lies with a man as one lies with a woman, both of them have done what is detestable. They must be put to death; their blood will be on their own heads. -- Leviticus 20:13

This is the same book, mind you, which says eating pork is an abomination. Yet, for some reason, Jesus's sacrifice cleansed the animals and supposedly absolved us all from sin. Except when we love someone who is the same gender as us. Surely, God -- who loves us all, mind you, and gave his only son so that we can spend forever with him because of love! Love! LOVE! -- could see past the whole "eew, his pee pee touched his pee pee" aspect of a rote animal behavior to the true nature of why two people, of any gender, race, creed, background, whatever, might put past themselves their own selfish nature in order to share life with another person.
No. "I'm God, and I made my kid hang from a crucifix for three days, starving and bleeding from the side until he died. You think I'm going to let your dicks touch and get away with it?"

That's not my idea of God... An all powerful, all knowing hypocrite.

Most Christians believe that God made us in his image. If this is true, that means God is, at least in some part, gay. Either that, or he is imperfect. Which is it?

Furthermore, why do Christians selectively decide this is a law of God which must be followed in this day and age, but others shouldn't? Here in its entirety, is the "Letter to Dr. Laura" which made the rounds a few years ago. The point it makes is exactly mine: Why do Christians selectively follow these laws and rules?

> Dear Dr. Laura,
>
> Thank you for doing so much to educate people regarding God's Law. I have learned a great deal from your show, and I try to share that knowledge with as many people as I can. When someone tries to defend the homosexual lifestyle, for example, I simply remind him that Leviticus 18:22 clearly states it to be an abomination. End of debate.
>
> I do need some advice from you, however, regarding some of the specific laws and how to best follow them.
>
> a) When I burn a bull on the altar as a sacrifice, I know it creates a pleasing odor for the Lord (Lev 1:9).The problem is my neighbors. They claim the odor is not pleasing to them. Should I smite them?
>
> b) I would like to sell my daughter into slavery, as sanctioned in Exodus 21:7. In this day and age, what do you think would be a fair price for her?
>
> c) I know that I am allowed no contact with a woman while she is in her period of menstrual uncleanliness(Lev 15:19-24). The problem is, how do

I tell? I have tried asking, but most women take offense.

d) Lev. 25:44 states that I may indeed possess slaves, both male and female, provided they are purchased from neighboring nations. A friend of mine claims that this applies to Mexicans, but not Canadians. Can you
clarify? Why can't I own Canadians?

e) I have a neighbor who insists on working on the Sabbath. Exodus 35:2 clearly states he should be put to death. Am I morally obligated to kill him myself?

f) A friend of mine feels that even though eating shellfish is an Abomination (Lev 11:10), it is a lesser abomination than homosexuality. I don't agree. Can you settle this?

g) Lev 21:20 states that I may not approach the altar of God if I have a defect in my sight. I have to admit that I wear reading glasses. Does my vision have to be 20/20, or is there some wiggle room here?

h) Most of my male friends get their hair trimmed, including the hair around their temples, even though this is expressly forbidden by Lev 19:27. How should they die?

i) I know from Lev 11:6-8 that touching the skin of a dead pig makes me unclean, but may I still play football if I wear gloves?

j) My uncle has a farm. He violates Lev 19:19 by planting two different crops in the same field, as does his wife by wearing garments made of two different kinds of thread (cotton/polyester blend). He also tends to curse and blaspheme a lot. Is it really necessary that we go to all the trouble of getting the whole town together to stone them? (Lev 24:10-16) Couldn't we just burn them to death at a private family affair like we do with people who sleep with their in-laws? (Lev. 20:14)

I know you have studied these things extensively, so I am confident you can help.

Thank you again for reminding us that God's word is eternal and unchanging.

Your devoted disciple and adoring fan.

Hypocrisy.

And that's why I am so hard on Christianity. I've read the Bible, cover to cover (not all in one sitting, mind you). I've read the Quran. I've read the Torah (which, I'll save you the trouble, is just the Old Testament Bible with a few extra Shaloms). I choose not to accept these books as law books for my life, because I also choose not to accept the description of God they've provided.

God, as I understand him, is not a "him", it is an "it." It's the tie that binds; the force which drives the universe to keep expanding and for atoms to bond and form molecules. It's the underlying energy which can neither be created nor destroyed. It's the space between; that omnipresent glue which holds everything together.

The Greek philosopher Democritus once said, **"Nothing exists except atoms and empty space. Everything else is just opinion."**

I believe God fills that space. It is the glue that holds us together. And the more I see trends in human evolution, even as simple as concepts and ideas that seem to arise in separate locations at the same time and spread like wildfire... The more I believe in that connection. And I think that being in tune with that connection is being in tune with God.

God talks to me all the time; most especially in moments when I'm tuned as completely into my surroundings as I can be -- on hikes, or when the very tip of my pen touches the paper, or when I'm trying to "feel" the light on a subject I'm trying to draw. I especially feel God in music. When those perfect vibrations are found by a talented musician and it not only fills our ears but sweeps our bodies in waves and we feel it... That's part of God talking to us. Because it's part of one person's soul talking to us in a language we all understand.

God is in us all and binds us together. God IS the universe. God is existence. It's corporeal and exists and is the harmonic hum which vibrates within us all (and within all things). And I do believe in it. I'm still trying to come to terms with it and research it and understand it.

I don't worship it. I don't worship anything. I don't think that an all-powerful, all-knowing force requires my subservience. I don't believe that anything with unlimited power would require that mortals revere it. More than that, I don't think that an all knowing creator could make the mistake of creating a being which willfully denies it and then punish it for doing exactly what it was created to do.

I do not believe that there may be, somewhere in the multiple layers of reality, some being sitting on a mountaintop lobbing lightning bolts of judgment at gay people. I believe that this entity exists in the minds of people who need a higher power which justifies their beliefs. "God says it, so it must be true, so it's okay for me to hate."
And to get to where I am now, at 33 (almost 34), I had to do a lot of learning on what I didn't believe. And that's why I've read what I've read, gone to services where I've gone to services, talked to whom I've talked to... I'm no better than

anyone else who believes a thing because they were taught it. Belief is belief. It's the acceptance of a thing in the absence of that thing's existence.

I believe that my best friends are not robbing a bank right now instead of working. I can't be there to check on each one of them for certain, but everything I know about them guides me to this conclusion. You believe that God is the creator of all things, that he gave his only human son in sacrifice that you may live a life free from the confines and condemnation of original sin.

The difference between my beliefs and theirs? My beliefs allow for them to have their beliefs, and I'm not going to go impose my will on someone who isn't doing anything with their actions which will harm me or anyone else. Because ultimately, what you spend your time thinking about at home in your own time doesn't affect me one bit. But the second you act on it, I get to respond.

Stay away from my rights and the rights of others. Stop changing history to bend to the nature of what you choose to believe. Feel free to tell me to shut up, or hate what I say, just as much as I tell you to shut up and hate what you say. Just understand that when you take action based on your beliefs, I'm going to take action based on mine.

So there you go. I'm not an atheist. I'm certainly without religion, and have been ever happier the longer I stay away from it. And in the proper contexts, I'm just as critical of Islam, Judaism, and even Hinduism as I am on Christianity when the need arises.

Critical is not "anti." I call into question things that make no sense to me.

But here's the really, REALLY interesting thing: In my ten years of doing this, I've never once had an Islamic person, a

Jew or a Hindu email me and demand that I share my belief system with them, or else I'm an Atheist. It seems that Christians don't really dig "critical." So yes, the vast majority of my reactions on this blog and elsewhere are toward Christians... Because for some reason, it's only Christians who feel the need to "save me" constantly.

And what you get here, when you come here -- by your own choice, mind you -- is reactions to things. The day a Muslim sends me email or writes something that pisses me off, you'll get an earful on that too. Just hasn't happened yet. Tells me a lot.

I don't believe all Christians are bad people or that all of them are out there ready to impose their will on me. As I said before, I have a LOT of Christian friends. I love them. If you haven't figured out much else about me, surely you know by now that I don't waste time being around people I can't stand. I don't do that. Hiding yourself around people to be socially accepted is loathsome and disgusting and false. I genuinely like and love my Christian friends. They genuinely like and love me.

But I will say that I find the underlying tenet of Christianity to be hypocritical. And above all else, I loathe hypocrisy. This doesn't mean I loathe Christians. I judge all people based on their actions and not much else. Those who act according to Jesus's teachings, I find to be wonderful people. They act in accordance with their beliefs. That itself is not hypocrisy. Believing in the tenets of Christianity is not hypocrisy. The act itself is not hypocritical. It just so happens that the foundation of the religion to which they ascribe, to me, is.
I just feel that, if you're going to choose something from the Bible to build your life around, how about starting with this:

Thou shalt not hate thy brother in thine heart: thou shalt in any wise rebuke thy neighbor, and not suffer sin upon him. -- Lev 19:17

I just think that your beliefs should stay the hell out of my rights and life. That goes for everyone, including (and in some cases, especially) Hitchens Atheists. You're not actually Atheists, you're Anti-Theist. Just for the record -- you guys are a religion. You have organized yourselves around a belief -- that there is no God. You're pushing your will on others in the name of fact and truth. Welcome to your religion-based crusade. You're on Jihad. You're everything you profess to hate.

Hypocrites.

So there you go. A question I've been asked no fewer than 20 times a year for the past 10 years, which I've successfully avoided or ignored until now. And why now? Because I think that as time moves forward and I keep doing what I'm doing (whatever it is I'm doing here; I still haven't figured that part out yet), lines need to be drawn in the sand. You need to know what you're getting into when you pay attention to me. There's no secrets. For the past 10 or whatever years that I've been writing on the internet, I didn't mean to keep my religious beliefs (or lack thereof) a secret per se. I just never thought they were important.

The more I criticize religion, however, the more important they become. And so, that's where I stand. I believe in a higher power. I call it God for lack of a better term. I believe God to be love. I also believe it to be unifying, cleansing, enriching and wonderful when you pay attention to the grand nature of how delicate every creation is. When you look at the structure of cells and beyond them, molecules -- and beyond them, atoms, protons, neutrons, electrons, strange behavior at a distance, quarks, quantum events and so on...

And I'm not going to blow you up, fly airplanes into you, or protest your wedding to make you see I'm right.

FUCK YOU AND YOUR PHD IN ENGLISH LIT

POSTED JANUARY 6, 2011

If you follow me on Twitter or Facebook, you might remember this tweet:

@joethepeacock: Just got into a fight with an English Lit PhD about publishing. He's not and wants to be, and just bashed my advice because I have no degree

We're all pretty friendly at my gym. You see the same people all the time, and thankfully, the vast majority of regulars are all pretty friendly, nice, good people. We get along. Some of us do stuff together, like cycling or running events.

What's really interesting though: most of us don't really know what each other do outside of the gym. For the most part, we all pretty much exist as the people we are when we're working out, and that's great. Occasionally, though, someone will find out what I do and we'll talk about it. Sometimes, it's about web development. Other times, graphic design. And of course, there'll be times where folks find out I write.

So, a few weeks ago, a dude who works out at my gym chatting me up about publishing and whatnot. He'd been casually mentioning writing and whatnot the past few workouts, going out of his way to say hi.

This is a guy who, previous to this newfound interest in me, shared nods and a few smiles now and again. Occasionally, he'd make a comment about what I was lifting, or a cute girl. But that's about it.

Apparently, one of the people at my gym who reads my blog and stuff told him that I write for a living (which is only sorta true, because I also do a lot of other crap). He asked for my phone number so we could meet up and he could buy me coffee, which is bullshitese for "I really just want to get as much info as I can out of you to accomplish my own goals."

And that's fine. It happens. And I'm 100% okay with it, because that's part of my whole mission: telling people how to do this whole thing for themselves and get their writing out there.

And he did call to ask if we could meet up. But I couldn't make it out that day, because I had an assignment for a client due (which is actually kinda cool, and I'll share it with you guys on Monday). So, instead of understanding my situation and doing what he should have, which was say "Oh, no big deal man, when is good for you? Let's reschedule" (which I would have done), he just starts asking the questions he wanted the answers to. He probably thought it was one hell of a great thing that I couldn't make it, because I just saved him the price of Starbucks to get information.

Now, I don't want to be a dick (yep, contrary to what you may think, I actually do try to be a decent person), So, holding my phone between my shoulder and ear as I resumed working on the project, I said "Really, the only advice I have for everyone is just to sit down and write it out. Even when you think it sucks, or you have no idea where it's going, or how to get it there, just write. You learn on the way."

His response? "Well, I'm okay on how to actually write a book, I do have a PhD in English Lit. I wanted publishing advice."

Oh. This.

So, I told him that it was actually really easy -- he could go to cafépress, lulu or lightning source and set up an account, and put the sucker out there. Basically, all the stuff I put in the No Bullshit Guide.

He got really snippy. "I'm not interested in vanity press," he said with a snide bit of verbal italics around the words "vanity press."

Of course, I tried to educate him on the difference, and it wasn't' doing much good, he wanted contacts at Penguin or advice on how to make some. "Can you introduce me to your editor?" He actually asked.

So I explained that I made my contacts was writing my book on the internet, asking everyone who read me to tell their friends, publishing the paper book myself and selling thousands of copies to people who supported me. "Penguin came to me, I didn't go to them," I told him.

He was silent for a moment. "So it was luck?" he finally asked.

"Isn't everything?" I replied. "I'm lucky that people got behind me and supported me."

"Well that doesn't do much good for those of us with more skill than luck, I guess." He actually said that.

Wow.

I began grinding my teeth. "And that means..." I sort of asked with my trailing verbal ellipsis.

"You admitted yourself, you dropped out of college," he said.

"So you feel that having a degree makes you skilled in writing a book?" I asked pretty bluntly.

"Well, yeah," he answered.

"And that skill cost what, 40 grand? 50 grand?" I asked. And before he could answer, I said "Glad I paid absolutely nothing to learn to write and instead bought all those rabbits' feet."

"Wow..." he said. "That's kinda rude."

"Yep," I said. "And you're in luck. I just flipped a coin and it came up tails, which means I get another book deal. Look for this story in it when it comes out."

He sat there, stunned.

"I'll sign it for you, if you want," I added. "Do you want me to add the 'PhD' at the end of your name?"

He hung up.

So, today was the first day since that conversation that I've seen him at the gym. He came right up to me and said "Dude, I have to apologize..."

"Hey, doc," I said, interrupting him. "Get your book out yet?"

He chuckled that fake ass chuckle people chuckle when they'd rather be slapping you than chuckling. "Nope, not yet," he said, then continued on his original track. "I apologize, I was pretty rude the other day."

"Not at all," I said. "I've met self-important entitled people in the past. I know what you lot are like." I started putting weights on a bar so I could actually do something useful while in the building besides wasting my time with the guy.

He sorta stammered, then blurted out, "So, when can we get that coffee?"

I looked up at him. "Got a quarter?" I asked.

He patted his pockets. "No?" he replied.

I looked around the gym and caught the eye of a guy we both know. "Hey, got a quarter?" I asked him. He dug into his bag and produced a nickel. "Good enough," I said, and I took it from him. "Call it," I said to the good doctor, and flipped it into the air.

"Heads," he said with a strange look.

It came up tails.

"Sorry man," I said, "Looks like you're going to have to rely on that talent of yours, cause you're just not lucky enough."

He looked me up and down, smirked, and walked away.

ON SAFE PLACES
POSTED JUNE 14, 2011

There's actually no such thing.

There are no safe places. There are only places you go to hide. And there's value in that. But never make the mistake of thinking that you have a truly safe place in this world, where you're protected from all evil and nefarious crap.

You must be strong. You must be stronger than that which affects you. You must persevere. When you go to write, you can go to a place where you feel safe... But don't think that that protects you from the effects of what you write, the memories it dredges, the feelings and the thoughts, and most of all the reactions of others. When you go to draw, it's the same thing. And especially in life -- there's no place truly safe.

You cannot turtle up. You cannot hide from life forever. You can trust no one and no place to be your safe place. You can go places you feel safe. You can be around people you feel safe around. But eventually, you WILL have to face things on your own. And when you do, you need to be strong.

I am not being cynical, I am being honest with you. And you need to know -- the world is tough. As my friend Casey says, "Life is hard, wear a helmet." Because you WILL take lumps. You will fall down. You will get hurt. You will collapse. And when you do, if you are lucky, there will be people there that will pick you up and dust you off.

But it's your legs you stand up on. Get them sturdy and strong. You'll need them if you intend to get anywhere.

JUST BECAUSE

POSTED JULY 7, 2011

Just because you feel it, doesn't mean it's how things are.

Just because you're hurting, doesn't mean you're wounded.

Just because you say it, doesn't mean that you mean it.

Just because you heard it, doesn't mean you understand it.

Just because you know it, doesn't mean you've accepted it.

Just because you've accepted it, doesn't mean it's okay, right, correct or how things should be.

Life doesn't work in absolutes. Period. There is no such thing as black and white, right or wrong, good or bad. There's how you feel about things and that's pretty much it. We're predisposed to reject pain and accept pleasure. That's our basis for determining right, wrong, good, bad, black, white.

Sometimes, you're supposed to get hurt. Sometimes, you're supposed to take a shot right to the jaw. One you never saw coming. You're supposed to know what that feels like, so you can know how to recover from it, and how to look for it next time.

That's what makes you stronger. Smarter. Whole.

Metamorphosis is painful. Just because it hurts, doesn't mean it's not a good thing. Let go of preconceptions of good and bad and accept that pain simply reminds you of how good pleasure can feel and vice versa. You will say things you don't mean to reject pain. You will pretend you've accepted things to just move past them and stop having to deal with them. You will languish in periods of pleasure and let things that cause pain slide or go without addressing them.

Just because you don't see it doesn't mean it's not there. And just because it's there doesn't mean you have to go seek it out and face it. When you get hit, accept that you got hit... And then don't get hit the same way again.

TATTOOS = EX-CON
(OR, YET ANOTHER JOE-ON-
AN-AIRPLANE STORY)

POSTED JULY 22, 2011

So you know how I was all kinds of annoyed that nothing happened to me at the airport or on the airplane on Monday? Well, Wednesday totally made up for that.

On my flight home from LA, I was in the very back row, on the aisle, and a family boarded. The mother and daughter took the two seats next to me (window and middle), and the father sat in a middle seat further up the row. So, being the gentleman I am, I asked the flight attendant if there were any open aisle seats near the front.

LO! And behold, there was. So, I gave the father my seat so he could be next to his kin (and he was very thankful!) and moved on up, to a seat next to an older woman and someone I assume was her daughter. And as I sat down, I heard them discussing the various celebrities in their shared copy of People magazine:

"Oh, she's MUCH prettier than Lady Gaga," said the younger woman.

"Yes, much... She's slimmer," said the older one.

It was then that I knew, this would be nowhere near as fun as my trip to LA. And sometime shortly after I tweeted the above conversation, I caught in the corner of my eye the elder woman looking me up and down, then holding a newspaper to her face and leaning toward her daughter.

And it wasn't very hard to make out what she was whispering:

"He must be an ex-con, with all the tattoos..."

She kept whispering about how uncomfortable she felt sitting next to me. So I snapped the above pic and Tweeted, Facebooked and GooglePlussed it. Because I'm social, is why. Plus, I think everyone knows by now, the second I mention I'm anywhere NEAR an airport, they tune right in and just wait for the hijinks to ensue.

Later on in the the flight, she gave me a weird look when I pulled out my laptop, like "What are YOU doing with a laptop, you convict?" I assume that's what it was like anyway, since it was hard to understand the noises her face was making as her overly-made-up skin stretched and groaned against its own wrinkles to make that face.

Later on, she mustered up the courage (or, became so unbelievably bored she had no other alternative but) to ask me what the hell I'm all about.

"So, what do you do?" she asked.

"I'm a writer," I responded as I finished typing a sentence, and then looked at her.

"Oh!" she said, nodding. It was like she was allowing for the idea that convicts AND writer-types could have tattoos. She then asked, "So, what do you write?"

Without batting an eye, I looked right at her and said "My time in prison."

The look on her face was priceless. It was like I'd just peed on her cat; she was so disgusted and taken aback. Of course, I had to Tweet, Facebook and GooglePlus that too, much to the delight of a LOT of people.

Not much happened after that. She shrunk away from me and leaned toward her daughter to say something, but I couldn't hear what (not that I much cared at this point). A bit later, she decided to reach out again and be kind. She asked me if I wanted her Biscoff cookies.

"No thanks, sugar interferes with my medication," I answered.

It took her a little while, but eventually she asked "So what are you on medication for?"

"HIV," I answered plainly.

You could have cut her head off and used her gaze to peel the paint off a car, she was that horrified by my answer. But the internet was delighted.

Shortly thereafter, I confessed that I'd actually overheard her talking about my tattoos earlier and wanted to just have a little fun with her; that I was 100% healthy and had never been to prison. And she didn't really take that as a joke. She was angry. She didn't say another word, to me or anyone, the rest of the flight.

I had to let her off the hook. I couldn't just let her suffer thinking that the guy next to her was one aluminum can accident away from giving her THE AIDS. Or maybe I could have... But I just don't have the heart for it. But, maybe next time, she will think twice before jumping to conclusions about someone based solely on their appearance... Or maybe she won't. Maybe this actually justified the idea that tattooed freaks are actually liars and terrible people.

FINE BY ME.

THE NO BULLSHIT GUIDE TO SELF DEFENSE FOR LADIES

POSTED AUGUST 4, 2011

A few years ago, I wrote a guide on how to actually win a fist fight. The guide was geared mostly toward men and boys who had no fight training, who may find themselves in a situation where they have to defend themselves against a bully. It was a much bigger success than I ever anticipated. To date, I've received over a hundred emails from fathers thanking me for writing the guide that finally taught their kid how to stand up for himself, and young men who have faced bullies and other less than savory characters using the tactics I taught them.

Yesterday, completely separate from each other, two women asked me to write a self-defense guide for ladies, with the same no-bullshit attitude and tactics I used in the fist fight guide. I took this as a sign, and have done exactly that. It is my sincere hope that no woman ever has to use any of the information in this guide, ever. But unfortunately in today's social climate, hoping isn't enough.

This guide will very lightly touch on things that you can learn in just about every self-defense course, video and article I've ever seen -- namely, situational awareness, avoiding becoming a victim, and all of that. It will then dive very briefly into why you should carry a gun, and if not a gun, a can of pepper spray with military-grade tear gas -- and if not that, a knife.

And then, we get to the stuff I've never really seen anywhere: what to do if you need to defend yourself against a male attacker with only your hands.

So, if you already know all that situational awareness stuff and you find guns and knives and the like icky and gross, feel free to skip on down to the last section. But I'll go ahead and tell you the point of this entire guide, and hope you won't skip anything:

This is your life we're talking about here. Not just staying alive, but living it without having to face severe traumatic experience (read: getting raped). He is going to hurt you or kill you. You need to be prepared to hurt him first and escape.

So even if you know this stuff, it's not a bad idea to re-read it and refresh your memory.

Situational awareness

This is the "common sense" portion of the guide. And that phrase is in quotes because, even though sitting here reading this thing, you're going to think "well, DUH, of course I shouldn't walk down dark alleyways at night by myself," I guarantee that the vast majority of you have done exactly that, thinking "well, I'm in a hurry" or "it looks safe enough."

Nothing is ever "safe enough." It's either safe or not safe. Period.

Now, there's no need to go out into the world thinking everyone's out to get you. You don't have to be in a constant paranoid panic every time you go to the mall. But you DO need to keep your head about you.

In the car:

If your car gets stranded on the highway, **stay the hell in it**. Don't go anywhere. Keep a disposable cellphone in your car and keep it charged up with minutes (and juice). Most states have a DOT program that can help you with roadside assistance. Even if a person is wearing a uniform (even a cop), STAY. IN. THE. CAR. No police officer is going to ask you to get out of your vehicle if you've done nothing wrong, and even if you have, you have the right to request they call another officer or their watch captain / sergeant to the scene before you exit the vehicle.

On that note: police cars have blue and/or red lights. There are no exceptions. No car without blue/red lights has the legal right to pull you over. DO NOT PULL OVER FOR ANY CAR WITHOUT BLUE AND/OR RED LIGHTS. For those that do, you can legally signal to an officer your intent to pull over by slowing down and turning on your hazards, which you should do until you get to a public, well-lit area.

Police cars may have red lights as well as blue, but they always have at least one of those colors. Typically, Sheriffs and state / federal vehicles (State Troopers, FBI) are blue-only (except in Michigan, thanks Erin).

Out and about / on foot:

Park your car under lights whenever possible, as near to any building as possible (that will be open when you plan to exit). Avoid recessed doorways and alleyways on city streets. Travel with people -- if you're by yourself, look around for a group of girls or guys and girls, and walk near them. Don't talk to strangers, especially men. Keep to yourself -- fuck all that "what will society think?" crap. If a scary man (of any race) looks scary, stay the hell away. Who cares if you hurt his feelings? The worst that happens is a nice guy has a bad story to tell his friends about how much his ego was hurt, the best is you avoid being beaten and raped. Pick the best option.

A quick anecdote: when I was active in martial arts (Judo, specifically), I regularly assisted in teaching self-defense courses. One of the students in my dojo -- a girl named Sandy -- was a black belt in Judo and studied Aikido. She was devastatingly fast and could handle just about every man in our dojo. In the self-defense classes, she executed every maneuver perfectly.

One rainy night, she was out on the town with two of her girlfriends, and they were approached by an attacker in a parking lot of a bar. The guy was waving a knife at them and demanding they surrender their purses. Guess what Sandy did?

a) A flying armbar which resulted in a severe dislocation while her friends called the police,
b) A super-fast saronagi (over-the-shoulder throw) which flung her attacker across the parking lot,
c) threw her purse at him and ran with her friends back to the bar?

Yeah, it was c. She was a highly trained martial artist. She was even armed with an umbrella. And she had the good sense to do the best thing she could have -- give the guy what he wanted and run.

I don't care how expensive the bag was or what you have in it -- it's not worth your life or your innocence. Toss the damn thing.

If you are approached and mugged, throw your purse (or wallet, or cash clip) in one direction and run the other. Trust me, if you're being robbed, they will choose the cash over you.

But if they're not out to rob you -- if they're there to rape and hurt you -- you need to know how to handle that. And that's why I recommend highly that you arm yourself. In order of effectiveness (and preference): a gun, pepper spray, a knife, a Taser / stun gun, a blunt instrument (those stupid key-bats you see on sale around town), hand-to-hand. I won't be covering ineffective measures, mostly because they're ineffective.

On weapons:

First thing's first: in my experience (and the experience of just about every self-defense instructor I've ever met), women's' ideas of effective self-defense measures are, in a word, not. Most women have a drastically inhibited concept of what effective self-defense is. So, I'm going to give you the only answer, and there is no variation on this:

You must be prepared to disable or kill an attacker who is intent on hurting you. And by disable, I mean to the point of being unable to pursue you. Kicking the nuts and punching someone in the nose? Sounds great. It's taught by mothers and fathers to daughters the world over. And guess what -- it's pretty much the least effective advice you could ever give anyone.

When physically confronted, men instinctively protect their genitals and face. It's inborn. We just do it. Then, there's the fact that adrenaline and endorphins block out the pain caused by being kicked in the balls or punched in the face (long enough to do you grievous bodily harm, anyway).

These measures aren't ineffective, mind you. They're just the least effective of all the advice you could be given. There are physical moves you can do to defend yourself, and we will cover those in detail in a bit. But my focus here is effective self-defense, and you have to understand that we are talking about keeping you from getting beat up, raped and/or killed. So, to that end:

The golden rules:

1) **Keep your head.** It's hard. You're scared. Try not to let fear turn into panic. Keep breathing. Keep your head up. Keep your eyes open. Don't fly into a blind rage. Don't lose sight of your escapes. Stay in control of yourself.

2) Make no mistake -- You're fighting for your life. Not just your ability to stay alive, but also your ability to live the rest of your days without the painful scars of a violent attack. This means you need to let go of any pacifist philosophy or maternal instinct you've got and get ready to get mean.

3) **Distance is your friend.** Bluntly, you cannot be raped if they can't get to you. You want as much distance as possible between you and your attacker. Escape is your absolute primary goal. Your best means of escaping an attacker is to have a great head start, and you want the guy to be completely incapable of pursuing you.

So my advice on weapons, in order of most effective to least:

Get a gun.

Now, I need to tell you that if you do opt for the gun -- and I sincerely hope you will -- there's a LOT to discuss. In fact, it's probably deserves its own guide. But the bottom line is that guns are not meant to intimidate or maim, they are meant to kill. Do not get a gun to scare off an attacker. Do not get a gun to shoot them in the leg. Get a gun to shoot them and kill them and save your own life. This will require, if not demand, that you go to a gun range at least once a month and hone your skills, as well as practicing your draw from wherever you decide to keep it (purse, night stand, waistband, whatever).

If you cannot face this, you probably shouldn't get a gun. But there's absolutely no getting around it: in the hands of a woman who has taken the time to learn how to draw, aim and shoot her gun, there's no better measure to defending yourself. Period, end of story.

If you don't want a gun, get pepper spray.

Let's assume you don't want a gun, legally can't get one, aren't prepared to be a responsible and effective gun owner (by going to the range and practicing), or you don't have the money. I highly recommend you get high velocity bear repellent for your home, and this SABRE spray for out and about. Don't bother with MACE -- some people aren't very susceptible to its effects, and even those that are will be much more susceptible to pepper spray + tear gas. The portable sprayer is pink. And that's nice. But they sell it in black, too, if you're into the stealth thing (or pink is just too stereotypical).

As for the bear spray, it shoots up to 30 feet and will flat knock a man down. When in the confines of your home, escape routes are fewer. You want as much distance as possible, and you want the guy to be completely incapable of pursuing you.

Keep a can of bear repellent near your bed, one near any door in your home, and one in the centermost hallway.

Now, if you're going to use spray, you need to be aware of a few things:
1) It's most effective in the eyes, nose and mouth.
2) You need to practice with it just like you would a gun. To not practice with it is folly. You will either fumble with it when you need it, or end up hurting yourself.
3) don't spray it into the wind, or you'll blind yourself, too.

Tasers / stun guns:

Tasers work... sometimes.

1) They're easily defeated by thick jackets and clothing. Ask a cop if you don't believe me.
2) You get one shot. True, they sell multi-shot Tasers, but if someone's wearing a thick jacket, the other two shots will just fail to penetrate as well, and then you're screwed.

Handheld stun guns have the same limitations, but with the added issue of proximity. Remember, distance is your friend. Stun guns require you be right next to the attacker.

Furthermore, while they do work, they don't subdue. They merely temporarily disable. The point of using any of these weapons is to render the attacker unable to attack -- and if you temporarily subdue them, then start running and they can get up and pursue, you've failed. And now, you're expending energy and oxygen and time while they pursue you, and if they get you again, you're in trouble.

Knife:

I recommend every woman carry a knife as a backup to their gun / pepper spray. I carry a knife myself. I've never had to brandish it, much less use it (thank god). But I have it, just in case. I'm a HUGE fan of spring-assist knives by SOG (specifically, the FLASH II). I recommend a solid aluminum handle. If you can get your hands on one, get a fully-automatic knife like a switchblade. Yes, they're illegal in many states, but so is rape. Your attacker isn't letting a pesky thing like "laws" get in his way. Don't let them get in yours.

I'm not knife trained in any real manner outside of the very basics, which I'm going to share with you:

1) Hold it blade-down, in an "overhand" grip. This would be like making a fist for punching, only there's the blade of a knife sticking out of the bottom of your hand.

2) If you're facing your attacker... What the hell are you doing? Run.

3) If your attacker has you from behind, plunge the blade of the knife into their thigh. Twist it. Remove it. This will keep the wound from closing and do some serious damage to his ability to chase you. DO NOT LET GO OF YOUR KNIFE, EVER. If you do, even if you've stabbed your attacker, you've just given him a knife. Don't make his job of hurting you any easier.

Don't wave your knife around like you see in movies (this really applies to every weapon). Don't threaten. Don't telegraph you have it. Your job is not to intimidate, it's to escape. If you pull out your weapon, use it. Don't pull it out unless you are absolutely going to use it. You run the risk of being disarmed, or worse, escalating an encounter to something far more serious by producing a weapon that the attacker is now prepared for.

Blunt instruments (bats, flashlights, those stupid "key bats" they sell so you can swing a keyring at a guy intent on hurting you, etc.):

Well, simply put, they require you be close to the attacker. That's what we don't want. But they're better than going bare-fisted. So if you have nothing else, or lack the good judgment to get a gun or buy pepper spray, get yourself an ASP (collapsible baton). Know that in most states, they require a law enforcement ID to buy, unless you go to a pawn shop or gun show. Also, they're considered a controlled weapon, like brass knuckles or a blackjack. But again, the law isn't really a concern when someone's trying to hurt you.

If it is a concern for you, then get a huge 4-battery Mag Lite and carry it everywhere. It doesn't rouse suspicion, it fits nicely under the seat of your car, and it is legal in all 50 states. It's also cumbersome. It probably won't fit in a purse. It's awkward to carry around stores.

But the truth is, short of a baseball bat, it's the most effective legal weapon you can possess... That isn't a gun or pepper spray, of course.

Your bare hands (AKA the last resort, AKA what to do if he gets you):

If you're facing your attacker, read up on my fist fight guide. It's long, and necessary if you're not going to heed my advice on weapons and running. Read it. The only difference is that it's possible a swift kick by you to the knees or genitals might help... But you need to keep in mind, kicking in tennis shoes or heels (or barefoot) can result in a broken foot, or miss and leave you off balance. You need your feet and your balance to escape.

If you are caught from behind and still standing:
a) Stomp instep. Over and over again, stomp right down on his foot, preferably on the instep. Break the foot if you can. It doesn't take much to do this, by the way. And don't be satisfied with one good stomp -- keep it up until he lets you go, or you break his foot.
b) Sling head backwards, over and over. Break his nose or dislocate his jaw. Either will cause his eyes to water.
c) Grab his fingers (not hands, get a single finger) and wring it like crazy. Break it if you can, especially a thumb. You'll know it's broken when you hear the "CRACK!" sound and his yelping.

If you're on the ground, the fingers thing is still important. Break his goddamn thumbs. If he's on top of you, get your hands to his face and gouge out his eyes. Did you know it only takes about 15 sq. lbs. of torque to dislodge the eye from its socket? If you clap your hands with any sort of velocity, that's roughly 60-80 sq. lbs. of torque. Trust me, getting your thumbs into his sockets and pressing VERY HARD will be effective.

If you can't quite get there, slap his ears. Cup your hand and rupture the eardrum.

If you can't get there, make your hand into a blade (fingers together) and chop / stab at his throat. Don't punch at it, your fist is too big to fit into the gap between the jaw and collar bone to be effective. You want to crush his windpipe.

If you can't do that, start raising your knees at high velocity and try to crush his genitals. This isn't the most effective of all the tactics, but it does work.

At any rate, the SECOND you can get away, do so. And whatever you do, don't drop your hands to your sides or let him stop them. Thrash. Go fucking crazy. Tear his face off. Never stop until you escape.

If none of that works, and if you can't get away, OR you're in a "date rape" type of situation (indoors and unable to just go nuts and run):

In a "calm" situation (indoors, date rape):

If saying "no" and then fighting him off hasn't worked, go with it.

I know. Gross. But trust me on this. Just relax. Get into it. Start running your hands up and down his shoulders. Work your way up to his face. Maybe even kiss him. Get your hands on both cheeks. Put your thumbs right into his eyes. Press like hell and dislodge the eyes from their sockets. If he's got glasses, just slowly try to remove them.

If you can't get to his face, try asking if you can help him with his pants, or even better, "Go down" on him. Get his pants to his ankles. Get his underwear to his knees. Place both hands around the testicles and yank as hard as you can -- try to pull the bastards off. A distended testicle will make him incapable of running, and is FAR more effective than trying to kick or punch the balls. It takes quite a lot of force to rupture one, but not much at all to yank it out of place.

With his pants around his ankles, he's not going to be able to chase.

If that's not possible, look for an alarm clock or the phone. Anything with bulk. Grab it and slam it against his head.

In any case, the second you can get out of the room, run. Get out of the house / building. Go to the nearest populated place (a neighbor's house, a store, a gas station). Shame has no place here -- swallow your pride and get running, even if you're disrobed and embarrassed.

Note: I want to make it absolutely clear that the first priority before "Go With It" is definitely saying no, making it very clear that you are not comfortable, and then if possible fighting him off. It's only after these tactics have failed that I'm advocating turning the tables and trying another tack. You're in a situation where you're already trapped and something you don't want to happen is happening, and fighting has failed. Rather than just giving up, try another tactic that may open an opportunity for you to escape).

All of this said, it's far better to have a weapon and be safe and distant.

Final thoughts:

The major major MAJOR point here is to be aware of your surroundings and not get attacked in the first place. If you are attacked, you need distance between you and your attacker, as quickly as possible. To that end, a weapon which incorporates distance is primary. One that incapacitates and keeps them from pursuing you is preferred.

It's unpleasant to talk about, but the truth is, there's no martial art in the world that can teach you how to defend yourself while unconscious. If he can't get near you, he can't choke you or knock you out.

If you have no choice, or weapons simply aren't an option for you, you need to keep calm and use the situation to your advantage however possible. If fighting can't get you free, turn the tables. You're already trapped -- instead of just surrendering, try a fallback tactic of going with it and attempting to get your hands on the most vulnerable parts of his body, the eyes and the genitals.

Above all else... Be ready to hurt him for real. Because he's ready to hurt you, and that simply won't do.

HOW TO START YOUR THURSDAY THE HEAVIEST, MOST SADLY CONFUSING WAY POSSIBLE

POSTED AUGUST 18, 2011

This One High School Guy (or, Guy, as I'm going to call him because it's getting annoying using the shift key on and off five times in a row to type that name) was always decent. He is a very smart guy. In all the advanced classes, as was I for about 2 months my Freshman year before my father pulled me out due to not trying hard enough ("You're taking a spot that another kid who really would try hard could have," he'd tell me. "I'm not going to let you waste something someone else could put to good use!" My father was a stickler for waste. He wasted NOTHING. He once made me sit at the dining room table for almost 12 hours to finish a huge mistake of a bowl of Grape Nuts).

Guy and I had very limited contact after that. We shared a few classes during the 4 years we matriculated, and when we left high school, we never talked. Still, he was pleasant enough and enough of an overachiever that I was that special kind of Facebook curious we get when we wonder just how closely our vision of what someone would achieve after high school matches reality. So, I accepted the request, and before I could really get into reading his profile, a message came from him. This is, in its entirety, the conversation we had:

9:58:57 AM [Guy]: Hey, Joe. I hope all is well. I don't know if you've had any contact with Mandy - I know you two were friends or dating at one time. She's on her third bout with breast cancer, and this time it has spread aggressively to her bones. It's stage 4, whatever that means, and terminal. She's "Mandy [married name]" now and lives in SC with two kids, unless I'm mistaken. Thought I'd pass the news along.

...I had no idea that Guy even KNEW who Mandy was. She didn't go to our high school, and was only loosely connected to people I knew through me. But there it is. I just found out that a girl I dated 14 years ago is in the final stages of life due to a horrible disease, from a guy I haven't spoken to in 16 years. Through Facebook.

Hurrah to the modern age, huh?

Now, people who have read my stories and books know the name Mandy. She's... Well, she's enough of a figure in my life to warrant a few stories about her being written in my books. But the summary: She's an ex-girlfriend whose emotions constantly got ahead of her to the point of neurosis.

- Her tantrums were so legendary that I once snuck out the back of a restaurant and scaled a 12-foot security fence, only to become ensnared and very cut up and bloody, because she demanded we go see Titanic the night it opened. And if I hadn't, she'd have cried all night. As it turns out, we missed the film, but the Emergency Room did give her a free Jell-O, on account of her missing dinner. Well, I say "free..." It did cost me a few hundred dollars.
- She caused me to miss a VIP, invite-only Prince meet-and-greet show because it was "date night."
- She once bumped into a guy at one of those Christmas stores in the mall and he fell into a Hummel display, shattering a few figurines. When he turned around and told her to "watch it!" she began crying and insisted I beat the

guy's ass. The two of us stood there in the macho-yet-confused moment that's probably happened to every guy where you REALLY don't want to fight, but feel like you have to -- either because some guy is threatening you in defense of his girlfriend's honor, or some girl is crying and insisting you engage in fisticuffs. We didn't fight, but only because security showed us the door.

- When the relationship finally ended (and it took a LONG time for it to do so), she became a bit clingy, prompting a few weeks of... Well, the only word for it is "stalking." She hung out with my MOTHER. For WEEKS. And this culminated in her convincing my mother that I was "gay together" with my best friend Mike. The damage waged during those weeks persists today. My mom -- regardless of the fact that she actually walked in on me making out with two separate girls in my teenage life and was AT MY WEDDING -- still believes, in some deep dark recess of her heart, that Mike and I boffed. And it's Mandy's fault.

And now, Mandy is dying.

So here I sit, writing this out because it's the only response I have right now. The emotions I feel... They're unlike anything I've ever felt before in my life. I am filled with grief borne from the idea that someone I knew and cared about -- regardless of how things ended -- is suffering and in pain and doesn't deserve what she's going through at all. And I want to reach out. And I can't.

The conflict here is fucking horrible. It makes me wonder how selfish I am. It makes me want to prove myself wrong and write a letter and offer to lend my support. And THAT feeling makes me feel so hypocritical it borders on disgusting. She made me miserable! I was very close to hating her.

Yes, hate. It's a strong word. And I almost used it when describing how I felt about her at one point. Because I felt victimized by her in some regards. But that's the other half of the coin here: I was actually to blame, if you really get down to it.

I was never honest with her. I never told her that I was only dating her because I really wanted to be alone, and my friends and family couldn't accept that, so dating someone who was away at college was the perfect excuse. I introduced distance as a precursor to having the relationship, because -- and I'm only able to be honest with this now after 14 years -- I was too much of a coward to tell my friends and family to leave me alone and let me be myself (after all, a late-teens/ early-20's male should WANT to be with a girl, right? Being alone is tantamount to being OMGGAY).

And that emotional distance, coupled with someone like Mandy who cared A. LOT. ABOUT. EVERYTHING. prompts some pretty irrational behavior.

Like crying when I acted distant. Or trying a little too hard to get my attention. Or insisting she be important in my life when she's around, if I'm going to call her my girlfriend and tell her I loved her. Demanding that, if she was going to drive down from college to hang out with me on a weekend, that I actually hang out with her and not brush her off for a Prince VIP something-or-another with my friends. Insisting that, if I promise to take her to a movie she really wanted to see, that I keep that promise.

On the surface, and in my head and heart at the time, I felt she was pushy and insistent and selfish. And what I come to realize, sitting here thinking about it all, is that she was because she felt she had to be. Because when you boil it all down, she cared about me. She loved me, insofar as one can love another person at that point in life. And that makes me want to reach out to her and apologize for how it all went.

But I just don't feel like I can. Why would I? I spent a few years actively avoiding this person whom I wasn't happy with.

Why, only now that I've found out she's dying and suffering, do I want to reach out? I mean, let's be fucking honest here: I'm only projecting myself as the antagonist here because it's what we do when we feel sorry for someone. She and I simply did not gel, and she did some truly crazy shit.

You see? The part of me who remembers her less than fondly is at odds against the real, caring, honest human side of me who wants to just comfort someone in pain, who I once knew. Someone who doesn't deserve what's happening to her at all. Someone who made some mistakes against me due to youth and an overabundance of emotion. Mistakes that are only mistakes in hindsight.

It's an emotional clusterfuck. And writing about it is the ONLY way I know to manage it.

The marks we leave on other peoples' lives remain in stasis, emotionally. They don't really mature along with us. We remember what other people said and did with the taint of how we felt about it with the mindset of when it happened. We never allow for perspective to alter our thoughts on those moments until, like now, we're forced to.

And that's when you begin questioning things like your own humanity in a situation where you want to be a good person... But only because you know you can't live with having been a bad one.

We both have a lot to apologize for in each other's lives. But it's only an apology when you actually feel remorse. Do I? Does she? Do I even have a handle on the breadth and width of the playing field that particular game would be played on?

I don't think I do. Because in all honesty, as much of a brat as Mandy was to me, and I was an asshole to her... Neither of us were sorry at the time. And 14 years have gone by without a single thought in my mind that I owed her anything whatsoever.

So do I owe her anything now? And why? Because she's at the end of a life, the majority of which has been spent without me in it, and I feel bad for some parts of the short portion we intersected? Because the truth is, I already let go of all the stuff she did. A long time ago. It doesn't bother me. It makes for entertaining stories in books and at parties and that's about it. I have nothing in my heart or mind that requires closure from her.

And so, the conundrum. Reach out and have that conversation to satisfy my own grief, or leave her alone and let her live the rest of her life in the peace she's found elsewhere and just let all that go?

That's the gamble. Does reaching out help her pain... Or my own?

Maybe that's what this is. Maybe this whole post is hedging that bet so I don't have to make it. Maybe someone she knows reads this and shares it with her. Maybe no one ever does and this is catharsis enough that I can live with simply knowing that I at least attempted to rectify how I feel about this whole very tricky and delicate thing in my head and heart.

This is not intended to be insulting or hurtful. It's the exploration of how I feel about a situation that, no matter how you slice it, is difficult. And in no way do I feel my pain is even on the same level as hers -- that's actually THE POINT. She's suffering. She's battling through a disease I've only experienced tangentially in my life, in that people I know have had people THEY know suffer and die from it. What she's going through; what the family is going through... That's HELL. It's horrible. It's deep and powerful and a strain on life to the point of ending it. And I know that.

But I don't know *her*. Not anymore. So all I have is the pile of swirling backwash left in the bottle of a relationship that ended many years ago; suddenly put in the sunlight due to a random message from someone I hardly knew in high school. And I'm dealing with that.

...Yeah. So how's your Thursday?

JOE'S RULES OF AIR TRAVEL
POSTED SEPTEMBER 13, 2011

There is absolutely nothing fun about air travel. From the second you arrive at the airport, you're being conditioned to be miserable. Lines of cars entering and exiting the various parking areas, all of which are overpriced. Random police officers on Segways and mountain bikes yelling at anyone who pauses for more than a second at the curb. The bewildering setup of most terminals, where one airline owns 90% of the place and if you're not flying that airline, you have to pull out an Ouija board and ask the spirits beyond how to get to your airline's ticket counter.

Quite simply, **it fucking sucks**.

But when you mix in inexperienced travelers, self-entitled dickheads and complete morons, the experience becomes hell. Not just metaphorical hell, where you pass off a really difficult situation as "hell." No, I mean fire and brimstone, suffering for all eternity, etcetera -- because it pretty much drives those of us who travel regularly to want to murder a bitch. And I'm not really up on my Bible learnin' these days, but one thing I do remember is that murdering someone sends you right to the devil's playground. I don't wanna go there, so I'm going to try to fix you instead.

The majority of this guide is pointed at those of you who are inexperienced travelers. I don't hold much hope that I can change self-entitled dickheads -- for one thing, they don't read blogs. They're too busy watching real-time updates of their stocks to go enrich their brain meat with the thoughts of others. Plus, it's the thoughts of others, which don't matter to them. And I've lived enough of a life to know that you'll never fix the moron problem without the handy application of a flamethrower.

But that doesn't mean I can't try.

Get there on time. Rule Number One. First and foremost, numero uno, without question the most important and, honestly, easy thing you can do to make air travel less painful for everyone is get there on time. Most airports will cut off checking of baggage at the ticket counter 45 minutes before departure time. Lines can take some time.

If you are checking a bag, get there an hour and a half before your flight leaves, minimum. If you're not checking a bag, please for the love of God check in before you get to the airport over the internet. This will let you walk right to security. But if you don't, remember that lines take time.

Don't break in line. I get it -- your shoes cost more than my car. I don't care. It doesn't matter how fucking important you are on the ground at your company where you sell whatever widget you sell. In the airport, we're all the same. If you were that important, you'd have your own private jet. You're here at the airport, though, so fuck you. Get in line. Wait in line. Don't bitch about how important the meeting is that you're going to be late for. If you followed Rule Number One it wouldn't be a problem. And also? I'm not your employee or your kid, so if you try to break in line in front of me, I'm going to call you out. Loudly. And I encourage everyone in every airport to do the same to assholes who do this. Trust me, they'll back down.

Before you even get to the metal detectors, put everything that isn't your shirt, pants, socks and underwear in your carryon. Not your pockets, your carryon.

Don't wait until you get up there to do it. I use a backpack with a front zipper pouch that I specifically leave empty, so that when I travel, I can dump everything into that one pouch. Phone, wallet, ring, belt, gum, chapstick... EVERYTHING.

Everyone has to remove their shoes. This may soon be changing, but until it does, you gotta take them off. And If you don't want your bare feet to touch the floor, wear socks. It's common knowledge by now. If you don't wear socks, it's not my fault. I don't want to hear about how dirty the floor is, and neither does anyone else in line. We're all annoyed already, you're just adding to the pain. And don't wear your calf-high Doc Martens which take a month to peel off your foot either.

Shoes go in their own bin, as do laptops / iPads / tablets. Some airports are more lenient than others, but to save everyone time in case you're at one that isn't, just put your shoes in their own bin, and your laptop / computing device in another.

Seriously, enough with the jewelry. You're flying, not attending cotillion. There's no need for 31 pounds of gold and platinum. This is actually the case all day, every day, no matter where you go, because you look like a guido retard. But that's another post. Walking through the metal detectors will get your metal detected. So take the shit off. Please.

Wait until the "security" person tells you to step through the metal detector / scanner. They will bark at you if you don't, and that holds up the line.

Save the protests / bitching / attitude with the TSA. That's what Twitter is for. We're all equally resentful of the process the TSA puts us through. If you really want to protest, pull a John Madden and stop flying. None of us in line are going to sympathize with your plight, because we're sympathizing with our own plight. Rise up and rebel if you're going to, just get the fuck out of line before you do, thanks.

PLEASE check the guidelines for what can be carried on before you try to carry it on. Don't know where to look? Here, I'll help. A two minute check of your carryon will save you massive headaches and postage fees mailing your Leatherman back to yourself.

If you want to change your seat, ask the gate agent BEFORE they start boarding. If you got there on time, this shouldn't be a problem. They're trying to board us, and we all want to board. Your middle seat is your problem if you didn't try to fix it before this point.

Don't crash the gate. Okay, so if you look at your ticket, you will see the word "Zone" followed by a number. They will call this number shortly after the number before it, unless your number is "1" which likely isn't the case because you're reading this, and Diamond Premiere Platinum Ultrazord flyers don't read blogs, as previously discussed. You will earn exactly nothing whatsoever by getting to the gate before everyone else. There's no need to stack up five deep at the queue waiting for them to call your number. You will get on the plane. It's okay to just chill. I promise.

Sit in your seat first. I'll admit -- I violate this sometimes. I'm HUGE. I hate sitting in middle seats, and sometimes I can't get a seat change. But when I do it, I take a seat before my own so if the passenger who rightly owns the seat shows up, I can just scoot to the row behind. Unless you're really good at that, don't take a seat that isn't yours, because you hold up the boarding process by needing to travel against the grain of the line to get on board.

Use YOUR overhead compartment. Not kidding here, it's bullshit to think you deserve more than one spot in the overheads, and when you do this, you end up crowding out people who board later. Which means you're taking compartments that aren't yours. If I get to my seat and witness someone putting their coat and handbag and camera case and other shit that can fit under the seat in front of them into my compartment, I grab it, ask "Is this yours?" and when they say yes, I say "Here" and hand it to them. Now, because I look how I look, I get away with this 10 times out of 10. You may have worse luck, you may not. But if you follow this rule, we won't need luck, because we'll all get along.

If you've got the aisle seat, you don't get both armrests. Even I don't do that, and as I've mentioned before, I'm massive. I also try not to sit with my legs splayed out which crowds the person next to me.

You should have pee'd and poo'd before you got on. You're supposed to be a big boy and/or girl. When you use the lavatory while the plane is taxiing for takeoff, you violate procedure -- and again, I don't care about how much bullshit you think the procedure is, it is the procedure. Your protests are your own business, when they don't affect my flight. If you get up when we're taxiing, you'll keep us all on the ground and we will lose our place in line to take off, which means we sit on the runway until we can get a spot, which means they turn off the engines to save fuel, which means the air conditioning turns off, which means we all sweat and the plane stinks and FUCK YOU FOR BEING THIS WAY. Stay in your damn seat until they say you can get up.

Listen to the flight attendant, please. She's not being a bitch. He's not being a dick. They're doing their job... Their shitty, shitty job of being a waiter in a cramped restaurant 30,000 feet in the sky. They have heard it all. They have seen it all. Don't be a dick, and chances are, they won't be one either.

Conversation is for those who want conversation. It's natural to want to strike up a conversation with someone you're going to be sharing a seat with for a few hours. It's part of the human condition, and a nice thing to do to pass the time. I've made several friends this way. But if I'm sending clear signals that I don't really want to talk, please don't push it. If I have my headphones on, guess what -- it's less likely that I really, really dig the song on my iPod and more likely that I just don't want to be bothered. It's nothing personal. Tap me on the shoulder if you need something or if I'm snoring, otherwise, just let me be.

Perfume? Cologne? Smelly fried food? SERIOUSLY, FUCK YOU. There's no real advice I can give you here, besides don't fucking do this. If you do, you're a dick. I hate you. I will knee the back of your seat the entire flight to pay you back for the hours-long assault on my nasal passages. Put on your smelly shit when you land, and buy food that doesn't stink -- it'll also keep you from being a fat slob, but again, that's another post. Also, shower before you fly, please... Especially if you plan to take off your shoes.

It's your kid, not mine. Shut it the fuck up. Seriously, what is it with people who have kids that suddenly they just don't feel beholden to the common rules of courtesy that are supposed to pervade this society? It's bad enough in restaurants and movie theaters. And I get that sometimes, you just have to fly with your baby, and air pressure changes hurt their ears. Crying babies aren't so bad until they just won't shut up. You could get up after the seat belt sign is turned off and take it to the back... That'd be nice. But if your kid isn't a baby and keeps yelling and yammering and throwing a tantrum, figure that shit out before I duct tape its mouth shut and hog tie it.

If you're going to listen to music, please use headphones. Most phones and music players come with speakers built in. I wish they didn't. I find them convenient while showering or folding clothes, sure. But the rest of the time, they provide a means for retards to annoy me. I don't want to listen to Lil Wayne. I don't. I really, really don't. Don't play him on your music player's speakers. Please. God. Just. Don't.

When the plane lands, try to be patient. Again, we're all going to get off that plane. There's no need to go shoving through the aisle and put your ass in my face while you wait for the terminal gate to dock.

Let those with connecting flights get off first. Especially when your flight arrives late. They're in a rush for a reason, try to help them out. It's already been a shitty experience flying with you, the very least you can do is help them not miss their connecting flight so they can get on another plane with another jerk who doesn't follow the rules.

AN OPEN LETTER TO WOMEN RE: "WHY YOUR GUY FRIEND TURNED INTO A JERK WHEN YOU DATED SOMEONE ELSE"

POSTED SEPTEMBER 14, 2011

About two weeks ago I asked folks on Facebook and Twitter what I should blog about. They pick the topic, and I'll go to town. There were quite a few good suggestions, and I'm going to end up writing them (such as "Has chivalry evolved, or is it just dead?" and "Scars") but the one that overwhelmingly won the polling, with a whopping 20 suggestions via both mediums and email, was the one Ashley Hemsath suggested first: "Why do so many guys call themselves 'nice' and generally act like entitled jackasses when their female friends choose to date someone else?"

I shall address this topic in the form of an open letter to all women.

Note: I'm not going to discuss other permutations of male/female relationships, such as how they evolve, whether or not men and women can actually be only friends (they can, for as long as both can put up with the other being with someone else), and so on. I'm simply taking the one topic -- why a guy freaks out when their friend that is a girl dates some other guy -- and explaining it out.

As for whether or not this applies to all friendships with all men and women: No. It only applies in the situation stated above. If a woman has a guy friend, and starts dating another guy, and the guy friend turns into a jerk, the situation applies.

Dear Women,

So, you have this guy friend. He's a good guy friend. He's funny and he's smart and he gets you and you can tell him anything. That's nice.

You begin dating a guy, and your guy friend turns into a big jerk. You're confused. "Why," you ask yourself, "would my friend suddenly turn on me? Isn't he happy for me that I've found someone I connect with and can have a relationship with?"

Well yeah, he was happy for you when it was him. Now it's someone else. You basically just cheated on him right in front of his face. Confused? Well don't be.

Your guy friend turned into a jerk because HE IS A BIG FAT PUSSY. And he's not your friend.

Harsh? I don't think so. As a former "guy friend" of a girl, I feel I'm in the appropriate place to call out every single "guy friend" who does this as being cowards. I am lucky enough to have married my best friend. But that's only because at some point, I fixed the problem I'm about to explain to you.

He's pissy because, while you saw him as great and wonderful and kind and smart and charming, you never took the step he was begging you to take. You never completed the dots and said "be mine." And it's your fault, in his eyes, because he doesn't get that you don't work like he does.

He poured effort into you. He showed you time and time again that he would care for you and nurture your every emotion and provide for you. He was so very sweet to you and was always there for you. Because he wanted you. "But he's not like that!" You're thinking.

Nope. He is. We all are. Period, end of story.

"But Joe, no, you just don't get it!" You're saying. "He said he wanted to just be friends!" No, no he did not. If you think about it, YOU put that out there. You may not have said it in those words, but at some point, somehow, you let it be known that you were very comfortable in the niche you've just carved out that you've labeled "friendship."

And because he's such a pussy, he was satisfied with that. He saw something in you he wanted to be around, and because he sensed that he might lose it if he was forward (or, was just too chicken to make a move), he settled for what he could get. He was so afraid of losing whatever bond with you that he had that he couldn't go the rest of the distance and let you know he wanted to be with you.

So, you found someone you found romantically interesting and your friend suddenly turned into a jerk. It's not jealousy and it's not thinking this guy isn't right for you... No guy besides HIM is right for you, in his eyes. And you chose someone else. That stings.

Men can (and will) pretend they're enlightened and beyond the animal needs of sex. In fact, they may even convince themselves it's true. If you ask them, they'll lie right to your face (and to their own) and say "no, I'm happy just being friends!"

But you introduced another man and they got angry. That should tell you everything you need to know. But it doesn't, does it? Because women CAN be emotionally connected and bond with other people without the concept of a committed relationship, while they see physical intimacy as something reserved for a mate (committed or not).

Men are the opposite. They invest emotion, but physical intimacy doesn't actually require that investment (for most men). If it sounds neanderthal and base, well... It is. We are animals, after all. And while it's true that there will be guy friends who don't freak out when you date someone else who still want to sleep with you (trust me... they do), the ones who do freak out are the ones who betray all their "nice guy" posturing.

I'm not saying you can't let a relationship build from friendship. But at some point, one of the two of you will come to the conclusion that you want more than what you're getting. You should just be up front about it. And when a man isn't, it's because he's a coward who is too afraid of being hurt and left alone and rejected to stand up and say "Look, I want this" and let the chips fall where they may. They don't realize that finding out you want something different than another person isn't the worst thing in the world. In fact, it's not even irrecoverable. It's difficult to hear at first, but it equalizes the situation and lets you both know where you stand, which is the only way that sound decisions can be made.

But yeah, that's why he turned into a jerk. Because he's a pussy. That's all.

Your internet guy friend,
Joe Peacock

And, having been a former "guy friend" in the past who finally grew a pair and figured out that being a spineless passive-aggressive wuss is no way to go through life, I figured I'd also include an open letter to all the "nice guys" out there:

Dear Nice Guy:

You're not a nice guy. Stop the bullshit. You're manipulating her. It doesn't matter that it's "nice" manipulation, it's manipulation. You're too cowardly to step up and ask her out, so you figure you'll win her over on "the things that matter."

You're a coward and a pussy. She's dating "jerks" because jerks step up and ask her out. They post a question which is answerable. It doesn't matter if she SHOULD be with him; she's with him because he gave her the opportunity to answer a question.

I get that you think you're doing the same thing but you aren't. You're not asking a question. You're setting a stage and hoping she acts how you want her to. That, my friend, is manipulation. And I hope to God hearing this makes you feel as dirty as I felt the day I finally realized it.

Trust me, life is SO MUCH EASIER AND BETTER when you stop with the games. The day I finally stepped up and told my best friend how I felt about her, she married me. Yours may not marry you, but how the hell are you going to ever find out if you don't give her the opportunity to work with data that can actually be quantified?

Just saying.

Also, that guy she's dating? He's probably not as big a jerk as you think. He's just not you. And you, my friend... You're really the jerk. Because you're the one jerking her around and trying to make her take the initiative so you don't' have to feel rejected. Think about it a little and decide if that's who you want to be. Either way, good luck.

Your pal,
Joe Peacock

SOMETIMES

POSTED SEPTEMBER 23, 2011

Sometimes, you say "Just lucky I guess" when you know fully well you worked your ass off and are very talented, and just don't want to sound like a prick.

Sometimes, you get credit for being talented and working hard and the truth is that you got lucky. Really, really lucky.

Sometimes, you're obsessed with being correct when you should be focused on being right.

Sometimes, you convince yourself you aren't good enough and don't deserve an opportunity; not because you're not good enough and you don't deserve it, but because you're scared to death of what it means when you do deserve it... And screw it up.

Sometimes, chocolate-covered chocolate things with chocolate bits in them really are better for your overall health and wellbeing than forcing a night at the gym.

Sometimes, you push me so hard that it's everything I can do not to just step aside and watch you fall on your face from the weight of your own shit.

Sometimes, you just hurt. It's not anyone's fault (not directly anyway). You. Just. Hurt.

Sometimes, you don't want to be fixed, because you know that the thing that other people see as broken, you see as the only thing that makes you not like *them*.

Sometimes, I see a man wearing a patterned bow tie with a button up Oxford and khaki's, and he doesn't even have to open his mouth for me to know that I want to choke him to sleep for being such an insufferable prick.

Sometimes, she doesn't want anything from you and isn't trying to mooch a drink -- she really is flirting with you.

Sometimes, the only cure for feeling useless is to find something useful to do.

Sometimes, you want to punch the wall.

Sometimes, you hear the words coming out of your mouth and you can't believe them, and you're still saying them, and you wish you could stop and you even try, but they just keep coming and it gets worse and worse.

Sometimes, someone forgives you that you know shouldn't.

Sometimes, you stand there and you know for a fact you won't ever forgive someone, and you tell them you do anyway.

Sometimes, the joke is on you.

Sometimes, the greatest display of strength is walking away.

Sometimes, you forget every anecdote and lesson and philosophical abstract you've ever read or heard and you forget about consequences and rear back and pop someone square in the mouth, because *they deserved it.*

Sometimes, *you* deserve it.

29 MOMENTS
POSTED SEPTEMBER 29, 2011

The way the air feels the very second before the first drop of rain falls

The way the air tastes as her lips hover near yours right before you kiss for the first time

The sound of the silence just after you've said the words which finally landed with someone whose heart you're breaking

The feeling just after you've made the decision to surrender and reach out for help from someone

The second squeeze of a hug from someone you don't want to let go of

When you realize that someone you've wanted to meet for a long time hasn't disappointed you and lived up to expectations

The pause before hitting the delete key on an entire day's work because you realize it's useless

That feeling right before you're going to cry, when you are trying your hardest not to and you know it's going to happen anyway

The goosebumps on your skin just after you step outside on the first day after summer when you need a jacket

The meeting of your eyes by a stranger just after you've been caught checking them out

The rage that explodes through you just after you've made the decision to hit someone

Knowing you're about to break a promise

The sensation on your tongue as you try chocolate and port for the first time

The first drop from the sprinkler / water hose on a hot summer day

The realization that you've forgotten, just for a little while, that you are in pain

The pause just before the click the last time you ever say goodbye to someone, and mean it, over the phone

The excitement just before the mailbox door opens wide enough for you to see inside when you're expecting a letter

The disappointment just after the mailbox door opens wide enough for you to see inside when you're expecting a letter, and nothing's there

The second you realize you're about to spend a long time bored

The surge of power when you've finally placed yourself in the perfect position to turn and pin the opponent

The snapping sound in your brain the second you realize you deserve better than what you've been getting and you stand up and demand it

The second you reach down to grab a piece of toilet paper, and the roll is empty, and you've not been shopping in a while, and you've just moved out of your parents' home, and you realize for the first time that you're truly on your own

Coming out of the confusion of the panic-induced haze just after you've been in an auto accident that was your fault

The pause just before a child cries because you accidentally hurt it

The anticipation of the needle on your skin just after the tattoo machine buzzes for the first time

The wave of satisfaction the moment you realize something you built, organized or conceived actually works

The fear-tinged rush shooting through your body the moment you realize you're going too fast and need to slow down

The rush of heightened awareness when you're sneaking into a place you're not supposed to be

The fear of hitting the "Publish" button

ON DISAPPOINTMENT

POSTED OCTOBER 30, 2011

"Disappointment is your own fault. You expected too much."

A person I considered a friend told me that once. I thought he was an asshole. Turns out, he's right. If you don't want to be disappointed, don't expect so much. That's not pessimistic, it's realistic. If someone disappoints you, it's because they didn't live up to your expectations.

They're YOUR expectations. Don't make them so high next time, you won't be disappointed.

But then, you'll also never be rewarded for anything, ever. It's called trust. And the more of that you have, the more opportunity you have to have that trust rewarded. And the more risk you have of disappointment.

And that's how things like being taken advantage of happen to me, because my entire methodology in life is to first do what I can for things and people I believe in, and then see where it takes me. I do favors first, without being asked. I offer. I give.

Nine times out of ten, I'm rewarded with a new friendship, and when I'm really lucky it becomes an old friendship. And every so often, someone takes me for all I'm worth. And I'm disappointed in them. My fault. I shouldn't do that.

I'm still going to.

HIDING AWAY
POSTED NOVEMBER 3, 2011

It is okay to hide away from time to time.

Sometimes, it all gets overwhelming. It's 100% understandable that you need a break. And it doesn't matter who you are -- one can only take so much of something for so long. Your job will weigh on you. Your family's needs will push and pull you around.

Life is that way. It's the accumulated experience of everything, every day. And the thing about "everything" is that it adds up. And depending on the amount of "everything" at any given time, that stuff can weigh a lot. So sometimes, you need to put that weight down and recover. I'm going through one of those moments right this very minute (I'm still getting work done, mind you -- I can't ever just sit completely idle. I'm just not spending as much time online. Expect that to end soon).

A secret most athletes and trainers know: muscle strength isn't built while you're lifting and holding the weight. It's built while you rest. The same is true about your spirit. You need to take breaks from time to time in order to restore; to consider. You need perspective on what you've been through and a chance to let your mind and your heart rest for a minute.

And that's the key. "For a minute." Because if you do it for too long, you go from needing a break from everything, to avoiding everything. And that's when things get dangerous.

It is NOT okay to hide away from life. You can't hide away from responsibility or your family or the great things that hard work brings to the world. Well, actually, you *can*, you're just a big pussy for doing so. And it's a sad, sad thing when you go from needing a break from things to being too weak to take control of your life.

Weakness isn't a bad thing when it comes from effort and exhaustion. And it's not a bad thing when something comes at us that's just too heavy to handle alone. We're all weak from time to time, no matter how macho or tough we pretend to be. Sometimes, we need to ask for help to carry a load, or we need to take that break from the effort for a minute.

But weakness as a way of life is a waste.

SOMETHING SOMEONE NEEDS TO HEAR

POSTED DECEMBER 1, 2011

Let's think about driving for a second. You get in the car with the full intention of pointing a certain direction and steering the thing however it needs to be steered to get wherever it is you decided you wanted to go.

What you don't do (at least, I hope you don't) is get in the driver's seat, crank the thing up, put a brick on the pedal and say "That's my car! I'm just along for the ride! I wonder where it's going to take me today..." And then bitch and moan when it runs right into a ditch. Or worse, another car.

That's your life. Literally. You're in the driver's seat. Stop just going along for the fucking ride. Steer the goddamn thing.

I'm not so naive to think that you'll think it's just that easy. But I would argue that you actually realize it is, you're just not empowered to do anything to about it.

You are. If you're unhappy, just fucking stop being unhappy. It really is that easy. It absolutely takes time and is a process, but the first step to not being unhappy is to take the first step in the process. If you feel overweight and unhealthy, go to the gym. Stop eating bullshit. Empower yourself to feel the way you want to feel. It won't happen overnight, but the change in your demeanor will be nearly instantaneous. You just took control.

The same goes with hating your job (start something at night and work at it until you can quit the job), feeling stuck with a boyfriend or girlfriend (just fucking break up with them, being alone isn't that bad if you actually like yourself), hating yourself (change! It's not you that you hate, it's how you perceive yourself, and you can easily change that perception by changing your behavior -- and if your perception is guided by what others think of you, well that one's simple enough -- change who you're around).

Start steering. And while there are miles of road between you and the goal, at least you're driving and not just along for the ride. Because there's no getting around this: when you die, it's YOU on that deathbed. It's you facing your past and thinking through things you wish you'd done differently. And if you're satisfied knowing that you're going to look back at right now and say "Boy, I wish I'd..." instead of saying "I'm glad I..." Well, that's on you.

But fuck you if that's true. Seriously. FUCK. YOU. You're wasting your life, and I cannot abide waste. Just like people on the road who don't know how to drive and get in my way and slow down the process of getting from point A to point B, I wish you'd just go ahead and pull over and get the hell off the road.

But my first wish is that you'd wake up and start steering your life toward where you want to be.

If you woke up this morning and asked yourself "Where's life going to take me today?" you asked the wrong question. You should be asking "Where am I taking my life today?" And if you woke up thinking FML (Fuck My Life) and that you have no control and that life sucks and everything is bad and blah blah blah... You need to realize two things: 1) you're in control of your own life, and 2) if you're miserable, you're doing it to yourself.

And don't delude yourself into thinking that accepting where you are in life is the same as being happy with who you are or what your life has become. You can accept all sorts of things about yourself -- who you are, your talent, your skill set; that certain things don't work for you. But never, ever accept the notion that you don't deserve better. Anyone who tells you that (or even suggests it) doesn't love you and never will.

No one's stuck anywhere. You feel stuck, sure. But you're not. There's a door in every room. Open the damn thing, walk through it, and go somewhere that makes life better. It's a cliché for a reason: The journey begins with a single step.

The secret to winning at life is not getting what you want, it's heading where you want to go.

UPDATE: 8:09 AM:

If you think I'm just filling you with platitudes, let me share with you something I just wrote as a response to Amber in the comments of this post. Amber (who is very sweet, despite not knowing who I was at NYCC) said:

Oh, Joe. ..Joe. Joe. Joe..... While I agree with you on the fundamentals about taking the baby steps needed for a change, I doubt you realize how difficult it is. LIFE does get prohibitive. Whether it's nature, the economy, or other outside forces, we do not have complete control. I realize you're making a generalized blanket statement but when people are out in these cities protesting about their student loans and no jobs and some of us are driving off to jobs that don't provide enough hours or medical benefits -- trying to make those desired changes is like pounding our head against a brick wall. I disagree with you. It is neither that simple nor easy.

To which I responded:

You act as if I wrote this from the perspective of a life led with no adversity. You're relatively new to knowing me, so I'll give you a short rundown.

We were dirt poor growing up (literally; I lived with my grandfather and my room was a dirt-floor basement). My mother worked two jobs to keep 3 kids fed. My birth father was a horrible alcoholic. I spent most of elementary school and junior high in clothes that wore out after 6 weeks, while all the other kids I knew were well off.

I mowed lawns in high school to afford decent clothes, until I got a job at 15 after football and wrestling practice from 6-10pm every other night. I worked horrible shifts in retail, three of them a day for the six short months I spent in college -- where I volunteered in the computer lab to learn HTML in my off hours so I could spend at least some of my time doing something I liked.

During the first dot com boom, I quit college (which drove a wedge between my adopted father and I, as his dream was for me to play football at a prestigious college -- and when I didn't do that, he settled for just "college") to chase a dream of doing web development for a living. And it worked out for me.

I travelled around the world and lived in some very exciting places, and did just fine -- until the crash, when I had to take a job paying 1/3 what I was making during the boom. But at least I had work -- and thank God, because my wife and I were close to $70,000 in debt (not including the house note) thanks to a sudden and continual drop in income all the way around.

So I started writing on the internet, hoping that after a year or two, I could hone the craft into something -- ANYTHING -- that would pay, since software development had long since lost its luster for me and I was miserable (despite working around great people). So once again, I volunteered my time to something I adored hoping -- HOPING, meaning "without a plan" -- that something would pan out. And it did. By freelancing for magazines and selling my own self-published books and consulting with clients I had built during my development days -- all while maintaining my day job which paid 1/3 what I needed to "survive" at the time, my wife and I paid off all of our debt.

I worked my ass off. I put in the hours. And today, we're in a great position. I've built a business that provides work to artists, I work for Fark.com and I write articles for CNN (or will, starting this month) and Huffington Post, I've published a book with Penguin and didn't like it so I went back to self-publishing (five times the work and one fifth the sales, but much more rewarding), I've lost all the weight I put on during the highly depressing dot com crash (over 100lbs!) and keep in the gym at least 2 hours a day, and somehow I still manage 6 hours of sleep a night.

So yeah, I know exactly what I'm talking about here.

Choose a direction and start going. Don't let anything stop you. You can't afford to pay your debts? Work harder. Can't find a job? Create your own. Can't afford where you live? Move.

It. IS. That. Simple.

So, yeah. There's that.

RANDOM THOUGHTS ON AN AIRPLANE

POSTED DECEMBER 6, 2011

There's a fly that somehow got on this flight. I bet when we get to San Francisco, he's going to get out and be all like "Whoa. Where the FUCK am I?"

There's something sweet and endearing about a child who is taken aback by the marvel of flight. When they go "Wheeee!" as we take off, I can't help but smile, because I know that little brat won't be crying and screaming the whole flight.

There's a girl sitting in front of me who could be very pretty, if she'd stop being a joyless, bitter bitch and smile a little. Just a little, mind you. I'm not asking for a wide tooth-filled grin. Just a little smile. Something to show she's not a robot built specifically to sit in front of me on an airplane and make me blog about her being a joyless, bitter bitch.

"I'm totally going to get 4 hours of work done on this flight to San Francisco." "Oh, wow, good, there's Wi-Fi on the plane. That'll help me get work done!" 3 Hours Later, I've made 7 status updates to Facebook and Twitter, blogged random thoughts I had on the plane, and finished a few more levels on World of Goo. It's just like being in the office.

Sometimes, it's hot on the plane, and my ass sweats. About a year ago, I figured out that I could go into the bathroom and sit on the john and flush it a lot. If you've never used an airplane toilet, it doesn't use water as much as it violently sucks everything down the hole, creating this refreshing vortex of drying wind around your nethers. And it just occurred to me what the other passengers must think, as they hear the toilet flush 10-12 times in succession.

I always ask for a can of Coke Zero, no cup, no ice. I always get a weird look from the flight attendant. I don't understand why -- I'd rather have room temperature Coke than watered-down-yet-cool Coke. Plus, if there's ever a terrorist event, I want the can so I can fold it over a few times, rip it in half, and SLICE THAT TERRORIST'S THROAT. Of course, they could do the same with their own can of Coke Zero. Which is why anti-terrorism actions like taking off shoes and limiting access to nail clippers makes no fucking sense. But hey, at least I *feel* safe.

Why do people with horrific birthmarks or skin ailments on their scalp shave their heads?

There has never been a single time I've ever entered an airport with a Sbarro's or California Pizza Kitchen that, while I'd NEVER entertain the thought at home or elsewhere, I don't want a Breakfast Pizza.

My deodorant smells a little like carrot cake. It didn't smell that way in the store. But dammit if it doesn't smell like it right now. And now, I want carrot cake. I'm pretty sure there is no carrot cake on this flight, and my tongue won't reach my armpit.

IF YOU'RE HURTING, SAY SOMETHING

POSTED DECEMBER 12, 2011

Goddammit.

That's all I can think right now -- fucking goddammit. I'm so angry. And I cannot process it, and I cannot get rid of it. All I can do is use it.

So I'm using it to tell you, reading this right now, that you have a responsibility to everyone you love to tell them when you're hurting. They have the right to know. Sure, it's your life, and you get to lead it any way you want -- but if you're part of a family, whether blood relatives or friends or a collective or a business, and you start to fall down, you OWE it to those around you to reach out and ask for help.

You fucking owe it to them. Because you're a part of them. No matter how much you want to fight it, the fact that you've got people caring about you makes you a part of them. And when you remove yourself from them, you're cutting a part of themselves out of them.

You have the right to remove from your life the people who hurt you. You have the right to those who take advantage of you. You have the right to be happy.

But when you're hurting and you isolate yourself, you're not removing people who hurt you or take advantage of you from your life, you're removing yourself from people who love you and care for you and are part of your world, which makes you part of theirs.

Say something. Goddammit, just fucking say something. It's scary and it hurts and you don't want to burden them... But trust me, the burden they feel when you share how you feel is nothing compared to how they'll feel if they never have the chance again.

TOUGH GUYS VERSUS REAL MEN

POSTED DECEMBER 14, 2011

There's this concept I've been struggling with lately; the concept of the Tough Guy. Not internally, mind you -- I long ago let go of the notion of being a Tough Guy. I mean, I'd consider myself tough, and I am pretty sure I'm a guy. But as far as the Tough Guy brand, I think the moment I started writing about my feelings on the internet, I cashed that check and moved on.

The Tough Guy is the guy who can't admit weakness. He can't tell his friends when he hurts. He can't cry. He can't admit that he doesn't know something. He must challenge everything as if it's an attack against him. He can't let go of the notion that there's a pecking order. He can't live his own life. He can't allow himself to appreciate beauty, art or grace, because that'd make him a faggot.

This syndrome is killing men everywhere. It's driving them insane. It's the major cause behind breakdowns and midlife crises. It's an obsession with the external view of their lives. By living outside of themselves at all times and trying to control the perception the world has on him, the Tough Guy loses touch with the most basic element of life: awareness of self. His awareness becomes with the self he invents to keep up the Tough Guy act.

And this doesn't extend solely to guys who drive big trucks and wear Affliction shirts and act like they can kick everyone's ass. This isn't a machismo issue. This is engrained in the male social dogma. This is what fathers who were raised from the 20's through the 50's instill in their children from day one. It doesn't simply manifest itself in hanging nuts off the trailer hitch of a truck. It's men behaving like men. Not acting like men, mind you... Just behaving like them.

You must stand tall. You must be strong. You cannot show weakness. You must be stone tough. These things are absolutely the hallmark of a Real Man. But the Real Man knows when to turn this on and off. He realizes that in times of hardship, he must lead those who need to follow to a place of comfort, and to do that, he must instill confidence and steer the ship through the storm.

But that doesn't mean he cannot be afraid. Avoiding fear is not the same as pushing through it. In fact, if you're going to actually handle fear, the best thing you can do is internalize it and accept it's there. At least then it cannot sneak up on you and affect you in ways you don't expect, because now you own it.

It does not mean he cannot admit weakness. Seeking help when weak and needing comfort is a human trait, and like it or not, men are -- by the very nature of existence -- human. The human psyche can only handle so much load. If you don't offload the weight periodically and reduce the stress and strain on the shelf which stores our emotions, it will eventually snap -- and when it does, there WILL be a mess.

It does not mean he cannot admit failure. In fact, admitting failure is the key to success. It shows you've learned a lesson. Even if you don't admit it publicly (which, if you don't, is just stupid, for the world at large is not dumb. They know when you fail, and not admitting it just makes you look like a dick...

Or worse, exposes the fact that you don't belong in a place to succeed in the first place), he must admit it to himself. It's only when we learn the basics of math that higher functions can be learned and used, and failure to accomplish a thing is just the basis of learning how to proceed with that task or goal in a new way. It's learning.

Real Men learn.

Real Men cry.

Real Men do not inflict themselves on others.

Real Men stand up for those who cannot stand up for themselves.

They do not admonish the weak, they protect them. They do not abuse the meek, they lift the load and get them where they need to go.

Tough Guys break. Their stone exterior is just a shell covering the softness inside. Once the shell is cracked, the insides spill out.

Real Men are carved from wood. Not made of; carved from. They are shaped and molded and formed from the lessons of life. They have flex and can weather the storm. They provide shelter and support. They hold up the structure. They are not impenetrable, but they are solid to the core.

Tough Guys act tough. Real Men are strong. Strength is not always being *correct*; it's always striving to be *right*. Even when it means admitting you're wrong, or that you're afraid, or that you can't accomplish something.

Tough Guys fit a mold. Real Men grow. There is no mold for a Real Man, for nothing holds him in place. He's too busy expanding himself to be held to rules.

I'm sure there's likely to be Tough Guys who read this and think I'm full of shit, or that I'm a pussy or a faggot or whatever. That's fine by me, because my goal is not to convince a Tough Guy to stop being a Tough Guy. The world needs Tough Guys to highlight the differences between them, and what a Real Man is. And my goal is to get to young men and guide them towards being a Real Man before the Tough Guys can get there and waste yet another life.

YOU GOT YOU HERE...

POSTED DECEMBER 15, 2011

You're driving your car, and you get lost.

You want to get to where you intended to go, but you just can't find your path. So you keep trying. At some point, you realize, you're really, seriously lost. Time is ticking, gas is running out, and you need help. What do you do?

Even the most macho Tough Guy on Earth will admit that, at some point -- even if it's the last second before he burns his last drop of fuel wandering blind -- he will get directions.

And if he doesn't? Well, he runs out of gas and has to walk and admit defeat anyway. Or, sit by the side of the road until he starves to death. Either way, he got himself where he is.

Now, replace the car with living your life.

At some point -- and for some people it takes longer than it does for others, but at SOME point -- you realize that the source of your misery and your pain and your suffering is you. Either you're willfully punishing yourself, or you're willfully sticking around someone pushing you, but at some point, after years and years of assessment, all the data comes back and you realize, you're the common thread.

So what now?

Maybe the answer is to stop trusting yourself for a moment, because it's obvious you're fucking up and don't know where the hell to go, and you need someone to tell you exactly where you are and how to get out.

You got you here. Are you happy? No? THEN QUIT FUCKING LISTENING TO YOURSELF FOR ONE GODDAMN MINUTE AND ACCEPT HELP. Because you're wrong. Period.

And if you don't, don't be surprised when you starve or freeze, alone.

These aren't just platitudes. I'm not just posting fucking anecdotal shit here. I WENT THROUGH THIS. I learned my lesson. It took forever, but I learned it. And there's far more to learn, I realize that. But this lesson? And all the other lessons I post about? Firsthand experience.

You know... In case you were wondering.

WE ALL FALL DOWN...

POSTED DECEMBER 30, 2011

Accept this one fact, and your life will become instantly easier:

You will fall.

Just like accepting you will get hit in a fist fight, once you're done worrying about whether or not you might fall and just accept that it IS going to happen, you can go about the business of actually trying new things and going about doing something with your life that makes you happy.

Once you stop being afraid of the inevitable, you can concentrate on the rest of what it takes to move forward.

And when you fall? Well, the natural inclination is to say "Get the fuck up." But reality disagrees with that, in my experience. If you just snarl and get up and start plowing ahead again without thinking, at least for a moment, about what went wrong and how not to do it again, you'll likely just do it again.

So no. No need to be a hardass about it. Take a moment. Indulge in the most natural and, frankly, satisfying instinct we have as human beings: feel sorry for yourself. Analyze what went wrong and blame yourself for it and cry if you want to. But spend no longer than you absolutely must for that instinct to show up and for you to recognize it and get past it.

Just as falling down in life is inevitable, so is feeling sorry for yourself. So you need to accept that part of it too, so you can concentrate on moving past it as quickly as possible and getting back to life.

That's the thing that separates the successful from the self-pitying whiners. Everyone -- EVERYONE -- goes through the cycle of fail - pity - move on. But the whiners' method of moving on is to let everyone in the world know why it is they couldn't pick themselves up and dust themselves off and go back to it, while the successful get past the self-pity and use it as motivation.

Because pity is the single worst thing that can ever be felt about you. When people pity you, they see you as incapable. It's not your fault. You're not able to take control and fix it.

And when you feel it about yourself, you can very quickly get caught in a downward spiral which leads to self-loathing. And you don't want to go there; not if you want to actually enjoy your life. So the trick is to let it happen, and then the moment you begin finding all those reasons you're weak and can't handle life, get stronger there.

The old saying is an old saying for a reason: a chain is only as strong as its weakest link. Failure exposes those weak links. It's up to you as the owner of the chain to identify them and fix them.

Or, just let the chain of your life lay broken and mangled in the dirt. Either way; it's up to you. But know that at the end of your life, you're going to realize that you're the only person on Earth who was ever capable of fixing yourself.

Use the self-pity to do that. Find those weak spots. Double and redouble your efforts to get stronger where you are weak. Take the time it takes to repair and rebuild and move forward; don't waste a second longer than you must on it. Just like in the gym, before you can get stronger anywhere, you must figure out where you are weakest and get stronger in those places.

As it turns out, just like in the gym, most everyone starts off weakest in their heart. And so, that's the first place you should focus on getting stronger. And that's what this and all the rest of my December posts have been about. And I hope they have helped.

We all fall down. When you do, remember what the old Japanese proverb (and Courage Wolf) says:

"Fall down seven times, stand up eight."

LIVE

POSTED JANUARY 1, 2012

Get up.

Right now.

I'm serious -- stand up out of your chair and finish reading the next few sentences, and then actually do what I ask:

Go out of the room you're in, go out of the building you're in, and do something new. Brand new. Something you've NEVER done before.

Pack a soda and a sandwich and visit a new park. Take a walk somewhere you've never been. Buy a new toy that isn't what you usually get -- if you collect figures, get a bike; if you buy games, buy some running shoes. Talk to strangers. Buy a book from a store you have never been to on a topic you've never read up on that you've always wanted to learn.

Live.

Especially if you're the resolution type. In the midst is making your plans for change and listing all the ways this year could be different, stand up -- RIGHT NOW -- and go make it different, if only for one day or one hour.

Change begets change. If you want to change, start changing.

THEY NEED YOUR PERMISSION TO MAKE YOU MISERABLE

POSTED JANUARY 14, 2012

Here's a little present for you. It's a trick I discovered somewhat by accident around Christmas, when someone who used to be close to me showed back up in my life and proceeded to try to make me feel bad for being who I am, and then again very recently when some uncomfortable silences became uncomfortable conversations.

It's a simple question you ask yourself when someone (or someones) has gotten you to the point of frustration, sadness or even depression:

"How long should I let this person control how I feel?"

Once you ask that question, your feelings stop being a burden and become a choice. And you get to decide if you want to be miserable because an asshole has decided you should be, or if you want to go ahead and let that bullshit go and be happy (or, at the very least, stop feeling miserable).

This doesn't mean you have to quit caring about the person if they're someone you love. It just means you're not going to let them convert your love for them into misery for you. They need your permission make you feel bad. Choose not to let them.

And that's really the simple truth of it all: *everything in life is a choice. Everything.*

If you feel helpless in a situation, whether it be how you feel, or who you're with, or what you're doing with your life, begin breaking things down into choices and decisions. The truth is, as hard as it is to swallow, you are responsible for your own life. If you are honest with yourself, you'll see it. And even if you can't choose to leave a situation, you absolutely can decide how you're going to feel about it.

That's how you take control and own your life -- you decide to.

AN OPEN LETTER TO ARTISTS: ON VAMPIRES (THE NON-SPARKLY KIND)

POSTED JANUARY 15, 2012

Dear Artists (and creators, and entrepreneurs, and anyone with a dream -- but mostly Artists),

Success is hard.

It's difficult to attain, as we all well know. Part of the reason is that it requires hard work, and hard work is... Well, hard. And because success is difficult due to requiring hard work, there's a rather large number of people who can't attain it. And they're the other part of the reason success is so hard. These people are the main reason I spend so much time writing about succeeding on your own terms and drawing your strength from within.

Because these people are a danger to you. They are vampires. They live off draining you. When you succeed at anything, two things you never thought would happen, will happen:

First, people you thought loved you and cared about you will begin pulling you down and holding you back.

You won't understand it. In fact, you may not recognize it at first. The reason they do this is because people you've grown up with or have known for a long time won't be able to process the fact that you're moving forward. They will be jealous because they cannot. They will be hurt because they feel left behind. They will be angry that you don't listen to them. They will accuse you of being self-important and selfish, and will tell you how you've changed.

This is because you've become selfish, self-important and have changed. Because you're working toward your own happiness.

These things are not bad things. You need to know this. Caring about you and putting yourself first is not evil. It's not even wrong. It's what every single person on this Earth does all the time. We get jobs to afford nice things. We feed ourselves every day. We work out ways to take time off work to do things we want to do. We put ourselves first all the time.

But when you do it to elevate yourself, you will hear those terms lobbed at you as an insult. Because the people saying those things are weak and jealous and hurt that you would dare leave their little misery club. Selfishness is okay, so long as it doesn't make anyone else feel bad for not having it. When it does, you're going to hear an earful.

These are *energy vampires*. They will sap you of the thing that drives you. They have to keep you like them, at any cost, because bettering yourself reminds them of why they can't (or simply won't) better themselves.

How you know your real friends: they'll give you the space you need to shine. The praise they give you will be genuine and not laden with backhanded compliments or reminders of how you don't care about them or that you've become too good for them. They know that you need to fly. They won't shoot you down.

Second, people you thought didn't like you and complete strangers will come out of the woodwork to graft themselves onto you.

Note I didn't say leech off you. No. It's worse than simply sucking your blood. They want to find treasure without all the trouble of following the map. They will attempt to integrate themselves into your life and be part of your process. Leeches you can identify and pick off. Grafts become part of your skin and can only be removed with cutting and lots of bleeding during the process.

They will ask from you products or services you create and provide with promises of future payment or success or opportunity. They will never pay this back. They cannot succeed without your work or your involvement. If you analyze the structure they've built, determine if the whole thing falls down if you walk away. If it does, you're likely being used.

They will constantly praise you for qualities you wish you had. Not who you are, but who you wish you would be. The things they say appeal to the ego and not the spirit or heart. Always remember: those who praise you for what you are not wish to take from you what you have.

They will be angry when you don't give it to them. Like, seriously angry. They will accuse you of using them, despite the fact they asked you first. They will insult you by accusing you of being everything they actually are, and make you feel terrible and guilty -- for if they can't get what they want through praise, they'll work on your guilt and sense of friendship to get it.

These are *physical vampires*. They want to live off the thing that you make. They want to use you to survive. And they will do whatever it takes to make you their thrall.

How you know the people you can trust: they want to know you, not use you. They want to collaborate, not assign tasks. You can hang around and the topic of your work or success never has to come up. If they do want you to do something for them, they will pay you. FAIRLY. Either with money or in kind. But no one who cares about you for who you are will ask from you what you do without compensation.

Now, it's very important to note that not everyone falls into these two categories. I'm not saying everyone's out to get you. I'm simply warning you that these two types of people are either in your life right now, or will seek to enter your life as you succeed -- and the more you succeed, the more that show up (or walk away due to the jealousy and anger). And there is definitely a fine line between people accusing you of behaving badly to hurt you, and you actually behaving badly and them calling you on it. And you know the difference. Deep in your heart, you know when you're being a diva or namedropping or bragging.

But for the sweet ones, the kind people who are talented and amazing and who see their star begin to rise, only to have it hurdle back to Earth in a fiery blaze because someone shot it down, either out of jealousy or to wound them when they can't live off them like a lamprey... This is stuff you need to know and be ready for.

I liken it to getting your first tattoo: no matter how much you prepare and get ready and stare at the inevitable, the pain is still going to come. And you have no idea what it's going to feel like until it happens. And when you get through it (and trust me, you WILL get through it), the scar that's left will be beautiful and remind you always of the beautiful pain of realizing a hard truth. It will be with you always, and as the tenderness subsides, you'll be thankful.

Yours,

Joe Peacock

RUN

POSTED JANUARY 19, 2012

The next time:

- You're sitting in your car in traffic, debating going to the gym or just going home...
- Or when you're trying to start the next chapter in the book you've been working on for a year (or two or three or five) and just can't make your fingers go and want to play Xbox instead....
- Or the next time you're sick of eating green stuff on the new health plan you're on and want a double Whopper with extra bacon because God, it sounds good...
- Or the next time you want to lay your pencil down and never draw again...
- Or the next time that great idea had in the shower three days ago seems too stupid to present in the meeting and you're scared of what everyone else has to say...

Realize this:

There are way too many people who see you as competition and want you out of the way for you to take *yourself* out of the race.

Do what they want and sit out, or achieve what you want and **run that motherfucker.**

THE TOP FIVE REGRETS OF THE DYING

POSTED FEBRUARY 8, 2012

The Guardian recently posted an article about Bronnie Ware, an Australian nurse who spent several years caring for patients in the last 12 weeks of their lives. Bronnie collected her patients' dying thoughts on her journal, Inspiration and Chai, and eventually used that material to create her new book, The Top Five Regrets of the Dying.

I can attest personally that there is a clarity that comes when you realize you're about to die (as readers of my books and this blog know, I've had that clarity, oh, four times now). And during her patients' moments of clarity, Bronnie noticed five common themes that came up again and again:

1. I wish I'd had the courage to live a life true to myself, not the life others expected of me.
2. I wish I hadn't worked so hard.
3. I wish I'd had the courage to express my feelings.
4. I wish I had stayed in touch with my friends.
5. I wish that I had let myself be happier.

Something that I realized for myself, perhaps much earlier than I should have: These aren't the top five regrets of the dying. They're the top five regrets of the living.

I posit that we, as human beings, are all the same. This isn't a Tyler Durden style "You are not a unique and beautiful snowflake" speech, because I also believe that each and every one of us is unique, and we are beaten into a form of social submission that makes us dress the same and talk the same and like the same stuff. But that's because, deep down, we ARE the same.

We want love. We want acceptance. We want to belong.

We also want to be ourselves. We want to express ourselves artistically, physically, emotionally. We want our own unique thumbprint to be left on our existence, such that people remember us and think that there's no way life would have ever been the same without us.

But we're scared. We often see people who are themselves left out in the cold. Isolated. Not one of us. Not one of the group. Not one with society. We get scared when we think about that possibility; that our peer group or social group or family or friends will abandon us if we don't follow the trend and go with the flow and be what they expect us to be.

So, men refuse to feel. They turn into Tough Guys. They shield themselves from feeling anything, and if they do feel something, they sure as hell don't let anyone else know it. They have to adhere to their fathers' standards of what a man is... Or their buddies', or their drill sergeant's, or their boss's.

And women feel miserable in their own skin. They spend an hour and a half every day getting themselves to look like the covers of the magazines that tell them how they have to look if they're ever going to live a fulfilled life with a handsome man and girlfriends who gossip over martinis. They smile in the right places and laugh at the right jokes at parties, so the other women in attendance won't ostracize them and the men in attendance won't see them as unlovable. They abuse themselves mentally with thoughts of being alone if they're not with the crowd, and they abuse themselves physically with social standards of beauty that no real man would ever concern himself with.

We all work way too hard every day to afford trophies that symbolize our success. Big TVs, Xboxes, nice cars, clothes, shoes, a decent house, a college degree... We go into debt to attain these things, which chains us to the job we have to work day in and day out in order to keep them. And of course, the newest device or car or gadget comes out and we have to have that, and the cycle repeats itself.

We let petty squabbles and differences in opinion ruin otherwise fantastic friendships, because our pride gets in the way and we'd rather be seen as strong than as rolling over for someone else's opinion. We let political maps covered in reds and blues tint our ability to like and accept people for who they are. We play teams with our morals and adhere to a nonsense line in the sand that says we have to believe everything our team believes.

And that is all 100% pure grade-A bullshit.

The only people that are worthy of our time are the ones who want us as we are. When we die, we die by ourselves, not as a team. No one from your local political rally is going to show up and die with you. No one from your office will off themselves because you did. Which means you're ultimately the only person you have to reconcile any guilt with.

So why not start off not having any?

If you're unhappy in your life; if you're sitting in a cubicle right now wishing you could be free from the confines of a life spent working paycheck to paycheck to pay down the credit cards you used to get your electronic trophies showing how successful you are...

If you're too scared to let someone know how you feel -- be it a family member or a friend or a group of friends or the entire internet -- because you'll be seen as a wimp or a wuss or be laughed at for expressing your feelings...

If you're so petrified of being alone that you live a life and act a way that isn't your own...

You can stop all of that right now by doing one very special, important thing: love yourself.

When you make the decision to love yourself, you begin to realize that half of what you do every day in your life is complete bullshit. You begin to see the cracks in the foundation of the world you've built up around you. You start to realize that you've settled. You wanted something, but you settled for something else that approximated what you originally wanted enough to dull the pain of not having it.

You quit wasting your time chasing acceptance, because you've accepted yourself. You're complete as a person. You know who you are and what you want. And you will see them -- those around you who are playing the game just as you did -- fall like flies. Some will outright abandon you; some will accuse you of changing to the point they don't want to be around you.

But here's the truth: they didn't abandon you. You abandoned THEM. You don't need the social reinforcement to live the way you want because you've already reinforced the only thing that matters: yourself.

If you want to be beautiful, be beautiful. Beauty is in the eye of the beholder, right? So behold your own beauty and love it. Show it. Stop regretting your life. Start living it. **Today.** *Now.*

A REPLY TO A SUICIDE NOTE

POSTED FEBRUARY 8, 2012

I'll give away the ending of this letter:

You don't want to die. You just want the pain to stop.

Trust me on this. I've been exactly where you are. It hurts. My God, it hurts so bad. The entire world -- your entire world -- has come crashing down around you. You realized the constructs you put in place that serve as relationships were false. You realize that you never truly connected to anyone. You've had your heart smashed. You've felt pain your entire life, with brief reprieves that came when you felt you found someone (or someones) who understood you; who accepted you.

And that's gone. And now you're alone. You're isolated. You've been trapped in a vast expanse of nothing, because you were cut loose. You've made damn sure that everyone you know knows you don't need help. You're no pussy. You're strong. You're in control. And to do that, you've put everyone in their place. You've kept them at bay. You've never told them what's going on with you. You've never asked for help. And when they finally stopped trying to help you, you took that as a sign that they don't love you and never did.

And you want out. You want it all to go away. You want it to be over. And you think death is the way to achieve that, because nothing you've tried and no one you've met has ever cauterized the wound in your heart that's bled since birth.

So you're going to do something drastic... Something final. And that's your right (at least, I feel it's your right. It's your life, and you own it, and if you feel that you deserve the ability to go out of it on your own terms, in your own way, that's your choice and I can't stop you). But here's something you need to hear, because it's something you need to know: As you lay there bleeding; as your eyes begin getting too heavy to hold open from the pills; as consciousness begins to fade... You're going to have a moment that you don't realize is coming, and when it hits, it's going to be the most horrific moment you've ever experienced:

You're going to realize you've slipped over the edge of a cliff you never actually wanted to jump from, and now you can't stop. You don't want to die. You just wanted the pain to stop. You just wanted them all to realize what life would be like without you. You wanted to matter, if only for a moment. And all of that is about to happen, but in the worst way possible, and you feel for the first time that there are alternatives. Sure, you knew all along that there were, but now you actually feel it. It's in you. It's clear as a bell. And it's too late, because you're about to die with years left on your tab. Regret is going to set in. You're going to scream and you're going to cry and you're going to beg for someone to save you or for the pills to wear off or for your wounds to clot... And they won't. And your last moment alive will be spent in anguish and regret.

And then it's over. You're gone, forever. And we get to pick up the pieces. We get to clean up your blood and handle your remains and pack up your apartment and move your furniture and tell the world of your demise. We get to call everyone in your phone book and tell them what happened, and try to hold back the pain and the tears and the crying as we have to be the strong one in that conversation, over and over.

We get to hold your mother as she cries for days. We get to explain what your last weeks and months are like. We get to figure out, without any real answers, what happened; what we could have done differently. We get to live the rest of our lives knowing we couldn't save you. And now, we get to live the rest of our lives without you.

Thanks for that, you fucking asshole. That's right, I called you an asshole, because right now, you're being an asshole. And what a waste, as you never wanted to die in the first place, you just wanted the pain to stop.

It can stop. Right now. Right here. All you have to do is talk to us. All you have to do is pick up the phone, no matter how many times you have in the past, and say "I need my friends right now." All you have to do is ask. We realize you're hurting. We realize you're weak right now. We realize you need help, and that you're not crazy, you just can't do this yourself. That's what we are here for.

But you see us as the enemy. You've spent the past few weeks or months or even years pushing us away, because you can't trust anyone. And that's because you can't trust yourself. You can't admit to yourself or anyone else that you are the reason you're alone right now, because you turned your back on those who love you and every time they chased you, you slapped them away.

Because you feel like you have to. Because you know no better. And it's just sad that you can't, because it's all so easy. All you have to do is put down the blade. Throw away the bottle. Toss the pills. Take the first step. Admit to yourself that you don't want to die, you just want to stop hurting. Ask for help.

My fear? That this might stop you temporarily, because it filled enough of the hole in you to make you realize you're not alone; that you're not unloved... Until it's not enough.

And you convince yourself that I am just saying this to be nice, or because I feel like I have to.

Of course I have to. I love you. You're human, and you're here. You're alive. You have so much potential and so much access to so many wonderful things. You have a thinking mind that conceives of powerful concepts. It's just turned the wrong way right now. And I feel like I have to at least try to turn it the right way.

Please turn it the right way. Because when you are really honest with yourself in those moments where your fear can't hide behind bravado, you know you don't want to die. You just want to stop the pain.

So stop the pain. Call your friends. Get therapy. Stop being tough. Start being strong.

Or don't. I can't make you, and I can't stop you from doing what you are about to do. But I hope you won't. I really, really do. Because I want you around. It's entirely selfish. I don't want a life without you in it. I don't want a world that doesn't get to have what you bring to the table. But more than that, I don't want to live the rest of my life knowing that you lived the rest of your life in fear and panic and regret from making a decision you can't ever come back from, make right, or change your mind about.

But I'm not you. You're you. You're the only one who can stop you.

I eagerly await your reply. I can't wait to hear how you feel that suicide is your right. I want badly to hear your side of the discussion; to know why you've chosen this path. I want to discuss it with you over coffees had across multiple weeks. I hope we argue about this for years to come, because you'll be here to argue with me about it.

And I think deep down, you do too. Because the truth is -- and this is harsh, but there's no getting around it -- you don't want to die, because if you did... You'd be dead right now.

You're not. Let's keep it that way.

WE JUST GO

POSTED FEBRUARY 16, 2012

I was chatting with a friend of mine (Hi, Christy) about tattooing. She mentioned that she's been wanting to finish the piece on her back for some time now, but realized that financially, she should wait.

I said back to her, "Just do it. The sooner you get it done, the sooner you can have it for the rest of your life. Money comes and goes. We? We just go."

There was this long period of silence, after which she said "That was profound."

I don't know how profound it is or isn't. It just popped out of me. I wasn't trying to be profound, I was trying to be honest.

It's not really a personal motto, but it's absolutely the underlying tenet of how I live my life. Some might attribute it to my having already died once and faced death a few other times. Who knows. I don't hold those memories in my mind, and I don't obsess over the narrative they provide. They're not something I bring up in conversation. I don't wait for the perfect moment during someone's story, reach out, lightly touch their shoulder, look into their eyes and say "You know, having already died once, I can tell you that life is precious and you should live it to the fullest!" and all that sanctimonious horseshit.

But I do have a very keen grasp on the fact that, day by day, minute by minute, my life is being lived.

This does affect my decision to do certain things. It made me realize that, if I don't organize and exhibit my Akira art collection, no one else was going to, and if I wanted the world to see it, I had to do it before I die. It made me write and then publish my first book, and before that, blog in front of an audience who could have very well torn me to shreds. It made me ask my wife out on our first date. It made me who I am right now.

And sometimes, that underlying tenet isn't enough to break the barriers down; not on its own. I still haven't shown you guys any of the graphic novel I've been agonizing over for, oh, 18 years -- because I haven't drawn any of it. In fact, the few drawings I've shown you were done explicitly as an exercise to help overcome my phobia of drawing. But I'm working on that. I'm working past it. It's slow. In fact, it's the one huge wall in my own brain I just can't seem to crash through like the Kool-Aid man and yell "OH YEAH!" as I enjoy a pastime I've ached to do since I was a child.

But it's getting me there. And at some point, I'm going to realize that in the race between my "getting there" on drawing and my life being lived to its terminus, life is winning. And I'm going to have to kick the drawing thing into high gear and keep up. Because here it is, writ plain before both you and me: you get one life, and it's happening right this second.

Whatever it is you've dreamed of doing; whatever it is you want in life... You need to realize that simple fact. Your life is being lived. Right here, right now, as you read this. Sitting in a cubicle at work; reading your phone or iPad on the subway; stealing a few minutes away from doing the laundry and housework by reading my blog...

The clock's ticking. And one day, it won't be. So get to it.

BREAK THE CYCLE

POSTED MARCH 7, 2012

Hate your job? Quit.

Tired of being treated like shit by the guy you're dating? Leave.

Sick of being put down by your family? Tell them your limits and stick to them.

It's not the world's responsibility to make you happy. It's not up to others to read your mind. No one is going to walk through the door and suddenly give you permission to be happy. They're YOUR legs. Walk away. They're YOUR hands. Put them to work. It's YOUR life. Live it.

Or shut the fuck up.

It's your choice.

CONQUERING YOURSELF

POSTED MARCH 10, 2012

I was lying in bed, considering just how nice it would feel to roll over and go back to sleep. I began to feel my thoughts drift from how nice more sleep would be, into that lucid conversation one has with oneself as their mind fades into sleep.

I mentally shook myself, sat upright, and got up. My legs felt like lead weights hanging from threads, but still I stood.

I sat at the kitchen island and spooned the last bite of Raisin Bran into my mouth, when I felt an urge to match upstairs, plop on the couch, turn on the Xbox and lose myself on Mass Effect 3. "I'm on target with work. I deserve a lazy day."

I started walking up the stairs and had to decide - turn right at top and go to the game room, or straight to the bedroom and get dressed out for the gym. I actually paused and had to think about it.

I went into the bedroom and into the closet, dressed, and exited -- and when I did, I saw my bed. My warm, comfortable bed. My nest. My escape from the day. "I could fall right back I to it. No one will know. No one will care."

I closed my eyes, took a deep breath, and left the room. I got into my truck.

"GameStop is just down the road. Plus, you have grocery shopping to do. That's a day's effort. Do that, go home. Play games."

I drove past GameStop. I drove past the grocery store. I headed to the gym.

On the way there, I got into a phone conversation with my friend John Tyler Christopher about comics and illustration and gaming and eventually to our mutual love of Tekken. He invited me to join him in a lounge game with our studio mate Dexter Vines. I was sitting in the parking lot of my gym. In the parking lot. So close. Almost there.

I turned around and began to leave. All day Tekken fest with my buddies? How can I resist?

I got to the exit of the parking lot. I shook my head. I turned around.

"I'll have to join you later," I said.

This is my day, every day. It's the gym. It's work. It's writing. It's designing Fark. It's going to drawing class.

Every single day, the struggle is in my head. It was when I was going to school, but I had parents to force me. It was when I was working for companies, but I had bosses to answer to and debt to pay off. it was when I was playing football, but I had coaches to respect.

Now that work and fitness are a decision and not a necessity, that voice in my head is even louder. And that's why I don't answer it. I don't argue with it. If I try to defeat it with words, it will win every time, because it knows exactly what to say to get me to agree. It's the greatest con job in the history of mankind: the ego, that thing inside you which aims solely to satisfy and protect itself, has convinced you that it IS you.

The only way to defeat it is action. You can't play the game by the rules, because the game is rigged. You have to change the game.

And In my case -- and I suspect yours as well -- it's a daily battle. Sometimes, it's even hourly.

If ever you hear a voice in your head which tells you you cannot, by all means, do. That voice will be silenced.

SHIT CONSUMERS SAY

POSTED MARCH 22, 2012

"You have too much time on your hands."

This means: I cannot conceptualize working on things that don't directly pay me an hourly wage, because I bought what was sold to me in public school and am a good worker bee.

"Get a life."

This means: my life sucks and I wish yours did too, because I can't handle that you found something you love and I haven't.

"It's a nice hobby, but you won't make a living at it..."

This means: If I can't figure out a way to make a living at it, you can't either. Give up.

* * *

This is the kind of shit I heard my entire teenage and young adult life. This is the language of Consumers. Now, we are all consumers in some form or another, as we all buy things we need. There are a very select few on this earth who make everything they need. But for the vast majority of us, we are buying food, buying soap, and buying clothes.

The difference with a Consumer, however, is THAT'S ALL THEY DO. Their existence is spent consuming. They produce nothing that isn't waste. They work at jobs to buy things. They buy their entertainment. They buy their happiness.

And they want you to be just like them.

There's something about being trapped on the ground that compels people to invent ways to shoot birds out of the sky. They are jealous. They see you working on things of your own design and they judge it, because they themselves are experts in what they will consume. They can't understand that what you do isn't for them.

They have to picture whatever it is you make in a shiny package with lots of Photoshopped logotype and effects because that's what it takes to get their attention. They can't understand the process, and why it is so magical. Because they don't make. They consume and turn whatever they devour into shit.

I used to get combative about it. "Where were YOU when the page was blank?" I'd ask. Now, I just feel sorry for them; for they will never know the magic of making something that doesn't get flushed down a toilet.

One of my favorite quotes of all time by Why The Lucky Stiff says it all:

"When you don't create things, you become defined by your tastes rather than ability. Your tastes only narrow & exclude people. So create."

(A caveat: if you ever intend to sell what you make to them, you'll need to understand them. Just try not to become them in the process.)

ON SOFTNESS

POSTED MARCH 25, 2012

Life demands a certain hardness of us. We experience hardship. We get lied to. We are left disappointed by people who should have done better by us.

As our skin (both the physical kind and our emotional skin) toughens, it becomes less receptive to feeling. This is by design. It's meant to protect you from pain. Less penetrates the outer layer. Fewer things can scar you.

But there is an aspect to hardness that leaves us incomplete. If you lose your ability to feel, you lose your ability to learn new feelings. You can't appreciate new experiences. You can't take in new information by touch or by emotional involvement.

This is why you should allow yourself to be soft whenever you can. Soft feels. Soft absorbs. Soft envelopes and wraps around and holds.

Hard becomes brittle. Sure, hard protects against most attacks, but hard shatters when attacked from an unprotected angle or when hit with enough force.

Soft rebounds. Soft heals. Yes, soft isn't on guard, and there's a greater chance for injury. But there's also no chance of feeling something new unless you allow yourself to remove those defenses which shield you.

And it should be noted that, while sometimes those new feelings are actually painful, there's no way to learn about them and how to handle them without letting them in. That's how we grow. Hard cannot grow and it cannot expand. Nature shows us this as insects and shelled organisms shed their skin to develop further.

Soft is not weak. Soft is stronger than hard, because it takes courage to head into new and unexplored places without armor.

Allow softness. Allow tenderness. Cry. Laugh so hard it hurts. Feel sorrow, pain, humility. They are the only way to know what happiness, bliss and pride feel like, for without contrast, there is no depth.

It may hurt, but it won't kill you. In fact, it just might make you actually feel alive for once.

"THAT'S WHY YOU DON'T HAVE ANY FRIENDS."

POSTED APRIL 22, 2012

Yesterday, I was at the gym.

...Don't worry. This isn't a gym story. This is a story about a boy who needed to hear something important. But it happened at the gym. So that's why I started with the bit about being in the gym. If you were hoping for a gym story... Well, you could call this one if you really wanted to. And if you hate gym stories, you don't have to worry, the ones calling it a gym story are just really desperate for a gym story.

Anyway, I was at the PLACE THE STORY HAPPENED WHICH WAS THE GYM. And I was working out, as I am usually doing while I'm at the gym. And as happens over the years spent going to the same gym, relationships form and people get to know each other, and groups form and jokes are shared and camaraderie takes place. And it was the same this day.

I was talking with a group of folks who are regularly in during the afternoons on Saturday. Among them was a 14 year old boy named Bradley (not his real name). He's a great kid. He's been coming to the gym with his parents for the past two or so years. While his parents walk around the track upstairs, he spends his time learning how to lift weights with us big guys. When he first started, he was wiry and awkward. He's still pretty awkward; being a teenager and all. But us big guys, we set him on a good path to maintain a healthy level of fitness.

We were cutting up and laughing. The guys made fun of me for liking hockey. "That's a Canadian sport, isn't it?" one asked. "What are you, part Canadian?"

"Only the part that likes real sports," I replied. "And maple syrup."

"I still don't get why you don't like college football," another asked. "You're in Georgia. SEC is bigger than NFL here."

"What can I say?" I asked. "Southerners like their little league sports. I prefer watching pros."

And so it goes, about the same way every Saturday. The topics change -- what cars are best, what sports are better than other sports, what teams are better than other teams, what shows are better than other shows (but never politics or religion -- something you learn really fast in a gym is to never bring up the two topics most likely to incite violence in a building filled with metal bars and heavy plates). Someone has a divergent interest, everyone else jumps on it, and laughs are had. And invariably, the topic turns to girls.

Husbands laugh about the young singles and their stories about weekend endeavors. Singles laugh at the guys stuck at home with their ball and chain. Whispers are shared about which girls in the gym are hot; warnings are issued by the more experienced about the dangers of dating people from your gym or your job (short version: it doesn't matter how hot the guy or girl is, it's stupid. Unless marriage is assured, don't do it.)

One of the guys asked Bradley if he had a girlfriend. If there were dirt on the gym floor, he'd have been kicking it.

"Nah, no girlfriend," he replied.

"Young strapping lad like you? Nonsense," I said, knowing fully well that not only did he not have a girlfriend, he'd have absolutely no clue what to do with one if he did. Because I was him once. But as a grown up looking out for a younger kid, you have to act like it's completely ridiculous that girls don't flock to him. It's the right thing to do.

"I asked a girl out to the spring dance," he said. He then said something that hit me hard. "She called me lame and said, 'That's why you don't have any friends. Because you're weird.'"

The words rang in my head. Those exact words -- I remember hearing them. A lot. He didn't explain why she thought he was weird. He didn't have to. I knew the feeling very, very well.

"Come on now," one of the guys said. "Don't let her get to you."

"No, she's right," he said. "I don't have any friends. Not at school, anyway." His face got really sad. "I really am weird."

I was weird, back before I realized I wasn't. And it resulted in some extremely lonely times in my young life. My entire elementary and junior high school tenure was spent with no friends. In tenth grade, I found my tiny group of four friends (you can read about some of our little adventures in this story, which is to date the only thing I've written that came out exactly how I wanted it to, and that I am proud of).

I dated the wrong girl (they're all the wrong girl, until you find the right one). The four of us fractured into two groups of two -- Mike and I split off from Walter and Rod (not his real name, by the way -- Rod was the name I gave Jay Naylor, who is actually a very famous furry cartoonist. Yup: not only did I go to high school with a furry, he was one of my best friends. That in and of itself is a long and crazy story I'll tell one day, but not today. Today I'm telling a not-gym story).

Then one day, Mike got tired of my bullshit and said those words to me. "That's why you don't have any friends," he said at very high volume. He deserved to say it -- I'd just told him to go fuck himself when he tried to explain why my girlfriend at the time was screwing someone behind my back. I called him every name in the book. So he bailed and joined up with Walter and Jay, while I spent the last few weeks of my high school career alone. Even the furry had more friends than I did.

And now, 17 years later, life is fantastic. I belong to a studio full of amazing people who were all weird, just like me. I get to meet freaks from across the nation who all love anime and comics, just like me. I get to talk to people who read my weird stories about my weird life and relate to it, because just like me, they're weird.

There's thousands -- no, hundreds of thousands -- of us. All weird. All strange. All over, everywhere.

We all went to school and hated everyone because they didn't understand us. We dealt with the bullying and the isolation and the feeling that we were the weird ones. You want to know what's weird? Spending hundreds of dollars on clothes and shoes and purses that everyone else thinks is cool. Spending hours of your life doing things that everyone else is doing because it's cool. Liking the bands that everyone else likes because you're a loser if you don't.

You want to know what's weird? Hiding who you are just to have the company of people you don't even like. That's weird.

I looked him straight in the eye. My normally grinning mouth turned stern. With as serious a tone as I could muster, I said "Listen to me, okay? What I'm about to say is something I want you to take in and think about and really hold on to."

He nodded. "Okay, he said."

"This isn't just conversation, this is important," I said. "You listening?"

He nodded again. "I'm listening," he replied with a look that convinced me that he was.

I took a deep breath. "Right now, you're in high school in a small suburban town," I started.

He nodded.

"Everyone you know looks the same and acts the same," I explained. "They may dress differently from each other or belong to different crowds, but they're all the same. Hipsters, brainiacs, jocks, so-called 'geeks' -- they're all so caught up with not being left out that they're changing who they are to fit in with whoever it is that will accept them.

"When you show up and you're not like that, it scares them," I continued. "They don't know what to do with you, because they have no idea what it's like to think for themselves. So they try to make YOU feel like the loser, because there are more of them doing what they're doing than there are of you. In such a small group of small minds, the nail that sticks up gets hammered down.

"To them, you are weird," I said. "But weird is good. No, screw that -- weird is great! Being weird to someone just proves that you are being you, which is the most important thing you can ever be. There's nothing wrong with *you*. There's something wrong with *them*. They can't understand what it's like to be themselves, much less what it's like to be you."

He smiled a little. "You really think that?" he asked.

I laughed. "Dude, look at me!" I said. "I'm 300 pounds of ex-football player covered in cartoon and comic book tattoos, who builds websites and tours the world talking to people about his anime cel collection. Trust me, I know all about being weird."

He shrugged and said "It just sucks, you know?"

"Oh, I know," I said with a smile. "And here's the little bit of bad news -- It's gonna suck for a little while longer. But one day, you'll get out of school and go somewhere besides the small town you're in and you're going to discover that there are groups of people just like you -- not that they do what you do or act how you act, but that they refused to change who they are to fit in, and that makes them just like you. And when you find them, you're finally going to feel at home.

"It might be college, or it might be visiting another city. Hell, it might even be on the internet. But at some point you're going to find them. And it's going to be great."

He smiled. "That would be awesome," he said.

"It WILL be awesome!" I replied. "But until then, it's going to be lonely and frustrating. You're going to do stupid things thinking it's going to impress them or change their opinion of you, and it won't, and you're going to get sad. Just know that it does end. It ends the day you realize that you never wanted to be them in the first place, because they are losers. They lost the battle to be themselves. You're the winner."

I paused for a second, because it had just occurred to me that, at some point during my little motivational speech, his parents had walked up and were waiting a short distance behind him. I presumed it was to give him enough space to let the conversation be his own, but I knew they had heard me, because when I looked at them, they both nodded and smiled.

So I put the cap on the whole thing. "And I know your parents are right there, but I'm going to say it anyway: **Fuck. Them.**"

I kept my eyes on him, but could see just behind him that his mom reacted a little to my vulgarity. His dad placed his hand on her shoulder and just let it be.

The guys in the group all nodded and agreed with me, and began talking to him about their perspectives on the situation (which, in previous conversations over the years, I knew to be similar to mine). His parents came up to me and thanked me for talking to him.

"He just thinks the world of you guys," his mom said. "He talks about coming here all the time to work out with you."

"He really needed to hear that," his dad said. "We try to tell him that high school is just that way, but you know how it is..."

"No teenager wants to listen to his parents," I said. "Hell, I'm an adult and I still don't."

They both laughed.

"He's a great kid," I said. "He's going to be just fine in a few years."

"Well, thank you," the dad said. "It means a lot."

"Hey," I said with a shrug, "That's what we're here for. We're his friends."

ON CONFIDENCE

POSTED APRIL 29, 2012

The person who says "Fuck everyone! I don't care what they think!" usually does. A lot.

It's an offensive defense. It's talking loud enough that it drowns out the voices in their heads that say "Oh, but you do... You do."

By boasting how much you don't care what others think, you're actually allowing their thoughts to control you. If you didn't actually care what they think, you wouldn't care that they know how much you don't care.

Confidence isn't not caring what other people think. Confidence is to not let what other people think change you. Every story I write, every picture I draw, every site I design, every idea I conceive... I care a LOT what other people think about them. I care that they'll like them. I care that they'll enjoy them. I care that they'll react well to them. Any artist, performer or worker who tells you otherwise is lying.

Everyone cares what other people think about them and the things they do. It's human. Somewhere deep inside, you care. I care. We all care. Confidence is staring down the thoughts of others about who you are, what you're doing or how you're doing it, and saying "this will work." Confidence is knowing there will be consequences and doing whatever it is you set out to do regardless.

You might be wrong. No one said doing something with confidence would necessarily equate to doing it right. But without confidence, whatever it is you're doing doesn't actually belong to you. It belongs to everyone you're trying to please. Your words, your actions, your behavior... All controlled by the invisible strings being pulled by everyone around you.

Cut the strings. Do what you do; be who you are. Do so with confidence. Let people react and let them own those reactions. You own your moments.

FRIENDSHIP VS. CODEPENDENCY

POSTED MAY 13, 2012

You don't feel worthy of peoples' friendship, so you go out of your way to make them dependent on you. Because if they don't NEED you, they may not WANT you. And then you won't have any friends.

Sound familiar? If it doesn't, then none of this applies to you. You can safely close the browser window now. But if it does, let's you and I have a little chat.

You're a giver. You give. Give give give. That's you. Giving makes you a good friend. It's who you are. Your heart is open and you give freely of yourself to those you love and care for. But what happens when they don't give in return?

You probably won't believe it's true. "They're my friend," you say. "I like giving. I like going out of my way for them. I love them."

This may not have gotten you hurt yet... But you need to trust me when I tell you, it will. I guarantee it. You may or may not be familiar with the term codependency. I'm not a psychiatrist or a psychologist, but I can tell you that's what is going on, and you need to face it.

It takes two people to be "friends." Friendship is, by its very nature, give AND take. Each party gives equally. If one person is continually giving and the other isn't reciprocating, what you have is not friendship. What you have is codependence.

You will NEVER have an honest friendship until you learn to respect and value yourself enough to take as much as you give. You will have users. You will have abusers. You will have passers-by that like you, that you perceive as caring far more about you than they actually do -- because *you* like *them* that much, so *they* have to like *you* that much.

You'll go so far out of your way for them, and you have. Time and again. And when asked why they haven't done that for you, you will reply "Well, I've never needed it" or "I couldn't let them do that, I can handle myself" or something that sounds similar. And to be honest, it's true. Those aren't lies. But they are justifications.

I tell you this because maybe you keep getting hurt, or maybe you keep feeling used, or maybe you just plain need to hear why it is you end up in the gutter so often. It's because you keep laying down in it and letting people walk on your back over the muck and the mud.

When they don't reach down and pull you up after your great sacrifice, ask yourself -- did they ever ask you to do it in the first place? Because if they didn't, they don't actually owe you anything. You chose to do that. That's your call. To expect the same from them is natural, but it IS unfair.

I'm not saying that you shouldn't go out of your way for the people you love. I'm just saying that, should you find yourself doing so constantly and ending up unrewarded for your valiant efforts, maybe you should ask yourself why you're doing it. I'm willing to bet everything I own that the answer, after a tremendous amount of digging, will end up being what I said above: you feel like the only way people WANT to be with you is if they NEED you.

And that's not healthy. Worse, it's GOING to end up in pain. Over and over again. There is no other way for it to end, because no matter what happens, you're pouring more energy into being needed than they could ever reciprocate.

Because you have no sense of self. Because there's no "you" in you. That's an infinite hole that cannot be filled by anyone except you. And the more of you you keep pouring out, the less likely it will ever be that you can begin filling that hole and becoming a whole person. You deserve to receive as much as you give. Start by giving a little to yourself.

A LETTER TO MY 16-YEAR-OLD SELF

POSTED MAY 15, 2012

Dear Joe:

Hey. It's me. You. Whatever. Only, I'm from THE FUTURE™. 2012, in fact. So, to answer your first question, no, the world doesn't end in the year 2000. Also, the whole Y2K bug you're going to hear about in about 3 years? Totally overplayed. You're going to make a TON of money helping fix it though. Learning COBOL will be boring, but trust me, it's worth wasting the year of your life to do it.

Listen -- I know that right now, things seem bleak. High school sucks. You're going to be saying that for quite a while after you leave it, because it really does suck that much. No, it doesn't get any easier as you become a Junior and a Senior. In fact, what's going to happen is you're going to become more and more aware of just how little you're getting from the experience. It's a waste of time. Except for the bits involving Mike and the student teacher you're going to have in English class your Senior year. Those are worth sticking around for.

But don't mistake your hyper awareness of just how futile high school is for some superior intelligence. You're not really smarter than everyone else, any more than someone who knows it's going to rain is smarter than the guy who failed to pack an umbrella. It seems that way, because you're better prepared. But you're not smarter. You just picked up on something quicker than the others. The only difference is that you won't regret being rained on. You're not smarter, you're just ready to go. Drop the attitude. You'll enjoy the next few years a little more.

You feel trapped right now, I know. But you're going to travel the world. In fact, I'm writing this from LaGuardia airport in New York. Yes, you get to go to New York, finally. You spend a few weeks there when you're 19, and you're going to be scared to death to leave your hotel room for almost a week. In fact, being scared to leave your hotel room will be a motif for the first few travel experiences you have. But that's because you do them alone.

It's going to be amazing, trust me. You'll have some great experiences. You're going to love figuring out new cities. It's going to be an addiction for a while.

You're going to move out of mom and dad's place in a few years. This will make your relationship with them ten times better. Try to respect them. It's tough. Mom's going crazy as you get older, because she's feeling like her job as a mother is coming to an end. It's hard to stop being something you've been for 18 years, you know?

No, of course you don't know. Duh. You're a 16 year old asshole. I mean that in the nicest possible sense, of course.

When you leave mom and dad's, you're going to spend about 6 months in college. Yes, you drop out. You already know you will, but you go through the exercise anyway. Don't skip that -- go ahead with it. You end up getting some pretty great opportunities from working in the computer lab. Oh, and as you may have guessed from my mention of COBOL earlier, that internet thing you play on at night? That's going to be a career for you. One of three, in fact. It rocks. You're going to get paid gobs of money to invent cool shit.

I know, right? But don't rush it. Take your time. The really cool stuff doesn't start showing up until 2000, and by then, you're going to be pretty sick of it. In fact, you take a break from it in 2005. And get this -- when you take your break, you become an author! A real life, no kidding book writer. It's nuts. As of the time I'm writing this, you have written two books. One of them, you put out yourself (yep, just like Henry Rollins does), and the other is published by Penguin Books. You're writing a third. But you've been sidetracked by -- and this is really the point of this letter -- your comic.

You finally start drawing a comic. I know you're drawing them now, but in a few years, you're going to hear something horribly hurtful from someone you care deeply about. It's going to sting worse than all the shit everyone says right now, and it's going to cause you to back away from the drawing table for years and years. I'm not going to tell you who, or what happens, because even though it's the most hurtful thing you go through in the next few years, it's also the path you take to truly becoming your own person. It sucks, but it's important. Know that I wouldn't hold this information from you if I didn't think it was absolutely vital you go through it.

And that's what I wrote this to tell you. Everything you are hearing from everyone right now is wrong. They're small minded backwoods redneck assholes who are jealous of what they know you will eventually become. They call you "fag" and "pussy" because you draw and love comics, because they themselves have been held back from truly loving what they want to love and are jealous that you still get to.

They are wrong. You are alright. It's okay to be a football playing comic book fan. It's alright to play Dungeons and Dragons in the lunch room with your "geek" friends. It's just fine to be both athletic and a fan of stuff that isn't supposed to be a jock's chosen interest.

You won't go to college to play football. You won't be a pro football player (you actually do get signed to a team when you're 32, but the league folds before you can play your first game. But it turns out, it's actually a good thing, because some really fucking awesome shit happens that year with your Akira collection. Trust me, football sucks compared to touring the world showing people your anime cel collection).

So go out there and make dad proud. Light fools up on the football field and revel in the fact that you legally get to pop assholes in the mouth full-speed. Just know that it DOES end, thank God. I know it sucks going out there every day... Just make the best of it. You'll be done with it before you know it. And when you finally do hang up your helmet and focus on living life for yourself instead of your father, know that the road is tough and worth every single step.

There are a few things I wish you would do different, though. Don't stop working out. You become a 375 lb. fat ass for a few years. Life is much easier if you don't. You learn nothing of any particular use from the experience, aside from just how expensive Big and Tall clothing can get. Really, you can do without this experience. Work out. Don't stop. Keep your fitness.

Also, don't trust anyone until they've proven they can be trusted. That gets you into trouble in life a few times. You're going to fall victim to trusting the wrong family members; the wrong "friends" and business associates are going to bleed you dry. You're going to lose some money -- a lot of it in fact -- to these people. It's alright though. Again, it's one of those experiences that actually make you a better guy.

You're going to marry your dream girl. You haven't met her yet, but when you do at age 21, you're going to fall head over heels in love. And you're going to have to wait for her, too. It's going to suck. You have to be her best friend while she dates a total fucking loser for about two years. There will be a few girls in your life during that time.

You don't realize it now, but you're actually going to be a total dick to a girl and it's going to feel awful. You won't want to, but you're going to. And it's going to be one of the few regrets you actually carry with you. But it'll make you a better husband to your dream girl. She's an athlete. She's gorgeous. And she's so amazing in every way. You're going to wonder every single day why the hell she chose you. But don't discount yourself. You treat her well. You deserve her, and she deserves you. It's the best relationship you'll ever have in your life.

The bottom line: it's all going to be alright. Don't waste another second wondering if it will. You have an awesome life so far. It's hard, and there's some insane crap that's coming in your very near future (enough to write both of those books I told you about). And even though it feels like you're going through hell at the time, each and every one of those experiences is going to make you into who you are right now, which is pretty damn great if I do say so myself.

Take a few deep breaths. Realize that what you're feeling right now is very temporary. You will escape it, and not via the desperate method you're contemplating right now. Of course, if we're honest with ourselves, it's just a test to see if you have the balls to do it. You don't.

But eventually, you'll actually face a situation in your life where you seriously do consider doing what you're thinking about doing right now. And it'll be the darkest, most lonely moment you'll face in your life. You will actually taste the gunpowder residue on the barrel of the gun. It'll taste salty and dirty. And it's because no one has ever told you what I'm trying to tell you right now: YOU ARE ALRIGHT. The shit you've gone through, it's awful. It's terrible. And you will bury it deep inside of yourself until you have no choice but to face it.

And you win. By facing yourself down; by not pulling that trigger, you win. You beat them all.

Know that.

Love,

Yourself at Age 35

CAN YOU LET THEM BURN?
POSTED MAY 19, 2012

We have all had situations in life where we've had to walk away from someone or something. Maybe it was a person who you thought was a friend, but realized was really just using you. Or maybe it's someone you loved who headed down a bad path with drugs or alcohol, and for your own good, had to let go of. Or maybe it's a job, or a club, or something else.

I've written a great deal about how to realize when you need to walk away, and how to handle it. If you've been reading my writing for a while, you've no doubt seen me reference my favorite saying on the matter:

"When you realize you've been standing in shit, you don't stomp on it to punish it. You just walk away."

It's hard to walk away. I know that. You know that. And we've all been in situations where it's the last thing you want to do. But at some point you get sick of it all and you straighten your spine out and you walk.

But what then?

A lot of us like to feel self-righteous. We have this grand vision of the day that "they" realize they screwed up and now you're gone and they say "oh no, whatever will we do?"

I'll tell you exactly what they'll do: what they've always done. They'll fuck up and expect you to come clean up the mess. Not because they're mean, but because they're them. And people don't change. They won't stop being them just because you walked away, and it' unrealistic to expect them to. It's also unrealistic to believe you will stop caring all of a sudden.

So days or weeks or even months go buy, and then suddenly, you watch as they pour gas on themselves. Always before, you'd say "No no, don't pour that gas on yourself." And sometimes, they'd stop, and you'd have to clean up gas.

But other times, they wouldn't listen. Instead, they'd pick up the matchbook and begin fumbling with them. And always before, you'd say "No no, don't play with the matches! It's a bad idea to begin with, but now you're all covered in gas... Stop that!" And sometimes, they'd stop, and you'd have to clean up dead matches and gasoline.

And then, there are other times when they'd actually light the match. And you'd yell "No! Put it down!" And they'd look right in your eyes and light themselves on fire. And without fail you're there with the fire hose to put them out... And sometimes you get burned in the process. And as they're walking away drenched and slightly burnt, you're stuck cleaning up the flood, all the ashes, dead matches and gasoline. And just as you get done, there they are, pouring gas on themselves...

So you finally got sick of it and you left. That's hard. But it's nowhere near the hardest part.

The test of whether or not you've got the stones isn't when you hear about them playing with gas again or when you see them pick up the matches. That stuff is easy enough to ignore when you're feeling defiant and self-righteous. The test is when they set themselves on fire again.

Your heart is now on the line. Who you are as a person is being called into question. Did you ever actually care? Can you let them burn? Or will you, once again, rush to put them out (and end up cleaning up their mess again... Or worse, getting burnt yourself)?

No one ever talks about this part of it, because no one wants to admit to themselves that their love for someone or something -- even when that someone or something is harmful to them -- will threaten their resolve. The last thing anyone wants to say when encouraging someone to stand up for themselves and walk away is "oh, and by the way, eventually you'll get tested and will have to be a cold heartless person and let them hurt themselves, and you'll probably fail that test and it'll all be for naught. But hey, you should still stand up for yourself!"

 You will know when you're serious about changing your status in life and caring about yourself when you can watch someone you love who is harmful to you stand in front of you, douse themselves with the fuel of their own mistakes, and light themselves on fire -- and for the good of both you and them, you let them burn.

If you're the kind of person who can love someone through thick and thin and put yourself at risk for the greater good, it will be the hardest test you'll ever face. The one thing I've realized that makes this a little bit easier: if they loved you (or at the very least respected you) they wouldn't put you in that position in the first place. They'd listen and at least try to change. And they most certainly wouldn't put you at risk of getting burned along with them.

People who love you, protect you. After all, that's what you keep doing for them. If they're not doing the same for you, they deserve to burn. Let them light the way to a better path.

USELESS WORDS, PHRASES, SENTIMENTS AND OTHER BULLSHIT

POSTED MAY 24, 2012

Useless words, phrases and sentiments, when someone else is hurting:

- It'll all work out
- It'll be okay
- aww, honey...
- Any song lyric or movie quote
- "I haz a sad"
- :-(
- Look on the bright side
- Tomorrow's another day
- Man up
- Grow up
- Do you know who really has it bad? The [demographic in third world country]
- [any words, phrases or sentiments that focus the attention on you]
- clicking any plus or like button

Non-useless words, phrases and sentiments, when someone else is hurting:

- How are you?
- Are you okay?

- What can I do to help?
- I love you.
- Thank you.

Useless words, phrases and sentiments, when YOU are hurting:

- Absolutely anything written on Twitter, Facebook, G+ or any other social network. Going to social networks when you are hurting isn't seeking relief, it's seeking validation.

Non-useless words, phrases and sentiments, when YOU are hurting:

- I am hurting.
- Help.
- Can I talk to you for a moment?
- (Over the phone) I need to make an appointment with [name of therapist]
- I need my friend right now.
- I need my [sister/brother] right now.
- I need my [boyfriend/girlfriend] right now.
- I need my [husband/wife] right now.

Know the differences. Useless words, phrases and sentiments simply fill the space. Actually useful things do more than fill space, they help. Passing by someone's page on Facebook for a few minutes and expressing via comments and likes, platitudes that do absolutely nothing to help anyone, is masturbation. It makes you feel like you did something to help.

On the flip side, posting your pain on Facebook and Twitter is also masturbation. It accomplishes nothing, because people's replies are useless for the exact reasons I describe above. Furthermore you're not looking to end the pain, you're simply an approval junkie looking for a fix to end the withdrawal pains.

Try not to be useless. Seek actual help when you're hurting, and provide actual help when someone you know is hurting.

THE LIGHT VS. THE DARK

POSTED MAY 26, 2012

"You can't do that."

"That idea won't work."

"That isn't how we do things."

Shutting down someone's ideas is snuffing the match before it can become a flame.

In a dark room, when a single point of light appears, it draws all attention immediately. It burns the eyes; it sears the synapses. And rather than let their eyes grow used to the light and use it to look around and see what they can see, the fearful shrink back, then scream for you to put that light out. Because it burns. Because it causes discomfort.

Don't let them put your light out. If the people in the room try to snuff your match, move to another room.

Shine.

ABOUT THE MAN WHO GAVE ME (A) LIFE
POSTED JUNE 17, 2012

In 2012, geekdom is a much more accepted thing than it was when I was growing up (and trust me, I'm VERY aware that it was easier when I was a teenager in the 90's than it was before that -- the ways have been paved by every generation previous).

To give some perspective, it wasn't cool at all to like comic books, comic book related movies and television shows, cartoons and animation, anything at all related to computers or even video games. You got teased if people found out you liked guiding plumbers around a mushroom kingdom, saving princesses from castles (well, really saving toadstools who gave you round after round of disappointing news).

But there was way, way more going on with me than just kids at school calling me geek and nerd as insults. I was a fairly damaged kid. My dad married my mom when I was 10 years old. He adopted my sister and I. He basically volunteered to pick up the pieces of our lives at that point and make something out of them. And those pieces... They were pretty jagged.

My birth father was a horribly abusive alcoholic. My mother left him twice -- once when I was three, and again when I was seven (after being convinced that he'd cleaned up and deserved another chance). The second and final time she left, all of my toys and belongings had been left in Taccoa, GA in the middle of the night. We ran to escape my birth father during what can only be described as a drunken rampage that, even though I'm in a particularly open mood and sharing things I've never written about before, I still can't bring myself to describe.

We lived in my grandfather's garage with no heat and no air conditioning for about two years. The winters were raw and the summers were unbearable. Then, my dad came into the picture and attempted to give us some semblance of a normal life. He married my mother and overnight, I was living in middle class suburbia. I had toys. I had cable television. I didn't have to worry about a drunk madman beating anyone up in the middle of the night.

And really, when you do the comparisons, that would have been enough to celebrate. But my dad didn't just go "here, life's normal, you're welcome." That was just resetting the needle to zero. He worked his ass off to straighten me up, which all by itself was a full time job. I was a mess, to say the least. He disciplined me in ways that drove points home, and never once did he raise a hand to me. His business started declining when I was 13, and the short glimpse into upper middle class life I had faded -- but his resolve didn't. He did everything he possibly could to give my sister and I a normal life.

I remember once going shopping for school clothes and trying on shoes in Marshall's. He sat down in one of the shoe-trying chairs and took a moment to rest, and when he crossed his leg over his knee, I saw that he had holes in the bottom of his shoes. When I asked if he was getting new shoes too, he said "Naw, sport, they don't have my size here. I'll get them next time."

We spent most of my high school life being what you could easily call poor -- and yet there was always food on the table and the lights stayed on. We didn't have cable TV anymore, but it didn't matter since I spent most of my days on restriction for getting in trouble somehow -- but the one thing he never took away from me was my art supplies (and he was the only person in my life who didn't find ways in varying shades of bluntness to remind me that drawing and art was for "fags").

In very real terms, he saved my life. And I love him for it.

It's been very hard to write this. There are lines that I told myself when I started writing that I would never cross. Talking about my rotten childhood and my birth father were two of them. But I really feel the need to celebrate my father and all that he's done for me, especially lately. It's been becoming clearer and clearer that I get to be the world-travelling Art of Akira Exhibit guy and the web consultant guy and the writer guy and everything else I am -- both "geeky" and in general -- because of my dad.

It's interesting; when you tell stories about your fucked up childhood to your wife and your close friends, and they say "Jesus, that is fucked up" and you suddenly realize... You know, it really was. When you're a kid, that's just life. You have no perspective. Your day to day experience is spent dealing with whatever's coming that day. You haven't the ability to look outward and survey the landscape of what life is supposed to be and say "I'm not getting what I deserve." You just take what you can get.

And then someone shows up and takes you by the scruff of your neck out of a pit and says "you're safe." And you can't appreciate that until much later, because when you're born into a life where good days include not getting beat up by the man who conceived you or running in fear from him or any day where it was less than 90 degrees and warmer than 50 so you could actually sit in your own bedroom... You don't really understand that that's not how it's supposed to be.

And that's what my dad gave to me. He didn't give me life, but he gave me **A** life. He gave me normalcy, and then he gave me permission to be myself (even if no one else did at the time). He gave me an actual Dad. So I wanted to pay him tribute in the column and share with the world what I see as being a model father. I wanted to share a geeky perspective of fathers that I feel is important and worth sharing. And today, I wanted to explain why being able to write that article means so damn much to me. I am the man I am today because of my dad.

Happy Father's Day.

IT'S YOUR FAULT

POSTED JUNE 19, 2012

If you are not what you want to be, it's your fault. Everything else you, I or anyone else can say about it is pathetic, boring bullshit. It's not your wife's or husband's fault. It's not your kids' fault. It's not your parents' fault. It's not a lack of opportunity's fault. It's not your current job's fault.

It's your fault.

"But there's not enough time..." **Bullshit.**
"But I don't know how..." **Bullshit.**
"But..." **BULLSHIT.**

A case study:

I left college after one and a half semesters to go build websites in the dot com boom. I taught myself how to use Photoshop and write HTML, then eventually JavaScript and Java. No one handed me any books and said "You'd be good at this." I got interested, I studied and researched and learned on my own, and then I went and got a career. I worked for some of the most forward thinking foundational companies in the early days of the dot com boom, and helped pave the way for all kinds of neat things.

Six years ago today, I turned in my notice to my full time job at the time. I was writing software for a medical training and education company. It was a nice job and I liked my boss and the people I worked with. But it wasn't what I wanted anymore. I didn't give a two week notice, it was simply a notice that, once I finished everything that was on my to-do list, I was going to leave the company and pursue my dream of being an author. It took until November of that year, but I did indeed leave to tour the nation in my pickup truck to support my new book.

By the time I'd turned in that notice, I already had a book written. I was working on getting it laid out and ready for print. I didn't have a publisher. I didn't need one -- I already had several thousand people who committed to buy my book, because I'd been writing it online and having them edit and vote on which stories would make it into the book for the past four years.

I left that job on very friendly terms. It was very scary. But I did it. And the way I did it was by realizing in 2002 that my aspirations of being an author rode on ACTUALLY BEING A FUCKING AUTHOR. No publisher asked me to do it. I didn't wait for an engraved invite to sit down and write the Great American Novel. I found the time to write while working and consulting on the side for extra income.

Over time, I went back to work here and there for clients that needed my help. Eventually I took a full-time job at Fark.com because it was one of my favorite websites, and I'd just finished a stint as the producer of a web-based video series based on news from the site. I started that show and sold it to Turner Broadcasting for their SuperDeluxe network without anyone asking me to -- I just went to Drew, said "Hey, here's a great idea -- I'll pay for it if you let me use your site for material." Then I went to Turner and said "here's a great show, pay me."

I started that project because I realized that my aspirations of being a writer for video rode on ACTUALLY WRITING FOR VIDEO. No one gave me a wad of cash or begged me to try it out, thinking I'd be good at it. I took it upon myself to shoot a pilot, get the nod from Drew, and sell the show to Turner. It turned out that I hated doing that job, so I gave the show to the crew that was working on it, wrote off my losses, and went back to consulting and writing my 2nd book. Eventually Drew asked me to work for him -- and that was a bit of a pipe dream in and of itself. But I'd proven to him I'd do the job to the best of my ability. He didn't call everyone he knew and beg them to work for him, he just saw my work and decided to bring me on.

I left Fark a few months ago to follow some new dreams. These days, I'm pretty much professionally curious. I write columns for CNN and Huffington Post while blogging and writing books. I also belong to a fantastic art and animation studio, Studio Revolver. I get to be around art all day long. I consult for some clients who need my help. I get to work with some extremely cool companies and do some extremely cool things with emerging internet tech and extremely talented artists, and I get to do it all on my own terms.

I wasn't born with a silver spoon in my mouth. My family wasn't connected anywhere. I knew no one in any industry I ever started working in -- All I knew is that I wanted to be something, so I went out and became it. This isn't patting myself on the back. Far from it, in fact. I'm not special. I'm not hyper-intelligent. I'm not immaculately talented. I simply possess the understanding that books don't write themselves. Websites don't code themselves. Shows don't shoot themselves. Careers don't build themselves. If I can do this, you can do this.

So, you say you want to be a writer. How many words did you write today? It doesn't matter what the fuck else you have to do today -- **you have to write to be a writer.** Same goes for drawing comics -- you can't draw comics without drawing. You can't be a musician without playing music.

Step one to being what you want to be -- shut the fuck up and do it. You can't be anything if you don't do anything. So do something.

"WHY DOESN'T ANYONE LIKE ME?"

POSTED JUNE 27, 2012

I spent a lot of time as a kid wishing people would like me.

I did stupid things to fit in. At the time they made sense... Mowing lawns all summer to buy a name brand shirt and shoes, listening to the same music and watching the same shows everyone else liked.

A lot of that aggravation manifested itself as aggression later in high school. Once I found a few guys like me who simply didn't fit into any kind of category, who liked me for me, I felt better. I found a family. But things still weren't okay. The days where we didn't have classes together and the nights spent alone at home; those hours were filled with backchannel thoughts of why I didn't fit in. "Why don't people like me? Why can't I just be normal?"

There were a lot of lonely nights. I didn't go to parties. I didn't do the prom thing. I drew a lot and wrote and played video games. I built models and listened to the same albums over and over again. I called what few friends I had on the phone now and again and we daydreamed about what we'd do if we could just get out of town.

And then, there's this invisible line we all like to pretend exists called "graduation." There's an illusion that the day we graduated high school, the heavens opened and a divine ray of light shone on us, filling us with everything we never knew about ourselves which made us powerful and independent. And of course, that's complete bullshit. Most of us carried every insecurity and neurosis we'd spent 18 years cultivating with us into college or the workplace. I know I did.

I was the youngest kid working at every company I worked at throughout the late 90s. There was a minimum of a 10 year age difference between me and the next youngest person everywhere I worked for years. I'd love to tell you that I had all this amazing confidence and that all my efforts and talent and whatever you want to call being on the rise of a trend made me awesome, but it's just not true.

It was like someone hit the reset button. I wasn't old enough to go to bars with my coworkers... Like I was even asked. The friends I did have were more of convenience than of camaraderie. And I'd love to lie to you and tell you I didn't spend a lot of time saying and doing things in an effort to get people to like me. So I won't lie to you.

And then, one day, something dawned on me: I'm me. I'm me at work. I'm me at home. I'm not changing... Not really, anyway. Why am I spending so much time on worrying about people liking me? What about me liking them?

It didn't change everything right away, but it was a huge step toward learning how to like myself (and it is a process -- if you don't already like yourself, you have to dedicate a lot of time and effort learning how to... But it's worth it. My God, is it worth it).

And that's the thing I want to share with you -- quit making all the concessions and the effort. Put it on them. Not that you should force people to audition for your friendship, that's pretty much bullshit. But you absolutely get to be half of the equation of the friendships you're a part of.

You are worthy of being someone's friend. And you are worthy of deciding if you want to be friends with them. If they like you, let it be YOU they like, not something you do or say or wear or are just to have a friend. And remember... You have to like them, too.

ON TRUSTING PEOPLE
POSTED JUNE 29, 2012

Every single person in your entire life will, at some point or another, disappoint you.

This is inevitable. No one is perfect. No one is capable of reading your mind. No one is 100% capable of meeting every need you have, at every moment you have them. We know this, because you are not perfect. You are not capable of reading anyone else's mind. You are not capable of meeting every need anyone else has, at every moment they have them.

What is true about us is also true about everyone else. And when this is the case, and we are flawed beings, that means everyone else is flawed. Which means, at some point, you're going to trust someone to do something and they are going to fail you.

Relationships, therefore, are built on two things: how often this happens, and the reason why.

If someone disappoints you a lot, and they don't seem to care, they're a pretty miserable friend. In fact, it's likely they're not a friend at all, and you're throwing yourself away on that person, like spending good money after bad on a car that simply will not work.

If someone disappoints you a lot, but they don't mean to and they feel bad about it, you're at fault for trusting someone to do something they're incapable of doing.

If someone is reliable for the most part, and then one day fails you and feels terrible about it, you have to decide if you're going to hold that against them or get past it and give them another chance. If it happens again, the same way, you have to figure out if you're willing to live with that one person never being able to step up for that one thing and always feeing terrible about it.

And of course, there are strata of circumstances in varying degrees of both trust and concern between (and beyond) those above. And in every single circumstance, one thing is consistent: you.

You have to be able to make the decisions on what to do in every case. You have that control. If you stand back and think "well, I can't do better than this man who says he loves me but beats me" or "I love her, despite the fact that she's disgusting and nasty and mean and what can I do?" Or "He was supposed to get me a job with that company, and because he didn't, I can't be a [whatever]" -- Well, you're in control of that feeling, right then and there. You're making a decision via apathy or despair or loneliness. But you're still making the decision.

At the end of the day, you are responsible for how you feel. You cannot outsource your emotions; no one else can feel what you feel for you, and thus they are not responsible for your emotional state. That doesn't mean they aren't wrong when they fail you, and it doesn't mean that someone's hateful, selfish or negligent behavior should go without consequence. But how you feel about it? That's all on you.

And it's going to suck when someone fails you -- I'm not saying that you shouldn't be sad, angry or disappointed. You have to be if you're human and not a sociopath. What I am saying, though, is that you can't carry that feeing around with you and have it affect your life in a destructive manner. You cannot give up on life and point to the person that disappointed you at some point and say "It's their fault." You have to get up and eat breakfast and get dressed and live out your day, day to day, no matter who disappoints you, where when or why.

Giving up on anything because someone else failed you isn't their fault -- it's yours. It's your life. Other people are aspects of your experience. Don't make them responsible for your successes, failures, feelings and emotions.

SO WHAT IF THEY SAY "NO?"

POSTED JULY 3, 2012

You really want that job. But you can't bring yourself to apply because, what if they say "no?" What then?

You've been talking to him or her for weeks now, and they're funny and they're bright and they're really cute when they do that thing with the pencil when they aren't paying attention and you just happen to catch them in the corner of your eye... But you can't bring yourself to ask them out on a date, because, what if they say "no?"

So what if they do? And why are you presuming to answer their question before even asking them? Isn't it only fair that you give them a chance to voice their own opinion?

The problem isn't that they might say no. The problem is that you may find out you're not qualified, in their opinion, to fill the role you wish you could. And you may not be.

But then again, you also just might be.

You know how you figure it out? You fucking go for it. All those old clichés about "no risk, no reward" and "fortune favors the bold" and all that? They're old sayings for a reason. They're the advice from the old, handed down to the young, because it's only after we've lost our chance that we realize we should have taken it when we could have. And everyone's bold in hindsight.

Lonely, sad, regretful and locked in a position in life you don't want. But bold.

Or, you could be bold *now*. And yeah, they could say no. But along with that comes an opportunity to find out why the answer was no. If a guy rejects you because you're not cute enough, you just found out that you spent some time liking a superficial person. If you don't get the job because you're not qualified, you just found out what it will take to become qualified. You can't always get what you want. But you'll **never** get what you want if you don't try. Quit rejecting yourself before anyone else can reject you.

And then, there's what happens when they say "yes." Oh, the nerves! But you just went for it and got it. And now, you have a chance to take things to the next level. You get to explore new ground. You get to learn new things. You get to grow and be someplace you only went in your mind, with people you only imagined knowing the way you get to know them now.

But only if you stand up, take a deep breath, and go for it.

Go on. Stand up. Take that deep breath. Smile -- you're about to do something great for yourself. Now, go and **be bold, motherfucker.**

WHY?

POSTED JULY 5, 2012

I try my best not to give unsolicited advice, especially to kids and teenagers (**update:** except for this book, of course -- but hey, you choose to read it, so that's on you). I hated hearing the thoughts and stories of the "elderly" when I was growing up, and I found most advice to be trite and completely useless for the situations I was facing.

Of course, that's not true. The advice was usually, if not always, spot on. The thing I'm coming to realize as an adult is that advice isn't a thing that older people give younger people in order to stop them from doing something (although we really, really wish they wouldn't do it). It's something we give to them so that, when they look back on the situation they just completely fucked up, they'll know one thing to be true: it has been done before.

While it doesn't stop the pain, it at least grounds them in the fact that at least they're not alone.

One piece of unsolicited advice I do give to every young person I get the chance to: Always, no matter what the situation, ask yourself one important question: "Why?"

"Why" is the single most powerful word in the English language.

Why? Because it has the power to compel a response which cannot be avoided, even from yourself.

Why? Because if someone can't answer why (especially yourself), you know one of two things: you're on the precipice of a discovery, or you're being conned.

Why? Because if someone is asked "why?" and they don't know the truth, they will stammer, they will cajole, they will deflect or they will lie. All of these things instigate a process we detect as humans. We can sense when we're being led somewhere we really shouldn't go.

If "why" is being asked about a process, a thing, an event or other thing, and the answer cannot be given, it's justification to investigate, and no one can stop you without betraying the fact that ignorance benefits them.

If "why" is being asked about your own actions and motives, you have no choice but to admit, no matter how momentarily, answer honestly. The justifications and fabrications your desires will convince you are true will inevitably kick in. But if you ask yourself "why" about what you're doing, how you're feeling or what you're thinking -- even if for a very brief moment -- you have the truth behind it all. Or, at worst, you've just discovered a part of yourself you need to reflect on and consider. You get a chance to grow.

No matter how old you are, what you are doing, where you are going, what you are thinking, what you are being told, what you are being sold, or what is being presented to you, always ask "why?" That is the one question which, no matter what the answer, tells you the truth about a thing -- especially yourself.

HOW TO HANDLE (AND BEAT) AN ADDICTION

POSTED JULY 31, 2012

These steps to handle (and beat) an addiction are not perfect, but they work:

1. Breathe in. Nice and slow. Count to three as you inhale.
2. Breathe out. Again, nice and slow. Count one, two, three as you exhale.
3. There. Six seconds. You just spent six seconds without it.
4. Now again. Breathe in. Breathe out. Ten times. You've just spent a minute. It didn't control you for a full minute.
5. Try to string together a few minutes. It's going to be tough. You're going to think about it. You can't help but think about it. It's powerful. It's got you. But not right now. Right now, you've got you under control. Breathe.
6. Has it been an hour? Check the clock. It's been an hour. Sixty minutes have gone by, and you've stood strong. Sixty minutes now belong to you.
7. Can you do that 23 more times?
8. You need to talk it out. You need to hold it together. You need to call your most trusted friend(s); the one who knows you well enough not to tell you everything's going to be okay. You need to talk to someone who will listen to the lies you've already told yourself and believe, and tell you they are lies. You need that person who knows you better than you want to know yourself right now.
9. If you don't have a person like that in your life, you need to find a group. Any group. Even if your addiction isn't alcohol or narcotics, go to the group. Go somewhere, anywhere, where you cannot lie to yourself, and you cannot escape truth.

10. You are alone now. It's night, or it's day, or it's a few days or weeks later. You're alone. You've beat it this long. Things are hard. You remember how it felt. You miss it. But you know it's no good for you... But if you can just get one fix, *just one fix*, you'll be alright. You've gone this long. You deserve a reward. You deserve it.

11. Did you see the lie? Did you call it out? You deserve a reward which is indulging in the thing you've kept from indulging in. It's a lie. It's like saying "if you can go x days without killing yourself, your reward is killing yourself." It's your ego. It's protecting you from the pain. It wants you to believe it's you. It wants you to believe it's got your best interest in mind. It doesn't, it just wants the pain to go away.

12. What have you replaced the time with? What are you doing with your days and nights now that you're not in the stuff? What are you doing? Do you have a replacement? Find a replacement. Write. Draw. Bike. Run. Swim. Talk to your friend. Go to your group. Let the clock turn in your absence; earn more minutes and more hours and more days clean. You're in control.

13. You've gotten past the pain. You've gotten past the cravings. You see an old friend from the scene, or hear a story from the old guard, or get a whiff of that smell; that familiar smell... LEAVE. NOW. They're not your friends. Addicts are addicts first, and whatever else they may be second. They are not your friends; they're fixers. Misery loves company. Don't know them. Don't want to know them. Leave. LEAVE.

14. When was the last time you even thought about your addiction? Remember? You should. Keep track. Know that you're STILL susceptible. Even if it's not the old stuff, you've got an addict's blood. You've got a predisposition for escapism. You've won so many battles by earning those minutes and hours, days and weeks, months and years being in control. To win the war: You must build a life you do not want to escape from.

15. What have you done differently? What's new? Who are you now? Do you recognize yourself? Do you even know who that person that inhabited your body was? I hope not. And I hope you never forget who they were.

If at any point you miss a step, close your eyes, take a breath. Nice and slow. Count to three as you inhale. Start back over at step 1.

ON FRIENDSHIP

POSTED AUGUST 28, 2012

Sometimes, people ask me what I think about stuff via email or Facebook or Twitter, and want advice. Sometimes, they make requests for blog posts. I don't always entertain them, but when I feel like there's something I can share about my perspective on life gained from my experiences that could help people, I try to share it. This is one of those.

I can point you to any number of essays, diatribes and bumper stickers that will tell you all about what a "real friend" is. My favorite summation: "Friends help you move; real friends help you move bodies."

That's not what this is. I'm not going to attempt to educate you on what a real friend is, because I've already done that in several other posts. Add to that the sheer volume of shit you'll get back if you Google "Real Friend" and I think there's really no need for me to write yet another opinion on what constitutes a real friend.

No, this is a little different. It's about a harsh realization that, if you haven't learned already, you will. It's one that everyone gets to learn, whether they like it or not. In fact, it's so harsh that there are people who have learned it but simply cannot believe it's true, so they refuse it. They make excuses for it, or attempt to hide from it, or otherwise delude themselves into believing it can't be true.

But it is, and it sucks... At first. And then, it becomes the single most wonderful thing you'll ever learn:

More than 90% of the people you know in your life -- and this includes your family -- are not really your friend.

I don't mean to say this to depress you, and I'm not being a pessimist. In fact, the goal here is to actually make your life better, and ultimately make you happy. But to get there, we have to wade through the darkness, which in this case is the realization that the vast majority of people you call "friend" will watch you burn and not even piss on you to put you out.

You may be a popular person. You may be well liked and well thought of. You may have 200 or 2000 Facebook friends. But make no mistake: they're not actually your friends. You may have tons of kids in school that you're friendly with; they're not your friends, either. Liking someone is not friendship, it's liking them. Doing favors for someone does not mean you are their friend, it just means you like them enough to do favors for them.

You will figure this fact out the hard way. There is no other way, because this is a very, very hard fact of life to face. You won't want it to be true. In fact, as I said above, a lot of people can't believe it's true, so they go on pretending it's not. But it is.

The shortcuts to finding this fact out: go to jail and see who visits. Get cancer or become a serious kind of sick and see who helps out. Have your house burn down and need a place to stay. Attempt suicide and see who shows up to save your life. Become addicted to something and see who stands in your way and stops you. Say something you feel honestly that is terribly unpopular and see who stands behind you (not "in agreement with" -- real friends don't necessarily agree with everything you think or say, but they do love you enough to get your back when you're being attacked for being who you are, thinking what you think or feeling what you feel).

Of course, I really don't want you to have to go through these things in order to find out who it is in life you can truly trust -- it's compounding a terrible fact of life with a terrible event you have to deal with, and I really don't want you to have to go through something terrible. At the same time, I also really don't want you to build your life around the wrong kind of people; wobbly legs that hold your emotional table up so long as you don't put any weight on it.

More than once in my life, I've had to recalibrate my understanding of what friendship is. This year, in fact. And I suspect I'll have to at least a dozen times more before I pass. And let me tell you from firsthand knowledge: it hurts to realize someone (or a group of someones, or most everyone you know) isn't really your friend, and it doesn't hurt any less with each iteration of figuring this out.

So here's where this all turns into a good thing.

You will go through a certain period of your life thinking you have all these friends, and some stuff's going to happen to you (or because of you) and they'll disappear. You're going to get into some trouble -- not necessarily that you've done something bad, but you'll need help. There will be people who you've talked to, opened up to, poured your heart out to, and when you need them most, they'll be gone.

"Where's the good thing, Joe?" you're wondering. Well, watch who sticks around. See who remains. There's the good thing. There's your friends. And if there's no one... You've discovered a very important fact, one that's even more important than recognizing who your real friends are:

YOU are your real friend.

Get to know yourself, and you'll begin realizing what it is you do and do not need from others. More importantly, you'll get to know what you will and will not tolerate in your life. Know that you can survive on your own. You don't NEED anyone to save you.

That said, don't go isolating yourself from humanity. Other people are valuable in life, when they're the right people. And there's the big trick: surround yourself with the right people. People who don't seek to gain from you, who don't want from you what you have, who don't need you to make them feel good. The flip side to that -- don't do that to other people. Don't tolerate it from yourself. That's how you build real friendships.

And when you find them, hold on to them for dear life.

I hope this helps.

9/11/2012
POSTED SEPTEMBER 11, 2012

(Update, 9.11.13: I wrote this a year ago. In that year, there have been some changes, including the wife mentioned in this story becoming my ex-wife. Yet more perspective on why moving on is healthy and obsessing over tragedy simply leaves you stationary and in pain.)

I woke up just like any other morning. The alarm went off on my cellphone. I hit the snooze and laid awake enjoying the moment. A cat jumps up onto the bed and walks up onto my chest, begging for some early morning cheek scratches. My dogs begin whining a little, reminding me that there's only a few minutes left before their bladders explode.

The alarm goes off again, and instead of hitting snooze, I go ahead and turn it off. Begrudgingly, my wife and my cat both lift themselves off me so we can begin the process of getting on with the day. I turned on the television to catch up on the morning news and, much to my horror, I was greeted with images of two majestic towers in flames and smoking.

Our nation had been attacked... Eleven years ago today.

My response was immediate. "Really?" I asked my wife as I watched file footage of the most horrific event our nation has experienced in my lifetime. "Do they honestly need to do this?"

"What?" she asked.

"Remind us just how painful that day was?" I said. "Do they need to actually show the buildings on fire? Do they need to show the planes colliding with the towers? Do they need to discuss the deaths and horrors of that day? Are those things truly necessary in order to honor the victims and remember what happened?"

She didn't have an answer. And I don't think I do, either. What I do know is if my father died in an automobile accident, the last thing I want to watch year after year is the video footage of the collision. If someone I loved died of cancer, the last thing I want to see is video of their last days in the hospital, suffering.

Two people I know died in Tower 2 on 9/11/2001. I don't want to watch that building burning and collapsing every fucking year. It reminds me that they were in there and they were crushed alive, simply because they went to work that day and 19 crazy zealots decided to make a point that ended with 2,977 exclamation points.

And yet...

It's on every news channel, on repeat. It'll be the topic of political candidates' talking points today. It'll be bandied about by every person in this nation who wants to prove their patriotism or make some point about foreign policy. It's everywhere... Just like it was last year, and the year before, and the year before...

I think that many (too many) people feel that, if you don't stop and make a public display of paying tribute, you don't care. And God forbid you don't care about a tragedy, lest you be thought of as a heartless bastard. It's like all these personal moments are made public simply so we don't look bad in public about our personal feelings.

At this point, we are past the grieving stage. We are not grieving as a nation. We are now posturing; making a presentation for the sole purpose of avoiding the appearance of not caring.

Paying tribute does not necessarily mean you have to bring up the tragedy of the event. You don't have to remind people of the pain they suffered that day in order to honor the fallen. My grandfather never told me stories of dropping bombs all over England and France after D-Day. Instead, he always told me funny stories about the things the crew of his bomber did. I'd ask him about the war, he'd tell me about the time they put soap in one guy's canteen. I remember very clearly the day I asked him why he never talks about the war. His words to me resonated only very recently: "If you keep picking scabs, they never heal."

Have we healed as a nation? No. Have I healed as a person? Mostly... I knew people who died in Tower 2 that day. They weren't close friends or loved ones, just people I worked with at one point -- and even now, I think of them and I am sad that they died in the process of going to work just like any other day. It fucking sucks to think about -- and they were just work acquaintances. I don't want to imagine what it would be like to have a family member or best friend lost that day.

And that's the point. Why are we, as a nation comprised by a vast majority of people who knew no one who died that day, bringing this out every single year as if we did? Do you think putting this out there every year in "tribute" helps the families of the fallen move on? Do you think it honors those who gave their lives, either willingly or unwillingly that day?

It's time to move on.

And it doesn't mean we forget -- we will always remember the events of that day, regardless of how many "Never Forget" stickers we see on the backs of jacked-up trucks in states hundreds or thousands of miles away from New York. We don't need that to remember... But I feel that the person inside that truck needs it. They need the branding as a "Real American" and "Patriot." They need everyone else to know just how much they care about that day. They need it known. For what reason, only a psychologist can truly discern.

I'm not saying don't mourn. I'm just saying that maybe, 11 years later, it's time we quit picking scabs and let the healing process truly take hold. Remember always the lessons of that day. Honor those who lost their lives, either by being part of tragedy or by willingly rushing into those buildings to save the victims.

But there's definitely better, healthier and more respectful ways than by dragging out file footage of burning & collapsing buildings and by metaphorically dragging the corpses of the dead out for public display every single year.

Here's some stuff you could do to pay tribute to those whose lives were lost on 9/11 that, while they won't get you any attention for being a Patriot and won't make you feel super awesome for clicking "LIKE" on someone's jingoistic image tribute on Facebook, will actually help:

- Make a donation to your local Fire Department's burn unit and charity drives
- Make a donation to the local Police Department's injured officer fund
- If you lost a loved one or friend and know what charity or cause they supported, donate to that in their name
- If you are so inclined, say a prayer for the fallen.
- Discuss the event with friends
- Send a care package to our troops stationed overseas -- they need movies (decent ones, and send DVDs, not Blu-Ray -- most laptops and station TVs don't have Blu-Ray players), magazines, books, Crystal Light packets for water bottles,

and if you're really crafty, you can dye some decent vodka blue and put it in a Listerine bottle. Trust me, they'll thank you.

- Vote this election season

STOP THRASHING

POSTED SEPTEMBER 19, 2012

"Don't go down without a fight."

That's been my life mantra for as long as I've been alive. Don't be passive. Fight. Stand your ground.

But what happens when the ground breaks down right under you and takes you into the water? The torrent sweeps you under and you're whisked away in the rapids? What do you do when life simply won't let you fight?

Fighting will wear you out; you will run out of breath and you WILL go down. When you have no ground to stand on, it's impossible to fight.

So stop fighting it.

It took me many years to finally learn this lesson, and I continually forget it. It goes against my natural instincts and all of the things I thought I knew about life. But when things get out of control, it's no longer a fight that can be won. In fact, it's not even a fight anymore. It's like driving your car into a river; steering and hitting the brakes won't help.

Sometimes, you have to surrender to survive. It's a horrible fact of life for those of us who never want to surrender. Surrender sounds like weakness. It's not. It's acceptance -- and acceptance is sometimes the most courageous act we could ever perform, because it goes against everything we know and everything we are.

Now, standing and fighting is about self-respect. Never lose that. Never let anyone push you around. But when life dumps you in the river, you're not facing a someone anymore. When life itself begins tossing you back and forth and forces beyond your control take hold, shaking your fist and cursing its name feels brave, but you have to realize: the river is the river. It's not that it's mightier or stronger than you; it's a force of nature. It doesn't care. It doesn't think. It's not there to beat you. It's just there. It's going to keep flowing whether you fight it or not.

Ride it out. Find the calm spot. Use the energy you saved to swim to shore. Get back on track. Rebuild. Keep on living.

That's the victory. Not drowning. Not being broken. Surviving to fight another day.

Going against your own instincts is scary, and courage is strength in times of fear. Accepting that you cannot control what's going on around you and accepting that you have to stop trying to swim against the river, turn with the tide, point your feet (not your face) forward and go with the flow is scary. It's also the only way to keep from slamming your head against the rocks in your path and surviving.

It's important to know that sometimes, giving up the struggle is actually the only way not to give up on life. And while you may want to fight it, sometimes the only strategy that makes any sense is to ride it out. In the immortal words of Paul McCartney, "Let it Be."

And when in doubt just remember to breathe.

ON FEAR

POSTED SEPTEMBER 21, 2012

"Where ignorance lurks, so too do the frontiers of discovery and imagination." - Neil deGrasse Tyson

Imagine the frontiers that Tyson describes above as borders. There's the land of where you've been, and the land beyond, which is the land which you've never been.

Some people see these borders and shrink from them. After all, they're borders. They're there for a reason. You're not supposed to go past them. Going past the borders is out of bounds, and that's *bad*.

The reasons for it being bad are myriad. Someone told you it was bad, so you believe it. Mom and Dad will be mad at you. Your family will disown you. Your husband won't be pleased. Your wife will complain. Your girlfriend will break up with you. Your boyfriend will hate you. Your friends will think less of you. God forbids it.

Fear is what keeps people from exploring those frontiers of discovery and imagination. It's always fear.

Fear of reprisals.
Fear of learning that everything they've ever known is wrong and they might have to relearn.
Fear of the work involved in trying to discover whatever it is just past those borders.

Fear of realizing their dreams and fantasies of what they wish they could be and who they wish they were are simply wishes. Fear of being bad at something.

Fear of being good at something, and realizing they have been wasting their lives doing whatever else they've been doing.

Fear of finding out Mom and Dad and family and husbands and wives and girlfriends and boyfriends and God just might not be who they should spend the rest of their lives with, because they're afraid of being alone.

To say "so stop being afraid" is the greatest lie any human could tell another. Because the truth is, we're all afraid. No exceptions. It's just that some of us are thinking in voices that are not our own, We're listening to the wrong audio track in our own heads.

The trick is not ending fear. It's staring it right in the face, gritting your teeth, and taking one step forward. And when that doesn't kill you, taking another step.

It's not easy. In fact, it's goddamn hard. It's hard to get up the courage to even go to the edge of what you know, whether it be a new subject, a new life endeavor, or even getting to know someone you've never known.

But it's okay to be afraid. Fear is natural. It shows up and forces you to be alert. You will be afraid. You will want to turn around. You will want to go back to comfortable, to warm, to familiar. And that's okay, too... Just don't lament your life when you do.

To get something you've never had, you have to do something you've never done.

Go on. Walk right up to that border. Look at it. Consider it. Take your time. And when you're ready, take one step.

THE SECRET TO CHANGE

POSTED OCTOBER 14, 2012

"Change is like a diaper. The new one takes some work to get into and chafes at first, but at least you're not sitting in your old shit anymore."

I wrote that as a note to myself a few years ago. It's still relevant. In fact, it's one of the few that I actually kept and didn't toss.

I'm going to do you a favor. I'm going to save you tens of dollars in self-help book purchases and just give you the real, honest, no-shit secret to change:

1) Don't do the thing you want to stop doing.
2) Do something else.
3) Repeat.

Yep. It's that simple.

This isn't being naive. This isn't being short-sighted. I know, because I've been through it. Multiple times. I've done the posturing. I've done the self-deception. I've done the "It's too hard..." crap. And then, one day, I just stop doing the thing that I don't want to do anymore, and instead, DO SOMETHING ELSE.

People don't like change. Patterns are easy. They're routine because they're routines. Wash, rinse, repeat. Disrupt the routine, and you glitch the system. Glitches suck. They shock. They cause discomfort.

If you want to stop smoking, you can start chewing nicotine gum, or get a prescription for Chantix, or buy any number of books or tapes or even software that will coach you in the process. To me, this is all bullshit. It's not something else, it's "something else." It's like that guy who's always telling you about the comic book he's perpetually working on, and today, he did a bunch of character roughs! But you've never seen a single panel. Or, the guy who is always "writing a book" who never shows you page one. Or, the girl who says she's going to quit smoking, who uses another delivery method for the drug that she gets in smoking until she finally realizes she might as well smoke.

You can do this bullshit.

Or...

You can do what my dad did and, one day, just don't smoke. And then continue to don't smoke.

I've never smoked, so I can't tell you I know how hard it is to quit smoking in particular. But I have, at one point in my life, been 375lbs due to overeating and being lazy, and I have faced several addictions. The funniest of them (and the one I don't mind talking about): video games. You might laugh at the idea of video game addiction, but it's real, and it sucks. "Who can get addicted to Mario?" Well, anyone who would rather play in a fantasy world than face their real world. Just like living in chat rooms online all day. Just like obsessively posting to Facebook and Twitter for validation via "likes" and retweets. Just like overeating. Just like drinking. Just like everything.

Every addiction is a seeking of normalization and control over self that isn't present in day-to-day life. You feel helpless, so you find something to control. Living in this world sucks, so you go to the other world. It's escapism. Gambling, alcohol, heroin, food and yes, even video games.

Bad habits are the same thing. They may not be compulsions to a behavior -- they may be lack of another behavior. But the result is the same. One day, you decide you don't want these things to control you, so you control them. Even for a minute.

And there it is, the secret to change: decide what it is you don't want to be, and then one day, just decide you won't be that thing. Even if it's just for that one day. And then the next day, don't be it again. And again. And soon enough, a habit forms. And then, it becomes your new routine.

Yes, people will notice. Yes, people will complain. I know about smokers' circles. I know about the socialization that occurs during lunch hours at work spent at buffets and Taco Bells and whatnot. I know about gaming guilds. I know about happy hour at the bar.

I know how hard it is to not show up to those things and have people asking "Hey, where were you?" And then 'where were you' turns into "Hey, what gives?" And then 'hey, what gives' turns into "Traitor."

And then you're on your own. Thank God, because you're free.

My father loves to tell the story of when he quit smoking, because he loves punch lines to jokes. It's almost comical -- my entire life, I've watched this man build stories up around his experiences, just so he could deliver that zinger at the end. And his zinger at the end of the quitting smoking story is that he never really had a problem with quitting smoking -- the hard part was figuring out what to do with his empty hand! His entire routine up to that point was spent doing everything he did with his right hand, because his left hand always had a lit cigarette in it.

That's the problem, isn't it? Filling that empty hand... Filling that empty time... Filling that empty space. You must fill it, or else you're just leaving open vacuums from which no desire can escape. You snack while relaxing. Instead, chew gum. You drink with friends at the bar -- go to the gym instead. You hate your job and disappear in video games all night and on weekends. Write a book instead.

Join a cooking class. Make stuff. Draw. Run a mile around your neighborhood. Take up biking.

Or, keep being miserable, because it makes you "happy." And keep posting to Facebook and Twitter how much you wish whatever you hate about yourself and your life would change, and follow it up with "FML" or "But what can I do?" or other helpless bullshit.

And make no mistake: it IS bullshit. Because you're not helpless, you're just lazy. Everyone has the power to help themselves. You can help yourself by going to a meeting at the local Whatever Anonymous than the bar or the buffet or game store. You can help yourself by working out. You can help yourself by talking about your attempts at change with your friends and family. You can help yourself by removing yourself from ANYONE who doesn't support you in those attempts.

Or, you can help yourself to another drink, cigarette, ice cream bar, or 12 hour gaming binge. The choice is yours, and it's always -- ALWAYS -- a choice. And when you make the one that leads you to ultimate misery, and you complain on your social networks about it, and everyone else commiserates with you and shares your lament because they're miserable and misery loves company...

313

Know that at any time you want to, you can just step out of this Hokey Pokey circle and **DO SOMETHING ELSE**.

THE CREATIVE MIND (AND WHY IT CAN BE TROUBLESOME)

POSTED NOVEMBER 6, 2012

Dear "normal" folks:

I'm writing this from a place that's trying to be helpful. It is, of course, woven from my perspective and experience, and so there's tons and tons of margin for error. It's just how I see things. But from my perspective and experience, it's profoundly true that normal people don't "get" creatives. And the closer they are to creatives, the more the questions impact them. Sometimes, it's in interpersonal relationships. Sometimes it's in behavior. But somehow, someway, there's almost always issues that arise between creatives and "normal" folks. And I'm going to try to shed some light on that for you.

I have a theory that creative people spend the vast majority of their day living in delusion.

Because that's what creativity is. It's delusion. When you're being "creative," you're deluding yourself with visions of how life, things, ideas, concepts can be different. You delude yourself into thinking you should change or create them. And then you hold on to those delusions while you make the thing you make, and once it's done, you delude yourself into thinking anyone's going to care.

It's only after it's made, put into the world, recognized and accepted that the delusion changes into "creativity" because creativity is the word that society has come up with as a nice way of acknowledging this behavior.

Let's face it. We call things "creative" because "crazy" is insulting.

You might be thinking that I'm equating creativity to a mental disorder. Well, it kinda is, for certain definitions of "disorder." It's certainly not the normal state of normal minds, as defined by the majority of minds and how they operate. Remember, "crazy" is defined by the masses and majority, because crazy is the antithesis of accepted thought and how things are normally. "Normal" never changed anything in the world (much less, changed the world), because normal is normal. It likes how things are. Even Steve Jobs agrees. "Here's to the crazy ones," his famous soliloquy begins.

Creatives spend their time inventing characters, stories, scenes, technologies, theories and other things manifested from the input they receive from their surroundings. They take the stimuli they receive, both from the past and the present, and mix it with what goes on in their brain. Then, it's output in some form. Writing, drawing, painting, singing, playing music, sculpting, inventing and otherwise shaping reality to meet their delusion, as best as reality can be shaped.

This becomes an issue when normal life stuff happens. The creative mind -- which is delusional, mind you -- deludes itself with visions of how it could be, what might be happening, what should be happening, and the distance between the two things. We get wound up in that. It's hard to just live in the moment and "be" when you're a "creative" because creatives can't help when they get creative. Even if it's about stuff that isn't art. Creativity manifests itself in expression. Artsy inventive scientific stuff is a channel of output, not the creativity itself.

The thing normal people don't get is that we can't just turn that off. For us who suffered trauma, our creativity, our panics, our mania... They're coping mechanisms. They're mental armor they've never worn. They're defense mechanisms they've never had to experience.

Creativity, in all its forms, is the charcoal filter that turns impure thoughts into something digestible, because all creativity comes from a dissatisfaction of how things are. Creativity is the method we use to soften the raw feed while not diluting the message. Without it, the raw feeling; the raw thoughts... They would chew a normal mind apart. We call this being rude, or blunt, or inappropriate in most cases. It's because it's not normal. It's not acceptable by the standards of the majority. It's "off." It's delusional.

While I don't think every creative mind was abused, or abandoned, or hurt in some way, I do believe that it spawns from the place that requires a coping mechanism to function. It is a channel of thought combined with emotion that requires that charcoal filter if it's to be expressed and understood by anyone who isn't us.

I hope this helps shed a little light on things.

ZOMBIE EMOTIONS

POSTED NOVEMBER 27, 2012

Everyone experiences emotions. No one is immune. We like to think we are... But we're not. We get scared. We panic. We love. We hate. We admire. We lust. We're human beings. We feel, and that's not a bad thing. The problem is, people just don't know how to handle them. So they try to suppress them, or worse, kill them off.

And that's the problem. Emotions do not die. You cannot drown them in alcohol. You cannot shoot them down with thoughts. When you bury them, they turn into zombies -- they come back uglier and harder to handle, and the longer you bury them, the uglier and meaner they are. And they're nearly impossible to handle in large groups.

You cannot help how you feel. All you can control is how you behave. So allow yourself to feel what you're feeling, lest they come back and eat you alive.

THE INSANE ENERGY DRINK EXPERIMENT

RE-POSTED JANUARY 25, 2013

Sometimes, my energy drinks bore me.

The trouble is, I've grown accustomed to how all of this stuff works, and my "cycles" are just getting boring. So I figured, why not have a little fun?

I drink Red Bulls in the morning. They've got a little caffeine, but they keep me riding strong into the day. This is the "long burn" energy.

I drink Redline when I need a big boost, usually before working out - the extra energy while working out turns into more repetitions and calisthenics. This is a subtle but steady climb, followed by a slow and steady decline.

When Redline starts to dull out (and I get tolerant), I switch to N.O. Xplode. This stuff is sorta like Redline, but the "shock" factor is way higher - you don't just soar up to cruising altitude, you fucking take off like a rocket. And you pretty much crash the same way.

And so, I mixed three scoops of N.O. Xplode into two cans worth of Red Bull, and finished off the water bottle with a bottle of Redline Xtreme. An energy drink cocktail of epic proportions. And what do you get when you mix these?

N.O. Xplode + Red Bull + Redline = OH MY HOLY FUCKING GOD.

Consumed at 5:30 PM.

Immediate effect: At first, nothing (of course). But once it hit my system, it was like jumping off a roof, in reverse. I got into my truck, began driving to the gym, and within 10 minutes, my heart was racing. I was physically shaking by the time I got to the gym.

During the workout: Holy jesus mary shit fuck. I was sweating like crazy, and where I normally begin to fatigue and experience some muscle tiredness around the 25th rep in a high-rep workout, I went on to 30... then 35... then 40 and finally stopped at 50, with almost no real "pushing through." ON EVERY EXERCISE. I was still racing when done with the weights (about an hour or so) and went into my cardio session thinking "I'll run as far as I can until the juice runs down." I normally run two miles, and at the end of the second, my body is ready for me to stop. I'm not "winded", just tired and ready to call it a workout. Tonight, I ran four miles, and could have done five, but was just fucking bored on the treadmill.

After workout: Just about everyone I talked to commented on my "good mood." I was pretty hyper driving home, but not heart-racing hyper. Just... hyper. Called a lot of people, got a lot of conversations done. Saw God. Told him hi for my mom, since she believes in him and I don't. Nearly ran over a cop on a motorcycle. He gave chase, I just plugged an IV from my arm into the gas tank and outran that motherfucker something fierce. Invented two new punctuation marks. Divided by Zero.

The rest of the evening: No "jitters" - but I've been working all night. It's now 4:06AM, and I'm not even the slightest bit tired. I've written two new stories for my book, invented Joetonium which is 100x stronger than Adamantium but only bonds to cartilage, and fixed a leaky toilet. Don't hate anyone. Like everyone. Love you. Thank you for reading my blog. I want an iguana. I had one when I was a teenager, but he was a bit of a mean fucker, he bit me all the time. I can totally do cartwheels, watch.

The taste: Like a fruit-flavored 9-volt battery. N.O. Xplode is already pretty "sharp" tasting, but mixing it with the carbonation from the Red Bull made it practically shock my mouth with every sip.

Will I do this again? You're goddamn right I will.

YOU KNOW THE FUTURE'S HERE WHEN YOU'RE SCARED

POSTED FEBRUARY 15, 2013

It's been 17 years since the first time I set foot in New York City.

I was 19 years old. I was jumping head first into the dot-com world. I was scared out of my mind. I'd been sent up to New York City to help a client install some software. I was supposed to be here two weeks. I lasted about seven days.

I rushed through the job. I did the job, yes. But I rushed it. I didn't want to be here. I thought I did, but the second I got off the plane and had to catch a cab to go into the city, I realized I wasn't ready. I was terrified. I'd never left home before. This was the first time I'd set foot out of suburban Atlanta, GA and I was in the busiest, craziest, most hectic city on the planet. If it hadn't been for the fact that I hadn't eaten or drank anything in nearly 24 hours due to my nerves, I'd have soiled myself.

I lived in my hotel. I did my job. I went to work, worked, and went back to the hotel. I was terrified of the city. And if I had to be honest with myself, I was terrified of my life. I didn't feel I deserved it. After all, I was the poor fat white kid from nowhere, GA who somehow conned his way into a decent paying software gig that took him to the biggest, baddest city in the world.

New York City. The start and the end of so many things.

After I completed the gig, I phoned headquarters and let them know I was ready to come home. "Stay the rest of the time," my boss said. "It's paid for. Go out and have some fun."

"I want to go home," I replied.

"Nonsense," he answered. "Enjoy yourself."

"I want to go home," I said.

I managed to change the ticket and fly home on my own. Figuring out how to get through Times Square, how to hail a cab, how to get through LaGuardia... Those things feel trivial now. But at the time? Monumental victories. And I was proud of myself. I was proud that I figured out how to leave my hotel room and go home, on my own.

Little did I know, that half-a-trip was the start of a new life. It was the start of something powerful and meaningful that shaped me into who I am. I took a trip. I took THE trip. Since I was a child, I dreamed of going to New York City. I wanted to be in the city of blinding lights. I wanted to walk the streets and ride the subway and see a Broadway show and eat real New York pizza and meet real New York people.

And eventually, I did. A few weeks later, in fact, when I was sent back up for another gig. But that first trip? The one I always imagined going so well and being so amazing and changing my life? It went exactly how it needed to, and it changed my life forever.

I did it. I went somewhere. I got out of my small suburban town. I did work I was told I wasn't capable of doing. I saw some bright lights. I saw the big city. It scared the shit out of me.

But I did it. And I went back to write more code and meet new people and ride in a cab and take the subway to Union Square and visit the comic shops I'd only seen advertised in the backs of comic books and ate real New York pizza and made new friends.

And it changed my life forever.

I'm thirty six years old now. And I am back in New York City. I'm here for a while, housesitting and walking dogs. But I'm not here to housesit, and I'm not here to walk dogs. I'm here because I need to be here. I'm here because I have the most amazing friends in the world. I'm here because my life is starting over.

I'm staying at least seven days. And even though I've been here dozens of times before, this trip, right now, scares the shit out of me.

I'm not scared of riding in a cab. I'm not scared of the subway. I've eaten the pizza and seen the lights and taken in a show (or 20). I've met friends. I've worked in these buildings. I've met these people. This is hardly new stuff for me.

But my life? My life is new. Things are different. And now, I'm back where it all began. I'm back in New York City.

I am sitting in an apartment in Chelsea. The dogs have been walked. Dinner has been had with friends, as well as drinks. Stories have been swapped. Tears have been shed. And now, I sit here and I write this, because I cannot do anything else. I can't go out. I can't ride in a cab. I can't take in a show.

All I can do is think about the fact that 17 years later, I'm back here in New York City, staring in one direction at a life that led me back here, and in the other direction at a life I know is going to be amazing.

And it scares the shit out of me. Because regardless of where I've been and where I'm going, right here, right now, I'm in New York City. Hiding out. Disappeared. Away from all things. Away from myself, so I can find myself.

I don't know where this week will take me. I don't know where the next week will take me, or the week after that, or next month or next year. What I do know is that, for the first time in 36 years, I know who I am. Finally, I know who I am. And I know what I'm worth, and I know what I'm here to do on this Earth.

And yes, I'm scared. I'm scared to death. You know the future is really happening when you start feeling scared.

I've known that feeling for a while now. The past few years, I've felt a very slow, creeping fear crawl into me and overcome me. The fear that I'm being left behind.

I don't quite know when it happened, but at some point over the past three years, I changed into a person who simply isn't satisfied by the old ways. My old ways, that is. Constant information bombardment. Constant exploration of new frontiers. Constant stimulation. Losing myself in news, games, and data.

At some point, I stopped worrying about being the first to know something. Or rather, I stopped being the first to know something, and as I was called upon to provide information or insight, I had to rush to find out what it was about and then quickly come up with an opinion. Then, I stopped rushing. Then, I stopped caring.

At some point, I was posting to Facebook, Twitter, Instagram, Tumblr and my blog somewhere on the order of 50 times a day combined. Today, I'm lucky if I get a blog post up every two months. Facebook has been set up to auto-post my updates to Twitter, which consist primarily of jokes and one liners and pictures of my dog. I've stopped using Tumblr, and Instagram is simply a cache of pictures of my cats and the occasional plate of food (which, I'm convinced, is what Instagram was created for).

And all around me, there are young, enthusiastic people who now know far more about what's going on than I do. When things happen, I hear about them second-hand. Just a few years ago, that thought would have given me hives. To not be the first to know... I might as well be castrated.

But now, I am not only comfortable not being the first to know things, I actually relish it. I don't need it. And that fact – the shift in behavior and desire – scares me.

I cannot sit and play video games for 8+ hour shifts anymore. I cannot lose myself in other worlds that way. I can't even conceptualize building a website. I can barely sit down and design something for my own company.

New technologies show up and I miss the announcement. Things which one enticed me and made me tingle with anticipation now barely get a "oh, cool" from me.

And that scares me.

My old self doesn't fit in to this future. It cannot keep up. It can't conceptualize what is becoming omnipresent. Social media does not hold the same enticing anticipation of meeting new people and sharing new things. Technology increments along and I'm not even watching.

And I think the fear that it creates in me is the fear we all get at some point in our lives: the idea that one day, we're going to die. And when we do, we will look back and wonder just how much of our time was spent doing something worthwhile.

And that's where my fear actually begins to subside. I don't know how much of what I've done was worthwhile, but I'm certain what I'm doing now has the potential to be – and I don't know what I'm doing. I'm winging it. And it's all new. The old rules do not apply. I do not show up, clock in, do what I'm told, clock out and move on to payday. I don't write silly stories and publish them and get a check.

I run a company. I'm in charge. It's all on me now. And it's all new and scary.

My marriage is over and I'm on my own -- completely alone -- for the first time in my adult life. Yet, I am surrounded by people who love me for the first time in my life, and they show me daily how much. This is my family. My studio. My friends. Not a drop of blood shared between us, no marriage certificates -- and yet, I wade headlong into war with them and love them dearly, and they love me just as much.

My instincts are the only thing that has kept me from freaking out. My instincts have always served me well. I've always been great with clients. I've always been able to predict, with remarkable clarity, what's next. It gave me a career four times over.

Make that five.

And when they told me life was about to start over, I questioned them. I thought I must be crazy. But lo and behold, I wasn't. I must NEVER question them, no matter who convinces me otherwise. Ever. No matter how much I agree with them.

Headlong I plunge into the unknown, filled with fear and wide-eyed with panic, excited for the first time in my life that I'm finally feeling what it's like to stop coasting and finally live. And I'm starting that life with some time in New York City. Beginning again, the way I did before. Only this time, the fear makes me smile. I welcome it. It's a fear I'm not hiding from. I welcome it, because it makes me realize for the first time in my life, I'm actually alive -- and aware of it.

I'm scared. And I've never -- EVER -- been happier.

ON FUCKING UP

POSTED MARCH 20, 2013

Look, you're going to fuck up. It is an absolute certainty. No one can avoid it.

No one is perfect. We are all human, humans are flawed, and that's what makes us all so very special: the mistakes. The mistakes contrast and highlight the great things that make up the best parts of who we are.

So embrace the mistakes. Know – not think, but know – that you are going to fuck something up somewhere at some point.

What matters most is what you do after you fuck up. Miles Davis said, "If you hit a wrong note, it's the next note that you play that determines if its's good or bad."

Step up. Take responsibility. Ask for forgiveness. Take action. Make it right (or, as right as it can be). Don't hide. Don't run. Own that shit.

The only thing worse than fucking up is running from it, and the only thing people love more than someone who never does the wrong thing, is someone who does the right thing. So do the right thing. Steer your ship into the storm, batten down the hatches, and cackle like a mad person as you embrace the suck of taking responsibility for your fuckup.

Or, you know, be a coward and run. I'm sure once you finally outrun your own shadow, you'll be very happy.

GAY MARRIAGE: I DON'T GET IT

POSTED MARCH 28, 2013

I consider myself a smart guy.

I actively seek understanding and knowledge, and to that end, I read (a lot). I ask a lot of questions. I talk to a lot of people. I watch videos. I listen to talks. I try to pay attention to as much around me as I possibly can. And I feel like I do a pretty fair job of accumulating data, parsing it and drawing at least somewhat educated conclusions about things.

But I have to come clean: There's one thing I just plain cannot understand, and that's why anyone gives a shit about gay people getting married.

Why is this a thing? Why does it matter? It makes NO sense to me whatsoever.

Two men or two women decide to tie the knot. What happens? Why are religious people and Republicans (usually one in the same) so up in arms about it?

To try to wrap my head around it, I've analyzed it step by step and see what effect it has on you (or anyone who isn't them).

1) They love each other. They have found another person on this planet -- a planet housing nearly 7 billion (that's 7,000,000,000) people -- that they not only get along with, that they not only feel emotions toward, that they not only share a bond with, but that they feel safe around and unified with. They love each other. Just like you love your spouse, fiancée, or significant other.

Who does this affect? Their friends, who are happy for them. Their family, who (we hope) support them.

Does this impact your daily life? No.

What should you do about it? Mind your own fucking business.

2) **They exchange vows.** They promise to love, honor, protect and support one another.

Who does this affect? The caterer, the event planner, the hosts, and the attendees.

Does this impact your daily life? No.

What should you do about it? Mind your own fucking business.

3) **They hand each other rings.** They place a band of metal (or string or what have you) on each other's hands as an external symbol that they are in a monogamous relationship with another person.

Who does this affect? The jeweler. They've made a little money.

Does this impact your daily life? Well, are you the jeweler? No? Then no.

What should you do about it? Mind your own fucking business.

4) They consummate the marriage. However they see fit. **Who does this affect?** Unless they're particularly loud about it and you're in the next room, no one except them.

Does this impact your daily life? It shouldn't. If it does, you're overly concerned about the private lives of other people and seriously, seriously, SERIOUSLY need a hobby that isn't counting rosary.

What should you do about it? Mind your own fucking business.

5) **They live together.** They decorate their home. They watch television or listen to the radio or knit or play video games. They cook food. They eat.

Who does this affect? Retail outlets in the community who benefit from increased domestic goods sales (because, let's face it, couples consume more than individuals in just about every regard).

Does this impact your daily life? If you work at a retail outlet where they shop, sure.

What should you do about it? Mind your own fucking business.

6) **They share benefits.** House, insurance, 401k, cars. Just like a man and a woman would.

Who does this affect? No one else.

Does this impact your daily life? Nope.

What should you do about it? Mind your own fucking business.

None of this computes for me.

So yes, I don't get it. I don't get the hypocrisy, I don't get the insistence on putting your morals on other peoples' daily existence, I don't understand how beliefs -- which by nature belong solely to you and pertain only to what's in your mind, regardless of who else could relate to them -- can manifest themselves in actions against other people's lives WHICH DON'T IMPACT YOU WHATSOEVER.

I don't get it. Please, explain it to me. Give me a reason that doesn't start with "my beliefs" or "the Bible says" because neither of those things matter when it comes to the daily lives of people. Give me reasons. Give me plausible, fact-based logical reasons why homosexuals shouldn't be allowed to bond themselves in legal union and share their lives.

Just one. I beg of you. Because of all the stupidity in the world, even the stuff I cannot relate to one bit, this is one thing I simply cannot get my head around.

HEY LADIES - LET ME FILL YOU IN ON A SECRET

POSTED APRIL 17, 2013

Fashion and "beauty" magazines Photoshop models to look like some overly-aggrandized ideal figure. This is not the secret. Anyone who's spent any time on the net has seen the bazillion or so sites that reveal model retouching with before and after photos, showing everyone from Halle Berry to Beyoncé to Megan Fox being retouched from "human" to "super OMG beauty goddess whatever."

The secret:

They, the magazines and make up manufacturers and clothing creators, do not do this because this ideal is what we men find beautiful. It's not.

They do this because **they want to convince you that this ideal is what we men find beautiful** - and that ideal they're pitching is so realistically unattainable (or, rather, is attainable, but only through 8 hours a day at the gym, a professional nutritionist, and many, many sessions at the plastic surgeon's den o' cuttery).

And it forces you to go out and starve yourselves on fad diets and buy stupid heaps of ugly makeup and magazines that teach you how to be what you never could (or should) be and expensive clothes, making you hate yourselves when you look in the mirror to the point where, in my own simple polling at the gym last night, eight out of ten women - all of whom I find devastatingly beautiful - said that they wanted some sort of body enhancement or reduction surgery.

Not "would consider" - WANT.

That's such complete bullshit.

Do you realize how little attention men pay to the tiny imperfections you've been psychosocially abused into thinking we care about? NONE. Except for those jock meathead fucksticks in New Jersey who can't even see past their own tiny dicks due to having their heads shoved all the way up their own asses. And if you're caring what a guy like that thinks, you're already broken to the point that I can no longer help you.

Regular men - REAL men - don't see that. Beauty is in humanity. To have curves and shape and form is to be human. To be without those things, to hold yourself to an impossible ideal... Men won't ever tell you this, but when they see women like that, there's a subconscious event that triggers that immediately makes them uninterested. They may be ATTRACTED, but ultimately, it's just to the glint and glitter of the smooth thing in front of them; a fleeting thing at best. They're not actually interested in pursuing anything meaningful with a woman like that, because after all, she's broken to the point of caring more about what other people think than in being confident in herself.

You're beautiful, naturally. Take good care of your body. Eat right and exercise. But do those things for YOU, because you love how you feel when you do it and because it's just right to protect and nurture yourself... Not because you think some dude wants to see a six pack. And for chrissake, stay the hell away from the surgeon, unless your condition is a detriment to you physically.

Stop reading any magazine you can buy while you're checking out at the grocery store. Quit holding yourselves up to some retarded social ideal of what you should be. Be beautiful by loving yourself. Confidence is one thousand times sexier than any physical attribute.

THE TRUTH ABOUT THE TRUTH

POSTED APRIL 19, 2013

The truth is not your friend. It's not there to help you and guide you to a better life. It's not going to greet you at the door with flowers when you decide to face it.

It's also not your enemy. It's not trying to tear you down or punish you. It isn't malicious or evil.

The truth is agnostic to your happiness and/or pain. It doesn't care. That's because it doesn't like or hate you. It's just here to do its job.

And that job? The truth is Reality's enforcer. It will ask you nicely to listen. When you don't, it will smile, nod, and kick your teeth in. And It will keep escalating until you finally pay attention, no matter how much blood it has to draw or who gets hurt in the process.

It's natural to want to think the truth (and its boss, Reality) is a sadist; that it gets off on hurting you. But that's not even remotely true. If you keep getting beat up by the truth, you're actually just a masochist.

Don't feel bad though. We all do it. That's what being human is all about: thinking we are smarter and better and more agile than reality. But we aren't. Eventually, reality gets sick of your grandstanding and sends its goon, the truth, to teach you a lesson.

Ignore it, and you will feel pain. But if you listen, it will help you. Because it's only role is to show you the rules. And once you know those, you can actually play fair.

Not to say you'll win. Again, the truth isn't your buddy either. But both the good and bad news is that it's fair. And that's something.

...Still hurts like a motherfucker though.

THE ONLY MOMENTS YOU KNOW YOU'RE ALIVE

POSTED MAY 13, 2013

You're in the moment.

You're right here, right now.

Your eyes may be wide open, surveying all before them. Or, they may be slammed shut, and whatever's happening outside is playing like a movie on a projector, shooting through smoky light the events life on the backs of your eyelids. You may be afraid. You may be happy. But you're here. Now.

You're no longer thinking.

You're not processing and responding.

You are *alive*.

You move with agility you never knew you had -- and you don't even realize you're doing it, because you're not thinking about it. Everything you say comes straight from the heart, bypassing the brain and exiting the mouth before any filters dilute the message. Every action ends with a punctuation reserved for only the most important of statements, both expressed and spoken.

You are scared out of your mind. You are happy to the point of full release. You don't just feel the air rushing into your lungs, you feel the life that the air you breathe gives you. You

340

feel it coursing through your veins as each blood cell rushes, as fast as it can, the oxygen you're drawing in to the furnaces it fuels to make you do what you're doing right now. You can feel every single artery contract and release, pushing this life through you. You can feel every vein drawing out the impurities, making room for more fire. You exhale and it almost screams.

Everything glows.

That moment -- that period between thoughts, whether it be minutes or seconds or even nanoseconds -- that moment is when you know you're truly alive.

This is not a dream.

This is not a fabrication.

You're feeling what you feel. You're doing what you're doing. There is no time for regret. There is no time for planning. There is only time for being exactly who you are, exactly how you are.

It is a shame, then, that we often only know these moments in hindsight. Looking back on them, whether they just happened or they were years ago, we realize we were not merely living; we were *alive*. And it's also a shame that more often than not, we treat these moments like mistakes.

These moments are NOT mistakes. These moments are quite possibly the only moments in your life you're not making a mistake. You're living true. You're living honest. You're ALIVE.

Trust THESE moments to tell you who you are. Not the rationalizations ex-post-facto. Not the second guessing. Not other peoples' opinions on what happened. Look at the moment. Look at how you acted.

That. **THAT.** Is who you are.

The moments you know you're not merely living, you are alive... These moments are the only ones that matter. Everything else is just a response. It's spin. Your brain will get in the way and try to run interference. Don't let it. Don't allow it to attach definitions and explanations and rationalizations. Trust these moments.

Hide from them, and you'll continually regret the moments your brain turns off and your body takes over and does whatever it does when you're truly alive. If you dismiss them, you won't be able to live through them. You'll continually feel regret and pain and hostility toward yourself. You won't be able to use them as tools to know who you are at your core. And that will lead to a life filled with disaster. Pain. Shame.

Embrace them, and you will find yourself. You will know yourself. You will know that, at your core, beyond the voices whispering yes's and no's into your mind's ear, who you really are. You will begin to see the framework that makes you. You can then trust it. You can release, slowly, the contrary thoughts and rationalizations and second guessing.

And when you lose yourself in the moment and wake up from it, whatever took place... It was you on display. The real you. The you you've come to know and to trust to be you.

And you have nothing -- NOTHING -- to be ashamed of.

WHEN TIME IS GONE, IT'S FUCKING GONE

POSTED JULY 7, 2013

Shit happens. And when it does, you're going to look back at all the time you had before the shit happened and how much of it you lost.

I have a best friend. His name is Jeremy Halvorsen. This guy is amazing. He's never let me down. Every time I've ever needed him, he leapt up and joined the fight, whatever that fight may have been. He's been with me through thick and thin for over 10 years now. And I only met his mother in person for the first time this past March.

Michelle Halvorsen raised my best friend. She is a terrific mother. She's taken good care of this guy I look up to and respect. She made him who he is today. And I only just met her three months ago. Sure, we've heard everything there is to hear about each other through Jeremy. We've talked on the phone a few times, and the love and respect for each other was there even without face to face contact on a regular basis. I felt that when I finally got to hug her. I loved her instantly.

Sadly, yesterday, she passed away from cancer. Three months after I finally met her and began visiting Connecticut regularly and could see her more often, she's gone. And that makes me sad and angry, both for the loss of someone wonderful that just came into my life and for the fact that I let ten years pass without meeting her.

Did I waste all that time? Well, in that ten years, there was work... Oh, there's always work. Books written, tours taken, websites built, companies run, money made, money lost... Work, work, work. It has to get done. I can't beat myself up for that, can I?

And then there were the times I wasn't working during my travels, where I visited lots of places and saw lots of neat things and needed to relax. I can't really punish myself for that. It's how life goes -- you tax yourself; you have to recharge.

Hours and days spent hanging out with Jeremy, in person and via Skype, working on projects and building cool things, playing video games... That wasn't wasted. It was bonding and it was fun.

So did I really waste ten years where I could have met and gotten to hang out with Mrs. Halvorsen? My brain wants to tell me yes. Over and over again, yes, I could have gotten up there and met her way sooner. But it wasn't a priority.

But that's unfair. It was my friend's mom. I loved her and respected her from afar. And now, I have no other choice but to do that, because this amazing and lovely lady has passed on. And I'm left to think about all the opportunities I didn't take to meet her, see her, get to know her, and most importantly, let her know I loved her for bringing my best friend into the world.

She knew that I loved her, even though we never hung out. I know that. But that's just not enough. It's NEVER enough. Sure, work got done, but there's ALWAYS more work. Money was made, but there's ALWAYS more money. Games were played, but there's ALWAYS more games to play.

You never, ever have enough time. When it's gone, it's fucking gone.

Don't waste a second of it.

Talk to strangers. Get to know new people. Share your stories. Laugh and cry with them. Make them your friends. When they are your friends, spare no opportunity to tell them how you feel about them and why. You don't have to obsessively talk about it, but you can absolutely show it in literally millions of ways. Help them. Be there for them. Take care of them, and thank them when they take care of you. Meet their mothers and fathers and sisters and brothers. You don't have to like them, but hey, what if you do? Get to a place in your life where you can understand what "family" really means. It's the only thing that matters. Blood does not make family, love makes family. Understand that, and you understand life.

And for your own sanity's sake, say "I love you" more than you think is necessary. It never gets old. Ignore that conflicting voice in your head that keeps whispering about how embarrassing it is to say and just say it (but only if you mean it). Because when their time runs out, you're going to wish you had... But more importantly, when yours runs out, they'll know exactly how you felt.

Rest in peace, Mrs. Halvorsen.

TEARING YOUR EMOTIONAL ACL

POSTED JULY 12, 2013

We are idiots when it comes to our emotions.

Yes, all of us. People, as a general rule, are dumb about our hearts and brains. We get hurt, and for some reason, we think the best solution to the problems of our days is to immediately plunge right back into a similar situation that got us into trouble in the first place.

Nowhere more is this apparent than in affairs of the heart. We get our hearts broken, and we immediately go out and try to patch the wound with the attentions of someone else, as if that is the actual problem -- the absence of a person, any person, from our life.

I've done it. You've done it. We've all done it. Because we're dumb when it comes to our emotions.

We're slightly less dumb when it comes to our bodies (for some of us, only SLIGHTLY less dumb, but still). When we suffer an injury, we usually have no choice but to give it the time it takes to heal. What if we treated our emotions and our psychological state like it was a physical injury?

Imagine it like being a pro athlete. Your knee was just slammed into by a 260lb linebacker, and you've torn your ACL. You can't walk. You're injured.

Of course, you're going to have to go to the doctor and get the bad news. Then comes the brace and the crutches and the surgery. This takes weeks. And the entire time, you're in severe pain. How do you alleviate that pain? Pain killers, sure. Anti- inflammatories. Video games and movies and ice cream. Lots of things that take the pain away.

But you most certainly don't deal with it by hopping on the field and playing four quarters. That's fucking stupid. And that's what you're doing with your emotions when you insist on treating your pain with the exact same thing that caused it in the first place, instead of letting them heal.

Now, the really hard part to swallow -- just because you had the surgery on your knee doesn't make you ready to hop right back into being the starting running back in the NFL. Far from it. You've got to heal from the surgery, then you've got rehab. Months of it. Just to get back to walking normally.

Then, in order to actually compete, you've got to hit the gym and rebuild the strength you had in that leg. You've got months and months of training to do before you're ready to get back on the field.

Imagine if you did that with your emotional state when you've been hurt or suffered a loss. Instead of patching, actually taking the time to repair and rebuild. Instead of marching right back in front of the train that hit you and continually ending up in the emotional Emergency Room, take a break and heal up. Then, do some research and study the patterns that put you in that place in the first place (yours, or someone else's).

What if we took the time that's necessary to actually get stronger, instead of constantly ripping the same hole in our hearts?

"ANYTHING YOU NEED..."

POSTED JULY 14, 2013

It's simultaneously the nicest and also the worst thing anyone can say to you when you're going through a hard time:

"If there's anything you need... Let me know."

Sometimes they even add emphasis on the "anything." They verbally embolden it, like "If there's **anything** you need..." Or maybe they capitalize it: "If there's ANYTHING you need..." The really helpful will repeat it, italicize it and make sure there's plenty of dramatic pause in there too: "If there's anything -- *ANYTHING* -- you need..."

It means a lot, really it does. You mean it when you say it to friends in need. And when you're in need, it really does mean the world that they want to help you.

But there's a major, major problem. When shit goes south, often times the one thing you really need, you can't have.

Friends will do just about anything and everything else possible to help you... Except that one thing that fixes it all. They can't bring back the dead relative. They can't make the spouse un-cheat on you. They can't make your boss un-fire you.

And that's where you, as the person who has to face the tough situation, have to realize that to place that level of requirement on people is just plain unfair. You will turn all of your friends away and push them out because they can't do that one thing that fixes it all... So you feel they can't do *anything*.

If you're like me, you will bottle up all of your emotions, push forward, put on a smile and pretend like everything is fine. You'll fix your own meals, you'll take care of your own house, and you'll do everything in the world for yourself, because if you can't have that one thing, you don't want anything. Or even *ANYTHING*.

It's a mistake.

Rely on your friends. Let them help you, even if all they can do is sit there and be in the room and make sure you're not alone. Let them cook you a meal. Let them clean up a little. Let them help you pack things if that's required.

Burdens are heavy. Lifting them alone risks throwing your back out... Then where are you?

And as the friend who offers assistance, your job is to be the passenger in the vehicle. Be there when they need you, point out hazards if you see them, but otherwise, they need to do the driving. Your job is to work the radio, unwrap the drive-thru food, and put the straw in the drink. Otherwise, your job is to keep them from steering into a ditch or playing chicken with oncoming traffic.

THE COFFEE SHOP CHRONICLES

POSTED OVER THE YEARS

(The collection of posts below are all about my favorite coffee shop, a Starbucks in Fayetteville, GA. I am drawn to this place. Regardless of where I work or where I live, I always come back here, because it's absolutley crazy.)

Ahh, Starbucks.

I know that I'm not supposed to, and all my left-wingy hipster friends give me shit about it, but I really do love this place.

It's so strange - all the other Starbucks locations I've been to across Atlanta are so pretentious... Retarded marketing dorks and executives enjoying lattes and whatever. This one, however, is a little well of eccentricity in the middle of southern suburban Atlanta. I've been writing here for about 2 months now, and there's always a pretty interesting crowd here. For instance, there's a guy sitting a few tables over from me writing a book on napkins.

No, not like a reference book on different brands of paper cleaning products. He's writing a book. And he's doing it on NAPKINS. He's been at this for about 2 weeks. One day, I'm going to ask him what he's writing it about.

ANNNNNNNYWAY, There was a chick who, a few minutes ago, sat down directly across from me. She was about 5' 6" or so, dyed blond hair, ruby red lipstick, etc. and so forth - as

350

close to Brittany Spears as a no-class redneck harlot can get...
Which means "Just like her".

I looked up at her and she smiled, and with this ridiculously
faux-sultry voice, she says "HIIIIIIIIIIIIII there."

"Hey," I respond, then return to my tip-tap-typing.

She places her index finger on the lid of my laptop and
pushes down, flattening it out and forcing me to look at her
chest. "Whatcha workin' on?" She says with a toothy grin.

Without batting an eye, I look straight into her eyes and
answer, "Why, my latest manifesto."

She puzzles over that for a moment. "Whatcha mean?"

"Well," I answer, returning the screen to its regular position,
"The Olympics start in 2 weeks, right?"

She blinked a few times and said "Yeah?"

"Well, someone's got to bomb them, don't they?" I said, then
went back to typing.

She left.

~~~~~

So… want to hear something totally fucked up?

Well, yeah, of course you do. You're here, right?

Ok, so I pull up to the Starbucks I always write at, and there's
this young African American kid with a half bored, half
determined look on his face standing right outside the door
to the establishment. He's rocking back and forth on his feet
and tapping out a beat on the front of his thighs, rapping a

little when I walk up to enter the store. I nod hello, and in response, he begins... Well, mumbling.

"Hmm?" I say, stepping in a little.

He reaches down and picks up two boxes of brittle – one cashew, one peanut. Again, he mumbles, but this time I can make out a few words. "You mumblemumblemumble buy mumblemumble brittle mumblemumblemumble school?"

"Nah, no thanks dude," I reply with a smile.

He shrugs his shoulders, drops the brittle into the cardboard box at his feet and goes back to a-tappin' and a-rappin. I nod and reach for the door. Just as I make contact with the handle, it slams forward and raps my knuckles pretty hard. Immediately, the head of the Starbucks' manager, Kaitlin, pops out.

"Oh, GOD! Sorry, Joe!" She said, her face turning from angry to concerned and immediately back to angry as she turns to the youth selling his wares. "HEY!" she announces to him as he picks up his box hurriedly. "I've told you I don't know HOW many times today, go sell your brittle somewhere else! You can't do it here!"

"Fuh Yuh, BEIOTCH!" he replies, flipping her off and marching away, brittle tucked under his arm.

"YEAH, fuck you, too!" She said, drawing the attention of a few customers inside. She immediately turned to me and said "Sorry, sorry... God, I'm SO sorry. Come in, come in..."

"Hmm... Seems like you have a bit of a solicitation problem, Kaitlin," I said with a smile, trying to alleviate her embarrassment.

"WOW!" shouted Mike, one of the workers behind the counter. "That was impressive!"

"Shut up, Mike," Kaitlin said as she returned to the counter. "That guy's been here like six times today. He just WON'T go away!" She reached out and took my travel mug and immediately began filling it with the darkest roast they have, then plunked it on the counter in front of me as I reached for my wallet. "No, no charge," She said, holding the open face of her palm toward me. "Not after that little display."

"Hmm… Well, you didn't do anything wrong," I replied, "But thanks!" And I took my piping hot mug o' Joe to my usual table, pulled out my laptop, and got to work.

A few minutes goes by, and I'm happily tip-tap-typing away on the Dell from Hell, lost in the transcription of the next part of Romance.net. I take a quick break as I read over what I'd just written, reaching out for my mug and placing it to my lips. Just then, I see a bit of movement just above and beyond the screen of my machine. I look up and watch as the most intense scene I've witnessed in, like, weeks begins to unfold.

I focus in on the movement which became a form, which became the youth from earlier who was running full-speed toward the bank of windows at the front of the shop. In his right hand is a half of a cinder block swinging back and forth. The look on his face is not unlike that of an Olympic javelin thrower as they sprint toward the mark where they release the implement and fling it as far as they can.

Which is kinda what he did with this cinder block, only it was a half-underhand, half-sidearm type of affair. I just sat there with my coffee mug to my lips as I watched this lump of concrete arc through the air toward the window. It seemed to hang for just a moment at the peak of its climb before it began descending. Then, my field of view glowed white as the brick smashed into the safety glass of the Starbucks window, dividing it into tens of thousands of pieces clinging together with protective film.

But that's not the most intense part.

In the time it took me to place my mug back on the table and look over at the counter to see the reactions of the employees present, Kaitlin had leapt the counter and bolted out the door. I twisted my head back to the bank of windows, leaning to the left to look through one of the more pristine sheets of glass and watched as this five foot eight inch woman in khakis, a black oxford and a green apron sprinted across the parking lot and landed the most beautiful open-field tackle I have ever seen, slamming headlong into the kid and bringing them both crashing down to the asphalt. She straddled him and began beating the ever-loving shit out of him as one of the employees called 9-1-1.

The kid was held at bay by 3 of us who went out at first to help Kaitlin, but soon switched over to saving this poor guy from having his ass handed to him by a girl. He didn't resist or anything, he just sat there and cried as the cops arrived. The blue brigade and the concrete shot-putter just left a few minutes ago, as did Kaitlin.

I just returned to my table and began writing this.

It's like I said. This place is a little well of eccentricity.

~~~~~

I've been thinking much lately on the prospect of buying a new vehicle, and much to my own chagrin, I've pretty much settled on an SUV. I've been browsing online at the various car shopping sites, checking out the pluses and minuses of various models, but one is sticking out in my mind - the Toyota 4Runner (limited edition). Why?

Because one is sticking out of the front of the Starbucks where I am writing.

Yep, the very same Starbucks what saw a teenage hoodlum toss a cinderblock through one of its gigantic front-facing plate glass windows is now in need of a few more sheets of glass, because a gigantic Toyota SUV thought it was too good to use the front door.

I'm not sure of the backstory, really, but from what I could gather from the resulting insanity that followed the truck plowing backwards into the store, apparently the driver was a 15 year old a few weeks into her learner's permit, out on a driving lesson with her father. The two were here for whatever reason, and when they decided to head home, she asked if she could drive. He agreed, she hopped into the driver's seat, buckled up (I know because that's the one thing he keeps praising her on), started the car, and applied just a wee bit too much pressure on the accelerator. Luckily, the spot the vehicle was parked in was directly across from the windows looking out from the "bar" area, elsewise there would have been a conversation with the owner of this franchise a lot like "Hey, you got SUV in my Starbucks!" "No, YOU got Starbucks in my SUV!" and then the 2 would take a lick of their respective products and smile innocently, resulting in some new abominable dessert / engineering fad.

And remarkably, the vehicle has taken very little damage. It's a hearty, robust vehicle and, given my predilection for gently nudging various objects such as fire hydrants and billboards and fence posts with my car, I think the 4Runner just might do me fine.

Can't say the same for a Starbucks franchise, though. Looks like the bar area's going to be closed for repairs for a little while. Again.

On a side note, I picked the WORST DAY EVER to leave my phone at home to keep it from distracting me so I could write.

Anyway, that's my Sunday. How's yours?

~~~~~

So.

The Starbucks I usually write at has had its share of oddness over the past few years. Strange things just seem to happen there, usually while I'm in attendance.

Tonight, however, I wasn't even able to get near the place. Why? Well, it seems that the movie theater in the same shopping complex as it has a robbery suspect holed up inside with the SWAT team surrounding it. The entire complex has been sealed off and no one can go inside. So, instead of writing from there about other stuff, I'm writing here about there.

That entire area is just plain weird.

~~~~~

I hope I get to make this post before I run out of time.

I'm at the Barnes and Noble across the street from the Starbucks I usually visit to escape the madness of my house (which is why I don't laugh - ever - when I see a writer at Starbucks trying to "catch the coffeehouse vibe" or whatever, because they might be like me - they might live in a zany, madcap house filled with annoying animals and messes that need to be cleaned and whatever).

I'm here instead of Starbucks because Andrea wanted to do some book shopping. She decided to do book shopping at the last minute, as we passed the store.

"What the hell," I said, "They have internet and coffee. Might as well."

The problem:

Andrea brought two books with her FROM HOME to read while we sat at Starbucks - a new Iris Johanssen book and a Sudoku book (she's a Math major and loves the stuff). When we go to Starbucks together, she reads while I write (or surf or whatever). It helps kill the time. Since we decided to change locations mid-stream, neither one of us thought of the potential impact of this.

So, we enter the Barnes & Noble store to the warm, soft sounds of an alarm going off - apparently, somewhere in these brand new pants of mine, is one of those RFID alarm tags that I just can't seem to locate, because this has happened at several stores today. No biggie, right? The clerk comes over, sees that we just entered, and immediately doesn't care.

We sit. We drink coffee. I write. She reads. Yay.

The trouble comes when I was trying to leave the first time.

Because of the goofy tag thing, I tripped the alarm.

They decide they need to look in my bag - which is cool, I don't mind.

They find Andrea's books. Obviously, since she brought them from home, we have no receipt. But they're very new, she got them about 2 weeks ago on our last book shopping trip.

And now, I'm sitting in the back room of the Barnes and Noble waiting for the Police to show up - I kid you not.

They didn't want to let me use my computer, but fuck them - they're Barnes and Noble employees and I'm the size of a Volkswagen Vanogan - they aren't going to stop me.

Anyway, I thought you'd all enjoy knowing this.

~~~~~

It's Asshole Day At Starbucks!

Whenever I have a lot of work I need to power through, I head to a coffee shop. Long time readers will remember that I used to go to a very special Starbucks over in Fayetteville. It was special because the oddest crap kept happening there, including one of my favoritest stories ever.

But I've since found that a few other Starbucks in the area have their own special qualities - and today, since it's sunny and warm and nice out, I went to the McDonough Starbucks due to its superior patio and friendly staff.

And when I pulled into the parking lot, this is what greeted me: A car double-parked.

And it's not an especially nice one, either - it's just a Honda Accord. But the asshole felt so superior, he had to take two spots. And while I was grumbling about that walking up to the place, I began hearing over and above the light jazz playing on the speakers a loud, obnoxious voice that could only belong to a conservative talk radio host.

I look around the corner, and sure enough, there's a car with its windows down, doors open, trunk open, blaring the finest thoughts coming out of the fringe right this early morning.

Now, I really wish I could have gotten a picture of the guy whose car this is - pink polo shirt which didn't cover his beer gut entirely, white khaki shorts, blonde Glenn Beck hair, and a fucking porn 'stache.

I went inside and ordered my coffee, then grumbled to the very kind clerk about the guy bumping the talk drivel in the parking lot.

"Oh, he's here every morning," she said. "It's a little strange," she added with a grin.

I walked out fully intent on getting my Flip HD camera and Gorillapod to film myself driving up beside the car in my truck blaring " Disciple" by Slayer, leaving my doors open, and sitting down next to him and just drinking my coffee - but as soon as I grabbed the camera, he began walking to the car.

Mark my words, dear readers: THIS. WILL. HAPPEN.

~~~~~

I am currently being witnessed to by members of the Gay Christian Alliance. Seriously, this is happening. Right now. I am writing this as they tell me about their church and why I should come and how open and non-judgmental it is.

e already explained that the religion thing isn't my bag,
hey've countered with how it wasn't for them either, due
ll the stereotypical judgmental aspects and how
mental it is. And their church isn't judgmental, and
y're not judgmental. So they won't judge me. I should
eally come to the church.

I'm not so sure I even understand the whole concept here.
Christ changed their life and turned them around, according
to both of these guys. They were headed down the wrong
path. And now they're "realigned."

What does that even mean? This is why I hang out in
stereotypically gay environments - so I don't have to hear this
shit. Homosexuals, you my homies! Don't be flippin' the
script or other street slang I really shouldn't be using!

And for the record, it's not the fact that they're gay and
Christian. It's the fact that they're gay and Christian and won't
shut the fuck up about it and leave me alone in my straight
heathenism. For a couple of non-judgmental dudes, these
guys sure are disapproving of my lifestyle choice of being
without religion by way of not relenting on their message.

THE SECRET OF MAKING THINGS HAPPEN

POSTED OCTOBER 21, 2011

I want to give you the one secret I have. It's actually the *only* secret I've got. And I'm going to share it with you. It's the secret of making things happen.

The reason I want to give it to you: recently, people have commented on how things are going for me, and how happy they are that things are going well. It means a lot to hear this from you guys.

And as always, the corollary to those comments is the sentiment that sounds somewhat like "I wish I could make things like that happen in my life." This is always the corollary to well-wishing, and has been true every time I release a new book or when I started working for Fark.com or get a new journalism gig or show for Art of Akira or when I joined Studio Revolver or any other wonderful thing that's happened to me.

Those things happen because of the work I have done and the record I've built for myself. That part isn't the secret. That part everyone knows: the road to opportunity is paved with effort. The part most people wish could happen is the bit where they get to do the job they want to do for an organization they admire, or go on a trip they've always wanted to take, or speak to the public about topics they love, or publish a book with stories they like to write.

The secret to making those things happen -- the only one I have in my life and the one I'm sharing with you right now is this:

Just fucking do it.

It's a shitty secret, because you already know it. But for some reason, you still find a way to convince yourself you don't know how or you can't. So the secret is to just GO. No one wishes for the experience of writing, they wish for the finished book. They don't wish for the learning of syntax and user experience concepts, they wish for the prestige of working for a huge website.

You want to talk to people about anime or comics? Or talk about the biological impacts of television on children? Or talk about animal welfare? Start. Go. YouTube.com is free to use. Cameras are cheap. Chances are, your laptop or computer already has one. Record your talks. Put them on YouTube. Share them with your friends. If you get good feedback, share them with a website or two that covers your topic (don't spam or annoy though).

You want to write a book? Come on... That one's easy. Open your word processor. Start typing.

Want to be a reporter for a larger organization? Blog. It's free at Blogger.com, Tumblr.com, or any number of other sites that will host your blog.

"But I don't know how..."
Stop right there. That's not going to get you where you want to be. If you want to make it to San Francisco and you live in Atlanta, the first step is to point west, the second is to get moving.

Sure, you can book a flight or a bus or a train ride. But keeping with the metaphor, you'll likely say "But I don't have enough money to buy a ticket..."

Point west. Start walking. If you REALLY want to get there, you'll do that before you do anything else.

The hard, honest truth most everyone doesn't want to tell you: the words "I can't" are fucking bullshit. There are Olympic class sprinters with no legs, people. The drummer for Def Leppard has only one arm. ONE ARMED DRUMMERS AND NO LEGGED SPRINTERS CAN. You can do anything you want. You just don't WANT to.

Start working. Figure the rest out along the way. When you open your word processor and start writing your book, you'll get to a point where you wonder how chapters should be formed and the book should be organized. You'll go research that, either by reading other books and mimicking their style, or by reading how-to materials. But you'll figure it out on the way.

Another secret, but it's not my secret, it's a universal secret: no one who does anything creative knows what the hell they're doing. No one. They just start. They copy what they like. They start finding their own path. And as time goes on, they don't learn the one way HOW TO, they learn many, many ways HOW NOT TO. And they let that experience guide them the in the right direction. But they still run into walls and get bruises and fall down a lot.

Those who are unafraid to take the bumps and feel the pain of forging their own path are the ones who make it to the finish line.

Trying to map out the route to your goal is honorable and noble. It's also yet another thing that feels like work, but isn't work. Dave Sim, the godfather of self-publishing in comics and author of a 300 issue, 6400 page story said it best: writing notes, organizing ideas, penciling doodles and concepts feels like work, but the work doesn't begin until you start penciling, inking and lettering panel 1 on page 1.

You WILL end up with a lot of trash. You will delete entire chapters or an entire book. You will scrap your videos. You will end up killing your own articles on your blog, because you feel they go nowhere. But you MUST realize that that's part of the process.

If you can't point west and start walking; if you're obsessed with process instead of delivery, you're like everyone else: you want the reward without taking the journey and battling the dragon. You want it handed to you on a silver platter.

Even Albert Einstein pointed out that, at a certain point, reading and researching too much is damaging to the creative process and ends up stalling the creator out:

Reading, after a certain age, diverts the mind too much from its creative pursuits. Any man who reads too much and uses his own brain too little falls into lazy habits of thinking.
~ Albert Einstein

As I said on my Notes to Self site: I attribute all of my success to luck. The harder I work, the luckier I get.

Go. Do. Don't sit there and wish. Wishing gets you nothing. It occupies the mind and feels like work. Making notes? It streamlines the process of what you want to do, but until you DO it, you're not working. You're streamlining. Research? Reading? Asking around? All of that stuff, while VERY helpful, doesn't write your book or get you speaking dates or publish your article or gets you that development / creative gig at a big website. It's necessary to improve quality and do things well... But before you do things well, you should just do things.

Another Dave Sim quote: Get good, then get fast, then get good and fast. But what Dave left out: Before you get good or fast, you have to start.

So start.

Thanks:

Victoria Evans, for producing this book.

Casey Edwards, Jeremy Halvorsen, Katie Black, Liz Stricklen, Shawn and Jessica Hill, and Michael Crawford for taking care of me when I needed it most.

Jen and John Christopher, Melissa and Jeff Oyler, Laura and Randy Martin, Stacia Caliano, Claude Atout, Riki LeCotey and Chris Donio, Brian Stelfreeze, Cully Hamner, Allison Sohn, Virginia Peacock Hall, Renee LaBarge, Andy Chang, Colette Bennett, Christy Ramsey, Genevieve Dempre, Drew and Heather Curtis, and Tiffany Eckert Lumsdon for guidance, support, motivation and advice.

Buck Wolf, for believing in me.

CrossFit Signal20 in Stockbridge, GA, CrossFit Uncommon in LaFayette, IN and The Foundry in Chicago, IL for giving me the knowledge and drive to take care of myself.

Special thanks to Todo Brennan at ABT Tattoo in McDonough, GA for the astounding pieces of art all over my arms and leg which have become famous around the world.

And very special thanks to you, for reading my stuff, buying what I put out, supporting me and keeping this dream of mine alive. This isn't just some closing line in a book. I genuinely mean it. Without you, I don't get to do this. And I love doing this. So thank you. Like, for reals.